BAKING RECIPES
FROM THE
WIVES & MOTHERS
OF OUR
FOUNDING FATHERS

**Authentic Baking Recipes
from the Wives and Mothers of,
& Trivia About,
the Signers of the Declaration of Independence
and Our Constitution.**

INFINITY
PUBLISHING.COM

ISBN 0-7414-1944-0

Published by:

INFI∞ITY
PUBLISHING.COM
1094 New DeHaven Street, Suite 100
West Conshohocken, PA 19428-2713
Info@buybooksontheweb.com
www.buybooksontheweb.com
Toll-free (877) BUY BOOK
Local Phone (610) 941-9999
Fax (610) 941-9959

Printed in the United States of America
Published September 2009

Part of the Pelton Historical

Cookbook Series

Includes the Following Titles

Baking Recipes from the Civil War
Historical Thanksgiving Cookery
Historical Christmas Cookery
Civil War Period Cookery
Revolutionary War Period Cookery

Includes the Favorite Recipes of:

Signers of Our Declaration of Independence, Including:

Thomas Jefferson

John Hancock

Benjamin Franklin

John Adams

Richard Henry Lee

Thomas Nelson, Jr.

John Witherspoon

Signers of Our Constitution, Including:

George Washington

James Madison

Charles Cotesworth Pinckney

Robert Morris

Roger Sherman

Alexander Hamilton

Thomas Mifflin

Dedication

To my early descendants, Barnabus Horton of Leichestershire, England, who sailed to America on the *Swallow* some time between 1633 and 1638 with his wife Mary and their two sons, Joseph and Benjamin. They landed at Hampton, Massachusetts, and were Puritans;

And also to my Great great-grandmother Huldah Radike Horton, one of the finest and most famous horsewomen of her day. She had the honor of entertaining Lafayette in her home and riding at his side in a parade in his honor in Newburg, New York, in 1824. The French General and friend of the young Republic was making his second and final visit.

Contents

1

Introducing Baking Recipes of Our Founding Fathers

Baking in the American Colonies was far from an easy task. The women of the house made quite an art out of baking tasty loaves of bread, pastry, pies, cakes, cookies, and all of their other homemade goodies. In those days, homemakers couldn't always buy good flour. Almost every sack or barrel presented new baking problems. Flour always had to be tested for quality before using.

Here's how Mary Chew wrote it in her old receipt notes ledger in 1765. Miss Chew became the wife of William Paca (1740-1799) of Maryland in 1761. He would later sign the *Declaration of Independence* on August 2, 1776:

"As good a test of flour as can be had at sight, is to take up a handful and squeeze it tight; if good, when the hand is unclasped, the lines on the palm of the hand will be plainly defined on the ball of flour. Throw a little lump of dried flour against a smooth surface, if it falls like powder, it is bad."

In those days, the wood heated oven was not nearly as efficient as those used today. The method of measuring oven heat in the seventeenth and eighteenth centuries was simple but effective. Baking was always a matter of guess. The homemaker relied on when it *"felt"* hot enough to bake in. If the heat was excessive, it scorched the inquiring hand.

Consider the fact that the first Colonial women didn't have any sort of an oven in which to do her baking. As pointed out in the **EARLY AMERICAN COOKBOOK:**

"Big ovens of brick, always ready for baking, had been left behind in their old homes by the settlers. In the new land bricks were scarce. There was little known clay obtainable for brick making. Certainly none along the desolate shores of the broad Atlantic where the Pilgrims landed. And the Colonists were not at first equipped to manufacture bricks. So the Pilgrim mothers did their baking either in Dutch ovens of tin, set facing the open fire on the stone hearth with a tin shield to ward off the flames, or in an iron kettle with squat legs and a depression in the cover for hot coals to give the top heat."

Cookbooks used in the Colonies were initially brought over from England. One of the first to be reprinted in the colonies was **THE COMPLEAT HOUSEWIFE, OR ACCOMPLISHED GENTLEWWOMAN'S COMPANION,** written by E. Smith. William Parks in Williamsburg, Virginia, reprinted this in 1742.

THE ART OF COOKERY MADE PLAIN AND EASY, by Hannah Glasse, was published in 1747 and became a favorite of Colonial homemakers for many years. It contained this recipe that is attributed to the mother of Sarah Hatfield. Sarah was but 21 when she married Abraham Clark (1726-1794) in 1749. Clark later gained a measure of fame as one of the 56 heroic signers of the *Declaration of Independence.* Here's how Sarah wrote it:

"Tasty Cakes of Ginger Bread. Take whole Pound Butter, three Pounds Flour, whole Pound Sugar. Beat 2 Ounces finely beaten Ginger till it is fine powder. . Grate big Nutmeg. Put with other ingredients; then take whole Pound Molasses, a Coffeecupful Cream. Heat Molasses and Cream together. Work dough for Bread till stiff. Lay on Board with little Flour. Roll to thin Cookies. Cut in rounds with small glass turned over or Teacup. Or roll to ball in hands the size of Hickory Nut. Lay on Bake Pan. Bake in slack Oven."

Then in 1772, Susannah Carter's **THE FRUGAL HOUSEWIFE OR FEMALE COMPANION** was reprinted in Boston. Paul Revere made the printing plates for her cookbook. This was most popular with, and could be found in the homes of, many of the wives and mothers of the men who signed the *Declaration of Independence* and the *Constitution.*

Colonial Virginia's most widely known cookbook was commonly used in the homes of those who signed the *Declaration of Independence* and our *Constitution.* Shipped to America from England, it was to be found in the kitchens of most wives and mothers of the Signers. It's incredible title read:

"THE HOUSEKEEPER'S POCKET-BOOK, AND COMPLEAT FAMILY COOK: CONTAINING ABOVE TWELVE HUNDRED CURIOUS

AND UNCOMMON RECEIPTS IN COOKERY, PASTRY, PRESERVING, PICKLING, CANDYING, COLLARING. ETC. WITH PLAIN AND EASY INSTRUCTIONS FOR PREPARING AND DRESSING EVERY THING SUITABLE FOR AN ELEGANT ENTERTAINMENT, FROM TWO DISHES TO FIVE OR TEN, ETC. AND DIRECTIONS FOR RANGING THEM IN THEIR PROPER ORDER."

Another excellent example of how old recipes were written is found in Amelia Simmons' 48 page **AMERICAN COOKERY** published in 1796. This cookbook was also widely used in great many Colonial kitchens. It was the first originally American cookbook to be published in America. A recipe for *"Molasses Gingerbread"* is believed to have originally come from the mother of Nicholas Gilman (1755-1814) of New Hampshire, one of three lifelong bachelors who signed the *Constitution*. It reads as follows:

> *"One table spoon of cinnamon, some coriander or allspice, put to four tea spoons pearl ash, dissolved in half pint water, four pound flour, one quart molasses, four ounces butter, (if in summer rub in the butter, if in winter, warm the butter and molasses and pour to the spiced flour,) knead well 'till stiff, the more the better, the lighter and whiter it will be; bake brisk fifteen minutes; don't scorch; before it is put in, wash it with whites [egg whites] and sugar beat together."*

One of the most popular cakes, as well as the only cake made without bread dough in the Colonies, was that called *"The Nun's Cake."* The recipe for this special cake was carefully cherished and handed down as a prized heirloom from prior generations. It was no doubt, most often handwritten, and bequeathed from mother to daughter. This particular version of the recipe is believed to have been an original from the mother of Joseph Hewes (1730-1779), one of the 56 brave signers of the *Declaration of Independence*. Here it is:

> *"Take Three Pounds of Double-Refined Sugar beaten and then sifted, and Four Pounds of Fine Flour; Mix together and let them dry by the fire as the other materials are prepared. Then take Four Pounds of Fresh Butter, beat with Wood Spoon until Soft and Creamy. Then beat Thirty-Five Fresh Eggs,*

and leave out Sixteen Whites, Strain off Eggs from the Shells, And Beat them and the Butter together till all look like Butter. Then Put in Four or Five spoonfuls of Orange-Flower Water or Rose Water, and Beat more. Now take the Flour and Sugar, with Six Ounces of Caraway Seeds, and Strew them in by degrees, Beating it up all the while for Two Hours together. Put in as much as you want of Amber-Grease or Tincture of Cinnamon. Butter your Hoop, and leave to Stand three Hours in a Moderate Oven. Carefully Observe Always, when Beating Butter, to do it with a Cool Hand and Beat it Always one way in Deep Earthen Dish."

As you can readily see, most recipes found in cookbooks of the Colonial period were written as a descriptive paragraph. The paragraph contained all the ingredients needed, correct amounts to use, and how to properly mix them. Unlike today's recipes, it didn't have an orderly list of ingredients followed by simple instructions for preparing the cake, bread, or whatever was to be baked. On the other hand, many recipes handed down through a family were merely a handwritten list of ingredients without instructions telling what to do with them. Homemakers in the Colonies, when given such a recipe by a friend or neighbor, was expected to already know how to correctly mix the ingredients.

The Colonial homemaker depended on homemade yeast that varied greatly in strength from batch to batch. She made both liquid yeast and yeast cakes. Liquid yeast was commonly made and then bottled and stored until needed. Three kinds of yeast were especially popular with the early American homemaker:

Brewers Yeast or Barm
German or Compressed Yeast
Patent or Hop Yeast

The most popular yeast in the Colonies was the frothy brown, sour smelling, *Brewer's Yeast*. Pasty, easily crumbled *German Yeast* was also often used. This particular yeast would remain good for weeks if kept in a cool place. *Patent Yeast* was the cheapest and most extensively used of these ferments. *Potato Yeast* was a type of *Patent Yeast* commonly used. This particular recipe comes from the Meredith family. Their daughter, Elizabeth, later became the wife of George Clymer (1739-1813) in 1765. He went on to be a signer of both the *Declaration of Independence* and our *Constitution*. Here's the old Meridith family recipe:

"6 potatoes   2 tbls sugar
"4 tbls flour   ½ cup good yeast
"Peel potatoes and put in kettle with eight cups cold water.
Boil potatoes until they break. Leave potato water on fire but take out potatoes.

4

Mash them to a pulp while blending in flour and sugar. Then gradually wet with the hot potato water until it is used up. Allow to cool and when lukewarm add yeast and stir. Set aside in open bowl and warm place to ferment. When mixture ceases to effervesce, bottle and keep in cool place. This yeast is very nice and white. It is preferred by many who dislike the bitter taste of hops."

Other homemakers of the day used hops (dried flower clusters from the hop vine) to a great extent, especially when making yeast cakes. One old recipe is attributed to the mother of Elizabeth Sherburne. Elizabeth, a lovely and spirited young lady, would one day in 1775 become the wife of John Langdon (1741-1819). He would later have the honor of signing the *Constitution.* Mrs. Sherburne gives these directions:

> *"2 handfuls Hops...............Flour to suit*
> *"4 cups pared .... 2 tbls good Yeast*
> ` *and Sliced Potatoes   1 cup Indian Meal*

"Tie Hops in coarse muslin bag. Put with potatoes in small iron kettle with eight cups ice cold water. Bring to quick boil and cook 45 minutes. Remove Hops bag while water still boiling. Strain potatoes and boiling water through colander into large bowl. Stir enough flour into scalding liquor in kettle to make stiff batter. Beat well. Blend in yeast. Lay towel over bowl and set in warm place to rise. When light, stir in Indian Meal. Put on board and roll to sheet ¼ inch thick. Take a drinking glass and use it to cut into 3-inch diameter cakes. Allow to dry in sun or very slow oven. Take care they do not heat enough to actually bake. When entirely dry and cold, hang them up in a bag. Be sure to keep these cakes in a cool, dry place. They will be good indefinitely if properly stored. Use one cake for fair-sized loaf of bread. Soak in tepid water until soft, add pinch of soda, and mix with recipe."

Elizabeth Pettit, wife of Jared Ingersoll (1749-1822), Pennsylvania signer of our *Constitution,* wrote this tip regarding yeast:

> *"Yeast sometimes acquires a bitter taste from keeping, which is quite independent of that derived from hops. To remedy this, throw into the yeast a few clean coals freshly taken from the fire, but allowed to cool a little on the surface. The operation appears to depend on the power of freshly burnt charcoal to absorb gasses and remove offensive odors."*

Of course, the burnt charcoal was to be removed before using the yeast for baking homemade bread and other oven goodies.

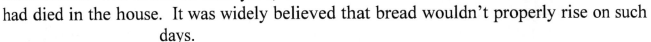

And here's a note of interest: Some homemakers in the Colonies were quite superstitious. They would refuse to bake bread at certain times. Sarah Hopkins, was the wife of Stephen Hopkins (1707-1785) of Rhode Island, one of 56 heroic signers of the *Declaration of Independence*. Sarah, as well as many other women of the time, would not consider baking bread whenever a dead animal was found in their yard, or when someone had died in the house. It was widely believed that bread wouldn't properly rise on such days.

Anne Carey Randolph was a lovely young woman who became the wife of Gouverneur Morris (1752-1816) in 1789. He had earlier signed both the *Articles of Confederation* and our *Constitution*. A baking poem written by her cleverly sums up the art of good baking:

"With weights and measures just and true,
"Oven of even heat,
"Well buttered tins and quiet nerves,
"Success will be complete."

2

Food in Colonial America

Of all the foods enjoyed by the early Colonists, oats were one of the first to be imported. Oats initially came to New England on a British ship in 1602. Settlers in Plymouth began planting oats. They soon became a food staple on Colonial breakfast tables and for baking. Oats were also extensively used as cattle feed.

The first wheat was sown in 1611 Colonial Virginia. And in 1626, samples of wheat grown in the Dutch Colony at New Netherlands were exhibited in Holland. Wheat was ordered from England in 1629 to be used as seed. It is probable that wheat was sown in the Plymouth Colony prior to 1629, although there is no record of this. In 1718, the Western Company first introduced wheat into the valley of the Mississippi.

Most people today know little or nothing about the vast availability of food in the American Colonies. Almost everything our early American ancestors ate came from the land in which they lived. Colonists planted seeds they brought with them from England. Indians introduced the Colonists to:

> potatoes...............pumpkins
> sweet potatoes........squash,
> peanuts...............wild rice

Indians also taught the settlers in the Colonies how to properly plant their gardens and grow their own crops. Every Colonist, with few exceptions, had their own family garden where they raised:

> sweet potatoes ....onions
> parsnips ....rice
> garlic ....carrots
> corn.......................turnips
> potatoes.................tomatoes

Tomatoes were known in the Colonies as "love apples." They were widely believed to be aphrodisiacs. Some Colonists were convinced the tomato was poisonous and, therefore, quite dangerous to eat.

Sweet potatoes, quickly became a popular favorite of the Colonists. They were included in a great number of baking recipes. Here's an old one for **Sweet Potato Corn Bread** as made by Mary Leach. She became wife of Richard Dobbs Spaight, Sr. (1758-1802) of North Carolina, one of 39 men who signed the *Constitution*:

"2 sweet potatoes.........2 tsp cinnamon
"2 sticks soft butter.......1 tsp baking soda
"8 eggs, beaten............2 cups cream
"1 cup maple sugar...... 4 cups cornmeal

"Take a fork and prick holes in the sweet potatoes. Put them in the oven and bake at 350 degrees for about 45 minutes. Set aside to cool. When they are cooled, peel off the skin and throw it away. Put sweet potatoes in a large wooden mixing bowl and mash to a pulp. Stir in the butter. Beat the eggs thoroughly in a smaller bowl. Add brown sugar, cinnamon and baking soda and blend nicely. Stir this mixture into the mashed sweet potatoes. Lastly, add the cream and cornmeal. Stir until a smooth batter is obtained. Pour into two greased 9 x 9-inch baking pans. Bake in moderate oven (350 degrees) for 50 minutes. The bread should be a golden brown when done."

Incidently, Margaret Brown, who became the wife of Thomas Stone (1743-1787), a Maryland signer of the *Declaration of Independence*, was a rather superstitious young woman. She believed, as many others in the Colonies did, that anything made with cornmeal should be eaten most often during the cold winter months. It was said to heat up the body. And she also would never fail to make a cross on top of her breads before slicing. This was to frighten Satan away from the family and keep him away from the home.

Fruit was readily available from local farms and orchards as well as from trees in the yards of the Colonists. Beacon Hill in Boston was the site of America's first apple orchard in 1625. Fruit trees were commonplace in the yards of Colonists, as were grape arbors. Wild berries were in abundance and easy to find. Therefore the Colonists had a nice supply of the following:

```
cherries…………..peaches
plums……………pears
apples……………apricots
cranberries……...mulberries
strawberries……..raspberries
gooseberries……..huckleberries
        blueberries
```

A 1717 pamphlet, **"DISCOURSE CONCERNING THE DESIGN'D ESTABLISHMENT OF A NEW COLONY TO THER SOUTH OF CAROLINA IN THE MOST DELIGHTFUL COUNTRY OF THE UNIVERSE,"** had this to say about food in the Colonies:

"Vines, naturally flourishing upon the Hills, bear Grapes in most luxuriant Plenty. They have every Growth which we possess in England, and almost every Thing that England wants besides. The Orange and the Limon [lemon] thrive in the same common Orchard with the Apple, and the Pear-Tree, Plumbs [plums], Peaches, Apricots, and Nectarins [nectarines] Bear from Stones in three years growing."

Domestic farm animals were raised on small farms and in the yards. These included sheep, pigs, cows and chickens. As a result, eggs, milk, cream and butter were plentiful and readily available for baking and the breakfast table. They, along with lard, quickly became household staples.

Butter made in the Colonies was always heavily salted. The woman of the house had to carefully rinse the salt from her butter before using it for baking. Butter was sometimes in short supply in the Colonies. When the woman of the house wanted to bake and had no butter on hand, she simply substituted finely ground salt pork as her shortening. Amelia Simmons,

how to purchase butter as well These pointers were long ago Meade. Miss Meade became the (1741-1811), signer of the from Pennsylvania. Here is how were worded:

"To have sweet the vegetable seasons,

in her 1796 **AMERICAN COOKERY,** told homemakers as how it was to be stored. given to Amelia by Catherine wife of Thomas Fitzsimons *Declaration of Independence* Catherine's original instructions

butter in dog days, and thro' send stone pots to honest, neat, and trusty dairy people, and procure it pack'd down in May, and let them be brought in the night, or cool rainy morning, covered with a clean cloth wet in cold water, and partake of no heat from the house, and set the pots in the coldest part of your cellar, or in the ice house. Some say that May butter thus preserved will go into the winter use, better than fall made butter."

Food, in some instances, was imported from England and the West Indies. Included were:

raisins.....................pineapples
almonds....................chocolate

In **REFRESHMENTS NOW AND THEN**, Patricia B. Mitchell offers this regarding chocolate in the Colonies:

"In the early 1700's, Rhode Island businessman Obadiah Brown established a 'chocklit' mill in which chocolate beans from the West Indies were ground. And in 1765 a chocolate factory financed by James Baker opened in Dorchester, Massachusetts. Thomas Jefferson praised 'the superiority of chocolate, both for health and nourishment.' "

A great variety of spices were also imported from the West Indies to add flavor to Colonial food preparations:

salt.......................nutmeg
cinnamon (cassia)..........pepper
marjoram...... ....mint
allspice ....caraway seeds
currants (raisins).........mustard
coriander...................parsley
sassafras...................dill
mace.......................sage
thyme......................rosemary

Homemakers made their own vinegar. Liquid yeast and yeast cakes were made by the Colonists with grape leaves as well as potatoes. One method for making yeast from grape leaves was given to my Great-great grandmother, Huldah Radike Horton, by Hannah Jones. Hannah would afterwards become the wife of William Floyd (1734-1821) of New York, one of the 56 heroic men who signed the *Declaration of Independence*. Huldah used this yeast on a regular basis when making bread for her family. Here is how Hannah Floyd had carefully transcribed the "*receipt*" in her cooking ledger:

"Use eight or ten leaves for a quart of yeast;
Boil them for ten minutes; Pour the hot liquor on the flour, the quantity of the latter being determined by whether the yeast is wanted thicke or thin; Use hop yeast to raise it to begin with, and afterwards that made of grape leaves. Dried leaves will be as good as fresh. If a dark film appears on the surface when rising, a little stirring will obviate it."

Following her fine yeast recipe, Mrs. Floyd then went on to offer this bit of information:

"Grape leaves make a yeast in some respects superior to hops, as the bread made from it rises sooner, and has not the peculiar taste which many object in that made from hops."

Since the Colonists didn't have refrigerators, root vegetables like potatoes and turnips were stored below ground in root cellars. Fruits were canned after making them into jams, jellies and apple butter. Cherries were often brandied.

Sugar and honey were available to the Colonists for use as a sweetener. In fact, a few short years after the American Revolution (in 1791), the first sugar refinery was opened in New Orleans, Louisiana. Prior to this, New England settlers initially imported all their sugar from Maderia and Holland. It was later imported it from the West Indies and Barbados.

According to Patricia Mitchell, this time in **PILGRIMS, PURITANS AND CAVALIERS**:

"The yellowish-looking sugar was formed in hard cone shapes up to two or three feet in length and weighing up to 55 pounds. The expensive cone, often packaged in blue paper, was covered with netting to keep flies away. Housewives sometimes strung smaller loaves from the ceiling in order to prevent animals and other pests from getting to them. A piece of tin was positioned on the string to prevent ants from climbing down from the ceiling."

Mrs. Mitchell goes on to explain how sugar was used by Colonial homemakers:

"To use the sugar, chunks were knocked off with a hammer or cut with 'sugar snippers.' Next the homemaker had to pulverize the sugar by pounding it or grinding it with a mortar and pestle. Some women soaked the sugar in water to soften it. (The custom developed of suspending a sugarloaf over the tea table so that guests could bite off sugar to use to sweeten their tea!)."

Maple trees were tapped to obtain sap. This sap was boiled down to make maple syrup and maple sugar. We owe the discovery of maple syrup to the American Indians. It is said that a squaw, short on water, boiled some sap instead and found the end result to be delightful.

Molasses was first imported in the late 1600s from the West Indies. It became a food staple in every home. The thick, dark liquid was poured over pancakes and eaten with other breakfast dishes. Molasses was also used for sweetening countless baking recipes including breads, cakes and cookies. And it didn't take long before it was being distilled to make rum for use as a flavoring agent in many baking recipes. Other drinks sometimes used to flavor a variety of baked goods in the Colonies were:

coffee…………….....beer

tea…………..………ale

cyder (cider)……….wine

Apparently, food never was in short supply in Colonial America. Read what George Percy had to say after he arrived in the Colonies in 1607. He recorded this observation:

"We found store of turkey nests and many egges. … This countrey is a fruitful soile, bearing many goodly and fruitful trees as mulberries, cherries, walnuts and vines in great abundance."

Jamestown, Virginia, had America's first cow in 1611. **LEAH AND RACHEL** was a seventeenth century publication that told of the availability of meat and other foods in Colonial Virginia:

"Cattle and Hogs are every where, which yeeld beef, veal, milk, butter, cheese … These with the help of Orchards and Gardens… certainly cannot but be sufficient for a good diet … considering how plentifully they are."

Yes, apparently food *was not* in short supply in the Colonies!

3

Bread Baking
in the Homes of the Signers

Eight Pointers on Making Good Bread -- Elizabeth Witherspoon's Suggestions

1. The first thing required for making wholesome bread is the utmost cleanliness. The next is the purity and freshness of all necessary ingredients. In addition, there must be attention and care throughout whole process of making and baking.

2. Salt is always used in bread making. Its flavor destroys the insipid raw state of flour. It is also used because it makes dough rise better.

3. In mixing with milk, the milk should be boiled – not just scalded. It must be heated to boiling point over pan of hot water, then set aside to cool before mixing. Simply heating milk will not prevent bread from turning sour while rising. Milk should be thoroughly boiled and scalded. It should always be used when just room temperature.

4. Too small a proportion of yeast will cause bread to be heavy. Insufficient time allowed for the dough to rise will cause same problem

5. Yeast used must be good and fresh if the bread is to be digestible and nice. Stale yeast produces a sour fermentation instead on one that is sweet. This will flavor the bread and make it disagreeable. Poor thin yeast produces imperfect fermentation. The result is a heavy, unwholesome loaf.

6. If dough is permitted to overwork itself -- that is to say, if mixing and kneading are neglected when it has reached the proper point for either – sour bread will probably be the consequence in warm weather, and bad bread in any kind of weather.

7. Kneading dough is one important key to good bread. Knead hard to manipulate every part of dough. Turn repeatedly over and around. Knead faithfully, from all sides, until dough rebounds after smart blow with fist on center of mass.

8. Placing it so near a fire as to make any part of it hot will also endanger the goodness of a loaf of bread. A gentle and equal degree of heat is required for its proper fermentation.

John Witherspoon (1722 or 1723 – 1794)

Heritage: Scottish. Born in small village near Edinburg. Descendant of the Great Reformer, John Knox. Immigrated to America in 1768.

Religion: Christian. Son of a Calvinist clergyman who was Minister of a Scottish church at Yester. Licensed preacher.

Education: Tutored in exclusive private school in Haddington. Theological studies at University of Endinburg when 14 years old. Masters degree in 1739. Divinity degree at age 20 in 1743.

Marriage: Twice married. First wife in 1783. She died in 1789. Wed again at 68 years in 1791 to a 24-year old widow.

Children: 10 children born in first marriage. Five died before the family immigrated to America. Had two more children with second wife.

Interesting Highlights: One of 56 men to sign the *Declaration of Independence*. Hancock was the *only* one to sign on July 4, 1776. Another 49 signed on August 2. Six signed at a later date – they were Richard Henry Lee, Gerry, McKean, Thorton, Wolcott and Wythe.

One of four Signers who had been trained for the ministry. The others were Hall, Hooper and Paine.

Held distinction of being the *only* active clergyman among the Signers.

One of eight foreign born Signers. The others were Gwinnett, Lewis, Robert Morris, Smith, Taylor, Thornton and Wilson.

One of only two Signers to have been born in Scotland. The other was the distinguished James Wilson.

Had no superior or match as a theological writer and teacher.

Served on more than 100 committees in the Continental Congress.

President of the College of New Jersey (presently Princeton).

Quotable Quote: John Adams called him *"A true son of liberty. So he was. But first, he was a Son of the Cross."*

Heroic Deed: Signing the *Declaration*. John Witherspoon knew that should the struggle for independence fail, an ignominious death by hanging would most certainly be his punishment.

Refused an offer of amnesty from British Governor Gage in June 1775.

Little Known Facts: Oldest son, James, served in Continental Army as an aide to General Nash. Killed during the Battle of Germantown.

Second son, John, went down with a ship at sea in 1795.

Lost eyesight two years prior to his death. Had to be assisted to the pulpit. Still able to preach a sermon with all the vigor of his youthful years.

Price Paid for Signing: When the British occupied New Jersey in November of 1776, they used Princeton to billet their troops and as stable for their horses. Everything was destroyed and all library books were burned.

Best Bread Baking Tips –
Given by Elizabeth Sherman

1. As a general rule, the oven for baking bread should be rather quick (375 degrees). The heat must be so regulated as to penetrate dough without hardening the outside.
2. The oven door should not be opened after bread is put in until dough has set or become firm. If cool air is admitted it will have an unfavorable effect on loaves.
3. The dough should rise and the bread begin to brown after about 15 minutes, but only slightly. Bake from 50 to 60 minutes. It should be brown, not black or whitish brown, but brown all over when well baked.

4. When bread is finished baking, immediately remove loaves from pans. Place them where the air will freely circulate around them. This will carry off the gas, which has formed within the loaf. It is no longer needed.
5. Never leave hot bread in pan. Never leave on a pine table or it will sweat and absorb the pitchy odor and taste of the wood. If you like crisp crusts do not cover the loaves.
6. To give the soft, tender, wafer-like consistency many people prefer, wrap while still hot in several thicknesses of bread cloth. A yard and a half square of coarse table linen makes best bread cloth. Keep in good supply. Use them for no other purpose.
7. When cold, remove cloth and put loaves in stone jar, tin box, or large stone pot. If cloth is left on it will absorb the moisture and give breads an unpleasant taste and odor. Keep box or jar tightly covered. Carefully clean out all crumbs and stale pieces before using. Scald and dry it thoroughly every two or three days.

Roger Sherman (1721 – 1793)

Heritage: English descent.   Born in Newton, Massachusetts.   Parents immigrated to the Colonies from England in the late 1600s or early 1700s.

Religion: Devout Christian.   John Adams described Sherman as *"...an old Puritan, as honest as an angel and as firm in the cause of American Independence as Mount Atlas."* Also see quote below.

Education: Early formal education extremely limited.   Avid reader.   Self-taught in mathematics, astronomy and numerous other subjects.
Always kept books open on the workbench while repairing shoes.   Studied law by reading books borrowed from local attorneys.

Marriage: Twice married.   Wed first wife, Elizabeth Hartwell, in 1749.   He was 28.   Little is known about Elizabeth other than she was a fine Christian young woman.   She died 11 years later in 1760.   Remarried, this time to Rebecca Prescott.   She was 20 and he was 42 at this time.

Children: Seven children born to first union.   Eight more born to he and second wife.   All but one lived to maturity.   Rebecca raised her own eight children as well as the seven born to Roger and Elizabeth.

Interesting Highlights: One of 56 men to sign the *Declaration of Independence*.   Hancock was the *only* one to sign on July 4, 1776.   Another 49 signed on August 2.   Six signed at a later date – they were Richard Henry Lee, Gerry, McKean, Thorton, Wolcott and Wythe.

One of six Signers who also affixed his signature to the *Constitution*.   The others were Clymer, Franklin, Robert Morris, Read and Wilson.

Seconded Benjamin Franklin's motion that congress be opened each day with a prayer.

Made an astounding 128 speeches at the Constitutional Convention.

Quotable Quote: *"I believe there is one only living and true God, existing in three persons, the Father, the Son, and the Holy Ghost ... that the Scriptures of the old and new testaments are a revelation from God, and a complete rule to direct us as how we may glorify and enjoy him."*

`**Heroic Deed:** Signing the *Declaration*.   Roger Sherman knew that should the struggle for independence fail, an ignominious death by hanging would most certainly be his punishment.

Refused an offer of amnesty from British Governor Gage in June 1775

Little Known Fact: Only man to sign all four of the main founding documents: *Articles of Association* (1774); *Declaration of Independence* (1776); *Articles of Confederation* (1777) and *Constitution* (1787).

Price Paid for Signing: All the Signers, including Sherman, suffered monetary losses because of their connection with the cause.   Some were brought to the brink of financial ruin, or even worse, abject poverty.

Homemade White Bread --
Mary Morris Made This for Robert

16 cups flour	1 tbls butter (or lard)
1 tbls sugar	2 cups warm milk
1 tbls salt	2 cups warm water
1 cup yeast	

Start this bread preparation in the evening before going to bed. Bread mixed at 9:00 P.M. will be ready to mold into loaves or rolls by 6:00 A.M. If bread is mixed early in the morning, it will be ready to mold and bake in the afternoon. Sift the flour into large pan or bowl. Put sugar, salt and butter in a separate smaller bowl. Add spoonful or two of boiling water, enough to dissolve ingredients. Add milk and warm water for wetting purposes. Now add yeast. Slowly stir in flour. Blend thoroughly and cover with heavy cloth. Set in warm place. Leave alone to rise for 7 to 8 hours. When properly risen, thickly flour kneading board and begin kneading. Be sure to flour hands to avoid sticking. Punch dough with palm of hand or fist until it becomes a flat cake. Fold over and knead some more. Keep kneading a minimum of 20 minutes. As a general rule of thumb, the more time taken for kneading, the better the bread.

Divide dough into four equal segments. Carefully form into 4 loaves. Put each loaf in lightly greased bread pan. Again set these in warm place and cover with heavy towel or cloth. Let rise until nearly double in size. When ready, place loaves in moderately hot oven, hot enough to brown teaspoonful flour in one minute (375 degrees). Bake for 40 to 50 minutes or until done. Test for doneness by sticking toothpick in center of each loaf. Toothpick will come out clean if bread is done. When finished baking,  immediately take out of pans. If crust is hard, wrap each hot loaf in thick towel or cloth as soon as it is taken from oven. Stand loaves tilted up against bread pans until cooled.

Robert Morris (1733 – 1806)

Heritage: English. His father, a Liverpool merchant, immigrated to America sometime in the mid-1700s. A very young Robert was left behind in the care of his grandmother. He was sent for at the age of 13-years.

Religion: Christian. His wife was the daughter of the late venerable Bishop of Pennsylvania.

Education: Brilliant young man. Placed in private school in Philadelphia. Chided by his father for his slowness in learning, Robert replied: *"Why, sir, I have learned all that he could teach me."* The 15-year old was immediately placed in the exporting business. With no more formal education, he became a resounding success and one of the richest men in the Colonies.

Marriage: Wed to Mary White in 1769. He was 35, she 20. Mary was from a wealthy, socially prominent Philadelphia family. She was described as *"tall, graceful and commanding, with a stately dignity of manner."* They were happily married for 37-years.

Children: Five sons and two daughters. Some sources disagree and say they had only four children – three sons and one daughter.

Interesting Highlights: One of 56 men to sign the *Declaration of Independence.* Hancock was the *only* one to sign on July 4, 1776. Another 49 signed on August 2. Six signed at a later date – they were Richard Henry Lee, Gerry, McKean, Thorton, Wolcott and Wythe.

One of six men to sign both the *Declaration of Independence* and the *Constitution.* The others were Clymer, Franklin, Read, Sherman and Wilson.

One of five to sign both the *Constitution* and *Articles of Confederation.* The others were Daniel Carroll, Dickinson, Gouverneur Morris and Sherman.

One of only two men to sign all three of our nation's basic documents – the *Declaration of Independence, Constitution* and *Articles of Confederation.* The other Signer was Robert Sherman.

Quotable Quote: Astonished and indignant upon hearing about the Battle of Lexington, he said this: *"I vow to dedicate the rest of my life to the cause of freedom."*

Heroic Deed: Signing the *Declaration.* Robert Morris knew that should the struggle for independence fail, an ignominious death by hanging would most certainly be his punishment.

Refused an offer of amnesty from British Governor Gage in June 1775.

Little Known Fact: One of two Signers of the *Declaration of Independence* who was born in England. The other was Button Gwinnett.

Price Paid for Signing: All the Signers, including Robert Morris, suffered monetary losses because of their connection with the cause. Some were brought to the brink of financial ruin, or even worse, abject poverty.

Wheat and Indian Bread –
Martha Devotion Huntington's Receipt

6 cups water, boiling	24 cups whole-wheat flour
1 tbls salt	or
White cornmeal to suit	28 cups regular flour
4 cups water, cold	½ cup yeast
½ tsp baking soda	

Put 6 cups of water in large pot or kettle over the fire. Bring to boil and take from stove. Add salt. Stir in enough white corn meal until a thick batter is formed. Continue

to stir for 10 minutes so the mixture doesn't burn. Then pour batter into large mixing bowl or pan. Stir in 4 cups cold water and allow the mixture to become lukewarm.

Put all the flour in another large mixing bowl or pan. Make hollow middle of flour. When the above corn meal batter is cool enough to bear your hand, pour into pan of flour. Add yeast to this. Lastly add baking soda dissolved in a little hot water. Blend all ingredients with the flour and work into smooth dough. Knead nearly an hour. Then strew a little flour over the dough, cover with thickly folded cloth, and set aside in warm place for 5 to 6 hours. When the dough is light [has risen], knead again until it is worked down. Cover and set aside in warm place to rise for another hour. When risen, knead another 30 minutes to an hour.

Break into 6 loaves. Place each loaf in well-greased bread pan. Again set aside in warm place and cover with heavy towel or cloth. Leave until loaves have doubled in size. When ready, put loaves into moderately quick oven (375 degrees) and bake 45 to 60 minutes or until done. Test for doneness by sticking toothpick in center of each loaf. Toothpick will come out clean if bread is done. When finished baking, immediately take out of pans. If crust is hard, wrap each hot loaf in a heavy towel or cloth as soon as it is taken from oven. Stand loaves tilted up against bread pans until cooled.

Samuel Huntington (1732 – 1796)

Heritage: English descent. Born in Windham, Connecticut, on July 20. Early family settlers immigrated to Connecticut from England sometime in the mid-1600s or early 1700s.

Religion: Devout Christian. See quote below.

Education: Father a farmer who saw little need for formal education. Samuel attended what were called "common schools" in the area. Yet through diligent study, he mastered fluent Latin, both in speech and writing. Studied law at age 22, using legal books borrowed from a local attorney (as did fellow Signer of the *Declaration of Independence,* Roger Sherman). Awarded honorary degrees from Yale, Dartmouth and Princeton.

Marriage: Married lovely 22-year old Martha Devotion in 1761. She was oldest daughter of a minister. Samuel was 30. Martha died in 1794 at 56 years of age. Her husband passed away two years later at the age of 65.

Children: None. Adopted three children of Samuel's brother. One child, Samuel, became Governor of Ohio in 1794.

Interesting Highlights: One of 56 men to sign the *Declaration of Independence.* Hancock was the *only* one to sign on July 4, 1776. Another 49 signed on August 2. Six signed at a later date – they were Richard Henry Lee, Gerry, McKean, Thorton, Wolcott and Wythe.

Presided over the adoption of the *Articles of Confederation* (1781) that initiated the formation of a new government when 13 semi-independent States agreed to form a *"firm league of friendship."*

An extremely shy man. Many people mistook this for haughtiness.

Led the battle in Connecticut for ratification of the U. S. *Constitution.*

Held variety of political positions under British rule. Resigned them all in 1774 as he began to side more with the Colonial independence movement.

Quotable Quote: An 1848 textbook reported that Huntington *"lived a life of the irreproachable and sincere Christian. ... Hence as a devoted Christian and a true patriot, he never swerved from duty, or looked back after he had placed his hand to the work."*

Heroic Deed: Signing the *Declaration*. Samuel Huntington knew that should the struggle for independence fail, an ignominious death by hanging would most certainly be his punishment.

Refused an offer of amnesty from British Governor Gage in June 1775.

Little Known Fact: Appointed President of the Continental Congress (1779 – 1781), which was at that time, the highest office in the new nation.

Price Paid for Signing: All the Signers, including Huntington, suffered monetary losses because of their connection with the cause. Some were brought to the brink of financial ruin, or even worse, abject poverty.

Rye Yeast Bread –
Elizabeth Heyward Fixed it This Way

4 cups warm water	17-1/2 cups rye flour
Flour to suit	¾ tbls salt
¼ cup yeast	½ tsp baking soda

This bread dough was usually prepared in the evening before going to bed. Bread mixed at 9:00 P.M. would be ready to make into loaves by 6:00 A.M. Take 1 quart warm water (4 cups) and pour into a large pitcher or pan. Stir in as much flour as necessary to make smooth batter. Blend in yeast. Cover with folded towel or other heavy cloth. Set in warm place to rise. This is called "setting the sponge." Leave overnight.

In the morning, put all the rye flour into large mixing bowl or tray. Make hollow in middle. Pour in sponge. Add salt. Lastly stir in baking soda dissolved in little warm water. Mix everything into a smooth dough, adding as much warm water as may be necessary. Cover with heavy towel or cloth. Set in warm place to rise for at least 3 hours. When dough has risen, place on thickly floured kneading board and start to knead. Be sure to flour hands to avoid sticking. Punch dough with the palm of hand or fist until it becomes a flat cake. Fold over and knead more. Keep kneading a minimum of 20 minutes. As a general rule of thumb, the more time taken for kneading, the better the bread turns out.

Divide dough into equal segments. Carefully form into 3 or 4 loaves. Put each loaf in lightly greased bread pan. Again set these in warm place and cover with heavy towel or cloth. Let rise until nearly double in size. When ready, place loaves in moderately quick oven (375 degrees) and bake 45 to 60 minutes or until done. Test for doneness by sticking toothpick in center of each loaf. Toothpick will come out clean if bread is done. When finished baking, immediately take from pans. If crust is hard, wrap each loaf in thick towel or cloth. Stand loaves tilted up against bread pans until cooled.

Thomas Heyward (1746 – 1809)

Heritage: English. Born in St. Lukes Parish, South Carolina, at the Old House Plantation. His father, one of the richest planters in the province, had immigrated to America from England sometime in the early 1700s.

Religion: Devout Christian. See below quote.

Education: Attended the best private schools in the area. Mastered Latin. Fluently read the works of Roman historians and poets in that language. Studied law under Mr. Parsons, a highly regarded attorney at that time. Then sent to England to further his legal studies.

Marriage: Twice married. Wed Elizabeth Matthew in 1767 or 1768 when he was around 21. She was a most amiable and accomplished young woman. She died in 1781. Remarried , this time to Elizabeth Savage.

Children: He and the Matthew girl had five children. All but one died as infants. His marriage to Elizabeth Savage produced three more children.

Interesting Highlights: One of 56 men to sign the *Declaration of Independence*. Hancock was the *only* one to sign on July 4, 1776. Another 49 signed on August 2. Six signed at a later date – they were Richard Henry Lee, Gerry, McKean, Thorton, Wolcott and Wythe.

One of the first men in South Carolina to openly resist the oppressive measures of the British.

From the ***Stamp Act*** to the ***Battle of Lexington***, he consistently and zealously supported and promoted the patriot cause. This activity made him a leader in the South Carolina revolutionary movement.

Last Signer of the *Declaration of Independence* to die. Passed away at 63 years of age.

Quotable Quote: *"The general and basic principles of Christianity are those identical principles on which our independence was achieved. I absolutely believe now, as I absolutely believed then, that these same Christian principles are eternal and they are as unchanging as the existence of God."*

Heroic Deed: Signing the *Declaration*. Thomas Heyward knew that should the struggle for independence fail, an ignominious death by hanging would most certainly be his punishment.

Refused an offer of amnesty from British Governor Gage in June 1775.

Little Known Fact: Held a commission in the Continental Army. Saw action with fellow Signer, Edward Rutledge, in a skirmish with the British while defending Beaufort, South Carolina.

Price Paid for Signing: Hunted down like a criminal. The British made great efforts to capture him, but to no avail. All the Signers suffered monetary losses because of their connection with the cause. Some were brought to the brink of financial ruin, or even worse, abject poverty.

Blood Bread Receipt –
Hamilton Family Hand-Me-Down

1 yeast cake   1-1/3 cups water, lukewarm
10 cups flour   1/8 cup salt
1-1/2 cups uncoagulated beef blood

Crumble cake of yeast in large wooden mixing bowl and blend with a little lukewarm water. When completely dissolved, add enough flour to make thin batter. Put balance of flour in large pan and make hollow in center. Pour batter from mixing  bowl into hollow space and sprinkle a little flour over the top. Cover pan with heavy towel or cloth. Put in warm place for ½ hour and let rise.

When ferment has risen (when the flour sprinkled over the top begins to crack), add lukewarm water in which salt has been dissolved. Lastly, add beef blood. Work into a soft, smooth and pliable dough. Place dough on heavily floured kneading board and knead thoroughly. Be sure to flour hands to avoid sticking. Punch dough with the palm of hand or fist until it becomes a flat cake. Fold over and knead more. Keep kneading a minimum of 20 minutes. The more kneading, the better the bread.

Divide dough into 4 equal segments. Carefully form into 4 loaves. Put each loaf in lightly greased bread pan. Again set these in warm place and cover with heavy towel or cloth. Let rise until nearly double in size. When ready, bake in moderate oven (350 degrees) for 40 to 50 minutes or until done. Test for doneness by sticking toothpick in center of each loaf. Toothpick will come out clean if bread is done. When finished baking, immediately take out of pans. If crust is hard, wrap each hot loaf in thick towel or cloth. Stand loaves tilted up against bread pans until cooled.

Alexander Hamilton (1757 -- 1804)

Heritage: Scottish-English-French. Born in the West Indies, the illegitimate son from a common law marriage. His mother was a planter's daughter of English-French descent. His father was a Scottish traveling salesman who deserted his family.

Religion: Christian. On his deathbed, he said: *"I have a tender reliance on the mercy of the Almighty, through the merits of the Lord Jesus Christ. I am a sinner. I look to him for mercy. Pray for me."*

Education: Most of his basic education came about through tutoring by a Presbyterian clergyman. A brilliant thinker, he taught himself to speak and write fluent French. Also studied law on his own and eventually opened a practice in Albany, New York. Attended King's College (presently Columbia University) in 1773 at the age of 16, but his formal schooling was interrupted by the Revolutionary War.

Marriage: Married Elizabeth Schuyler in 1780. She came from a filthy rich and politically powerful New York family.

Children: Eight children were born of this union.

Interesting Highlights: One of 39 men who signed the *Constitution*.

Unhappy as a child in the West Indies, he ran away and immigrated to America in 1772 when only 15-years of age.

Upon his arrival in the Colonies, he enthusiastically joined in the fight for American independence.

Although of modest origins, Hamilton rose to become one of the young Republic's brightest stars.

One of General Washington's closest friends and most trusted advisors during the Revolutionary War.

Served in every major campaign during the War in 1776 and 1777.

Hamilton's life ended tragically when mortally wounded in a duel with Aaron Burr, a man who was his deadly political adversary and a person he despised. Hamilton was heard to mutter: *"I have lived like a man, but I die as a fool."* He died in his late forties while in the prime of life.

Quotable Quote: *"The best we can hope for concerning the people at large is that they be properly armed."*

Heroic Deed: Refused an offer of amnesty from British Governor Gage in June 1775.

Little Known Fact: Only man to sign the *Constitution* who was born in the West Indies.

Price Paid for Signing: All the Signers, including Hamilton, suffered monetary losses because of their connection with the cause. Some were brought to the brink of financial ruin, or even worse, abject poverty.

Compressed Yeast Bread –
Mary Paca Made This for Her Family

1 ounce compressed yeast   12 cups flour, sifted
2 cups lukewarm water   1-tsp salt

Put yeast and lukewarm water a large mixing bowl. Stir just enough to completely dissolve yeast. Then add enough flour to make thick batter. Cover bowl with a thick towel or cloth. Set in warm place to rise. If the proper temperature, the batter (sponge) will appear foamy and light within 30 minutes. Now stir into this sponge the salt dissolved in a little warm water. Slowly add the rest of the flour and sufficient warm water to make dough stiff enough to knead. Put dough ball on heavily floured kneading board. Be sure to flour hands to avoid sticking. Knead from 5 to 10 minutes, longer if time permits. Divide into two loaves. Knead again for at least 10 more minutes. Put each loaf into buttered bread baking tin. Cover with thick towel or cloth. Again set in warm place to rise twice their height. When risen, put into moderately quick oven (375-degrees). Bake 45 to 60 minutes or until done. Test for doneness by sticking toothpick in center of  each loaf. Toothpick will come out clean if bread is done. When finished baking, immediately take out of pans. If crust is hard, wrap each hot loaf in heavy towel or cloth as soon as it is taken from oven. Stand loaves tilted up against the bread pans until cooled. **NOTE**: *This bread has a major advantage over other yeast breads. It is finished and ready to eat inside of 3 hours. Others usually require from 12 to 14 hours to properly prepare and then to bake.*

William Paca (1740 – 1799)

Heritage: . Heritage not known with certainly. Believed to be of Italian descent. Born at Chilbury Hall near Abingdon, Maryland.

Religion: Devout Christian. Was known best as *"a good Christian man of pure and spotless character."* Also see quote below.

Education: Privately tutored all during childhood and as young adult. Matriculated at the College of Philadelphia (now University of Pennsylvania) when only 15-years old. Upon graduation, was tutored in law by prominent Annapolis attorney.

Marriage: Twice married. Mary Chew became first wife in 1761. She was direct descendant of John Chew who had arrived in Jamestown in 1622. She died a year before the start of the Revolutionary War. Paca again married, this time to Anne Harrison in 1777. She died three years later in 1780.

Children: He and Mary had five children. Only one, their son, John, lived. He and Anne had one child that died in early childhood.

Interesting Highlights: One of the first men of any stature in Maryland to fearlessly and zealously espouse the patriot cause for independence from British oppression.

Won seat in Colonial Legislature and thereby became close friends with Samuel Chase and many others who were protesting British subjugation.

Elected to be a Maryland delegate to the Second Continental Congress convened on May 10, 1775, at Philadelphia's State House.

One of 56 men to sign the *Declaration of Independence*. Hancock was the *only* one to sign on July 4, 1776. Another 49 signed on August 2. Six signed at a later date – they were Richard Henry Lee, Gerry, McKean, Thorton, Wolcott and Wythe.

Served bravely in the Maryland militia during 1777.

Quotable Quote: *"My religion, simply stated, is genuine Christianity, the religion of Jesus Christ and His apostles. To this we attribute our free form of government."*

Heroic Deed: Signing the *Declaration*. William Paca knew that should the struggle for independence fail, an ignominious death by hanging would most certainly be his punishment.

Refused an offer of amnesty from British Governor Gage in June 1775.

Little Known Fact: He along with Samuel Adams and Thomas Jefferson were against the poll tax because it was being used to pay the salaries of Anglican clergymen who were representing the established church.

Price Paid for Signing: All the Signers, including Paca, suffered monetary losses because of their connection with the cause. Some were brought to the brink of financial ruin, or even worse, abject poverty.

French Bread –
Margaret Stone's Finest

2 cups milk	1/2 cup yeast
4 tbls butter, melted	1 tsp salt
or	2 eggs
4 tbls lard melted	8 cups flour

Thoroughly blend in large wooden mixing bowl the milk, melted butter or lard (or half butter and half lard), yeast, salt and eggs. Beat well and slowly stir in flour. Cover with heavy towel or cloth and set aside in warm place to rise. When dough has risen to double its original size, make into 2 large balls of bread. Lay both loaves on flat, well-greased baking tin. Cut diagonal gashes across top of each just before putting into oven. Bake for 30 to 45 minutes in moderately quick oven (375 degrees), or until done. Test for doneness by sticking toothpick in center of each loaf. Toothpick will come out clean if bread is done. When finished baking, immediately take from pans and set aside to cool.

Thomas Stone (1743 – 1787)

Heritage: Scottish. Born on father's estate, Poynton Manor, a plantation near Welcome in Charles County, Maryland. His family immigrated to America from Scotland sometime in the late 1600s or early 1700s.

Religion: Devout Christian. Denomination unknown. Great and zealous reader of the *Bible*. See quote below.

Education: Tutored extensively at home as a child and young adult. Was immediately thereafter apprenticed to a prominent Annapolis lawyer.

Marriage: Wed young woman named Margaret Brown, in 1768. She was from wealthy family. Her father had immigrated to America from England in 1708. Margaret died at the early age of 34-years in 1787.

Children: Three – one son and two daughters.

Interesting Highlights: One of 56 men to sign the *Declaration of Independence*. Hancock was the *only* one to sign on July 4, 1776. Another 49 signed on August 2. Six signed at a later date – they were Richard Henry Lee, Gerry, McKean, Thorton, Wolcott and Wythe.

His father had originally come to the Colonies with little more than the clothes on his back.

Elected to be a delegate to the First Continental Congress that convened on September 5, 1774, at Carpenter's Hall in Philadelphia. Adjourned on October 26 – a session of only 52 days.

Grief stricken when wife died in 1787 after more than a decade of failing health. Couldn't work and couldn't bring himself to attend sessions of the Continental Congress. Died a few months later, on October 5, 1787, while waiting for a ship in Alexandria, Virginia, to take him on a visit to England.

Quotable Quote: Stone, as did all the others who signed the *Declaration of Independence*, read, fully understood and agreed with this statement: *"For the support of this declaration, with a firm reliance on the protection of the Divine Providence, we mutually pledge to each other, our lives, our fortunes, and our sacred honor."*

Heroic Deed: Signing the *Declaration*. Thomas Stone knew that should the struggle for independence fail, an ignominious death by hanging would most certainly be his punishment.

Refused an offer of amnesty from British Governor Gage in June 1775

Little Known Fact: Extremely shy and unobtrusive man. This apparently prohibited him from being a more outspoken and prominent member of the Continental Congress

Price Paid for Signing: All the Signers, including Stone, suffered monetary losses because of their connection with the cause. Some were brought to the brink of financial ruin, or even worse, abject poverty.

Delicate Rice Bread –
Favorite of Samuel Adams'

4 cups warm water   2 tbls butter
¾ cup yeast   4 cups flour
1 tbls sugar   6 cups warm milk
2-1/4 cups rice flour

Pour warm water into large wooden mixing bowl. Beat in yeast, sugar, butter and flour. Cover with heavy towel or cloth and set aside in warm place to rise for 5 hours. When properly risen, stir in warm milk. Wet rice flour with little cold milk and stir until it becomes thin paste. Boil 4 minutes. Allow to cool to about 100 degrees and then stir into the previously made batter. If blend isn't thick enough to work into good dough, add a little more regular flour. Turn dough out on floured kneading board. Knead thoroughly for minimum of 15 minutes. Form dough into 2 to 3 loaves. Place in well-greased bread baking pans. Cover with heavy towel or cloth and set in warm place. Let rise again until loaves have about doubled in size and are light. When ready, put loaves in moderately quick oven (375 degrees). Bake 35 to 45 minutes.  Test for doneness by sticking toothpick in center of each loaf. Toothpick will come out clean if bread is done. When finished baking, immediately take out of pans. If crust is hard, wrap each hot loaf in a heavy towel or cloth as soon as it is taken from the oven. Stand loaves tilted against bread pans until cooled. **NOTE:** *If rice flour unavailable, boil 1 cup whole rice and mash to thin paste. Use in place of rice flour called for in the recipe.*

Samuel Adams (1722 – 1803)

Heritage: English. Born in Boston, Massachusetts. Ancestors were Pilgrims. Descendant of Henry Adams who fled from religious persecution during the reign of Charles 1. An ancestor was John Alden who sailed to America on the Mayflower.

Religion: Christian. He once said: *"The rights of the Colonists as Christians ... may be best understood by reading and carefully studying ... the New Testament."* Also see quote below.

Education: Tutored at the prestigious Boston Latin School for his college prep. Entered Harvard when 14 and graduated with honors in 1740 when only 18. Tutored in law for a short time.

Marriage: Twice married. In October of 1749, he married 24-year old Elizabeth Checkley. She died on July 25, 1757. On December 6, 1757, he remarried, this time to 29-year old Elizabeth Wells.

Children: He and his first wife had five children. Only two, Hannah and Samuel, Jr., lived to maturity.

Interesting Highlights: He and his cousin, John Adams, were two of the 49 men who signed the *Declaration of Independence* on August 2, 1776. Six others signed the *Declaration* at a later date. They were Gerry, Richard Henry Lee, McKean, Thornton, Wolcott and Wythe. John Hancock was only man to sign on July 4.

He once said: *"The right to freedom is a gift of the Almighty."*

Offered the resolution for a First Continental Congress that was convened in Carpenter's Hall, Philadelphia, on September 5, 1774.

Best known as "The Father of the American Revolution."

Quotable Quote: After signing the Declaration of Independence, he declared: *"We have this day restored the Sovereign to whom all men ought to be obedient. He reigns in Heaven and from the rising to the setting of the sun, let His kingdom come."*

Heroic Deed: Signing the Declaration. Samuel Adams knew that should the struggle for independence fail, an ignominious death by hanging would most certainly be his punishment.

Refused an offer of amnesty from British Governor Gage in June 1775.

Little Known Fact: Samuel Adams made this statement: *"The Constitution shall never be construed ... to prevent the people of the United States who are peaceable citizens from keeping their own arms."*

Price Paid for Signing: He and John Hancock were the only men not offered amnesty in 1775 by British Governor Gage. They were to be captured and severely punished because their *"offenses were of too flagitious a Nature to admit of any other Consideration than that of condign Punishment."*

4

Sweet Breads
as Made in the Colonial Home

Spiced Nut Gingerbread –
Anne Wythe's Specialty

1 cup butter	1 tsp nutmeg
2 cups sugar	1 tsp cinnamon
5 egg yolks, beaten	5 tsp baking soda (dis-
3 tbls milk	solved in hot water)
1 tbls ginger	1 tsp cream of tartar
1 tsp cloves	4 cups flour

1 cup walnut pieces

Cream butter and sugar in large wooden mixing bowl. Carefully stir in custard-like beaten egg yolks. Then blend in milk, spices and baking soda. Sift cream of tartar into flour. Gradually blend mixture with ingredients in bowl. Lastly stir in walnut pieces. Whip hard for at least 10 minutes. Pour batter into 2 well-buttered bread pans. Bake in moderately quick oven (375 degrees) for 35 to 40 minutes, or until done. Test for doneness by sticking toothpick in center of each loaf. Toothpick will come out clean if bread is done. Brush over finished hot loaves with white of an egg. Wrap when cold with heavy towel or cloth and keep in tight container.

George Wythe (1726 – 1806)

Heritage: English. Born on father's Black River plantation in Elizabeth County, Virginia (in the present Hampton). Parents immigrated to America from England sometime in the late 1600s.

Religion: Devout Christian. Denomination unknown. Moral training came primarily from the tutoring of his mother. Prayed nightly before going to bed and was often seen reading his *Bible*. Also see quote below.

Education: Acquired a good education in religion and the classics as well as moral training through home schooling by his profoundly capable mother. She also taught him fluent Latin. Attended a prestigious private grammar school operated by the College of William and Mary. Studied law under a prominent attorney Uncle in Prince George County.

Marriage: Twice married. Wed Anne Lewis in 1756. She was born August 30, 1726, the same year as George. Her father was a wealthy, prominent Virginia lawyer. She died sometime in the late 1760s. A few years later, he remarried, this time to a young beauty named Elizabeth Talliaferro.

Children: None from first marriage. One child that died as an infant from second marriage.

Interesting Highlights: One of 56 men to sign the *Declaration of Independence*. Hancock was the *only* one to sign on July 4, 1776. Another 49 signed on August 2. Six signed at a later date – they were Wythe, Gerry, Richard Henry Lee, McKean, Thorton and Wolcott.

Established America's first law professorship at the prestigious College of William and Mary.

Quotable Quote: In February of 1776, he helped John Adams and Roger Sherman write instructions for an embassy to be opened in Canada. The instructions said in part: *"You are further to declare that we ... promise to the whole people ... the free and undisturbed exercise of their religion ... And that all civil rights and the right to hold office were to be extended to persons of any Christian denomination."*

Heroic Deed: Signing the *Declaration*. George Wythe knew that should the struggle for independence fail, an ignominious death by hanging would most certainly be his punishment.

Refused an offer of amnesty from British Governor Gage in June 1775.

Little Known Fact: Made provisions in his will to free all of his adult slaves. A kindly man, he even provided for their support should they be unable to take care of themselves.

Price Paid for Signing: All the Signers, including Wythe, suffered monetary losses because of their connection with the cause. Some were brought to the brink of financial ruin, or even worse, abject poverty.

Currant-Walnut Loaf –
Dorothy Hancock's Special Treat

1 cup yeast	1/2 cup shortening, melted
2 cups sugar	1/2 cup butter. melted
3 cups milk	2 cups currants
Flour to suit	2 cups walnuts

1 egg

In the early morning blend together yeast, 1 cup sugar, milk and flour enough to make a thick sponge. Cover with thick towel or cloth and set aside in warm place all day. At night, add other cup sugar, melted shortening and butter, currants, walnuts and egg. Blend everything well. Add more flour as needed to stiffen mixture. Again cover bowl and set aside to rise overnight. The next morning, knead thoroughly and put dough into well-buttered bread pans. Let loaves rise until double in size. Bake in slow oven (300 degrees) for 30 to 40 minutes or until done. Test for doneness by sticking toothpick in center of loaf. Toothpick will come out clean if bread is done. **NOTE:** *Mrs. Hancock sometimes used maple sugar instead of regular sugar as her bread sweetener. Instead of currants, she was known to sometimes use dried blueberries or huckleberries. When a child, John Hancock sometimes made his own maple sugar with the sap he tapped from maple trees.*

John Hancock (1737 – 1793)

Heritage: English. Born near Quincy, Massachusetts. Family immigrated to America from England sometime in late 1600s or early 1700s.

Religion: Devout Christian. Father and grandfather were prominent Congregational ministers in Massachusetts. See quote below.

Education: Had only the finest tutors. Studied at the prestigious Boston Latin School. Graduated from Harvard College when 17 in 1754.

Marriage: Married beautiful Dorothy Quincy on August 23, 1775. She was a relative of John and Samuel Adams. He was 38, she 28.

Children: Two. Daughter died as an infant. A son, John George Washington Hancock, died when 9 years old.

Interesting Highlights: Delegate to the First Continental Congress that convened on September 5, 1774, at Carpenter's Hall in Philadelphia.

President of the Second Continental Congress that convened on May 10, 1775, at the State House in Philadelphia.

His wife, Dorothy, also an ardent patriot, matched the enthusiasm of her husband when it concerned freedom and independence.

Dorothy's father, Judge Quincy, also a fearless patriot, strongly supported his son-in-law's fight for American independence.

Boldly stepped forward, picked up the quill, and placed his name on the Declaration in large letters. Stepping back, he spoke those immortal words: *There! His Majesty can now read my name without spectacles, and can now double his reward of 500 pounds on my head. That is my defiance.*

The *only* man to actually affix his signature on the *Declaration of Independence,* July 4, 1776. There were 49 others who signed on August 2, 1776. Six signed at a later date – Gerry, Richard Henry Lee, McKean, Thornton, Wolcott and Wythe.

Quotable Quote: *We think it is incumbent upon this people to humble themselves before God on account of their sins. ... so God may be pleased to continue to us the blessings we enjoy, and remove the tokens of His displeasure.* Spoken on the eve of the Revolution (October 1774).

Heroic Deed: Signing the *Declaration.* John Hancock knew that should the struggle for independence fail, an ignominious death by hanging would most certainly be his punishment.

Refused an offer of amnesty from British Governor Gage in June 1775.

Little Known Fact: As a Major General in the Massachusetts militia, he led an expeditionary force to oust the British from Rhode Island.

Price Paid for Signing: All the Signers, including Hancock, suffered monetary losses because of their connection with the cause. Some were brought to the brink of financial ruin, or even worse, abject poverty.

Brown Bread –
Sarah Hopkins' Made it This Way

2-1/2 cups corn meal   1 egg
1-1/2 cups rye flour   1 cup molasses
      2 tsp cream of tartar   1 tsp baking soda
      Pinch of salt   4 cups milk

Blend all ingredients in large wooden mixing bowl. When thoroughly blended, pour batter into well-greased cast iron baking dish. Cover and place in moderately hot oven (375 degrees). Bake for 3 hours. Test for doneness by sticking toothpick in center of each loaf. Toothpick will come out clean if bread is done.

Stephen Hopkins (1707 – 1785)

Heritage: English descent. Born in Providence, Rhode Island. His parents immigrated to America from England sometime in the late 1600s or early 1700s. Exact dates unknown.

Religion: Christian. Quaker. See quote below.

Education: Received a token amount of formal education. Living on a farm, little educational opportunity was available to him as a child and young adult. Read profusely and was able to quite satisfactorily educate himself.

Marriage: Twice married. First wed in 1726 to a bright, industrious Quaker girl, Sarah Scott. Both were 19 years old. She died in 1754 after 28 years of wedded bliss. Not one to enjoy being a widower, he remarried soon after, in 1755. His new bride, Anne Smith, was 38, the daughter of a Providence minister. She died 2 years before her husband in 1783.

Children: Sara bore Stephen seven children, two of whom died as infants. His second wife, Anne, had three children who lived.

Interesting Highlights: Delegate to the First Continental Congress that convened September 5, 1774, in Carpenter's Hall, Philadelphia.

One of 56 men to sign the *Declaration of Independence*. Hancock was the *only* one to sign on July 4, 1776. Another 49 signed on August 2. Six signed at a later date – they were Richard Henry Lee, Gerry, McKean, Thorton, Wolcott and Wythe.

Seriously affected with palsy. After signing the *Declaration of Independence*, this heroic patriot, with visibly shaking hands, handed the quill to William Ellery. He said: *"My hands tremble, but my heart does not."*

His home state, Rhode Island, was first to publicly announce its independence. This was done on May 4, 1776.

Second Oldest Signer of the *Declaration of Independence*. The oldest was Benjamin Franklin.

Quotable Quote: An 1848 school textbook had this to say about Hopkins: *"He was a sincere and consistent Christian, and the impress of his profession was upon all his deeds."*

Heroic Deed: Signing the *Declaration*. Stephen Hopkins knew that should the struggle for independence fail, an ignominious death by hanging would most certainly be his punishment.

Refused an offer of amnesty from British Governor Gage in June 1775.

Little Known Fact: Once introduced a bill in the Rhode Island Assembly to ban the importation of slaves.

Price Paid for Signing: All the Signers, including Hopkins, suffered monetary losses because of their connection with the cause. Some were brought to the brink of financial ruin, or even worse, abject poverty.

Sweet Bread –
Dorothy Walton's Family Favorite

1 cup butter	2 tbls cream
2 cups sugar	2 cups risen bread dough
3 egg yolks, beaten	1 tsp baking soda
1 tsp nutmeg	3 egg whites, beaten stiff
1 tsp cloves	1 cup raisins, floured

Cream butter and sugar in large wooden mixing bowl. Add this to custard-like beaten egg yolks. Stir in various spices, cream and bread dough (take this dough from the second rising of your bread on a baking day). Then dissolve baking soda in a little hot water and add it. Stir thoroughly until everything is well blended. Then stir in fluffy, beaten egg whites. Lastly, blend in raisins. Beat mixture *very* hard for at least 5 full minutes. Place in 2 well-buttered bread pans. Cover and allow to rise for 20 minutes. Bake in moderate oven (350 degrees) for 30 minutes or until done. Test for doneness by sticking toothpick in center of each loaf. Toothpick will come out clean if bread is done. **NOTE:** *Mrs. Walton also used pure maple sugar or fresh honey from her hives in making this marvelous bread treat. Try one of these sweeteners in place of sugar.*

George Walton (1740 – 1804)

Heritage: English and Scottish descent. Born in Frederick County, Virginia. Parents immigrated to America sometime in the late 1600s or early 1700s. Anything more regarding his parentage is rather obscure.

Religion: Devout Christian. See quote below.

Education: Extremely limited as a young man. Worked full-time as a carpenter. His mentor believed schooling to be a waste of time. Thirsting for knowledge, Walton spent his nights reading while using a wood torch for light.

Marriage: Wed to Dorothy Camber. Taken prisoner by the British a year later. From his deathbed in prison, he wrote these words to his wife: *"Remember that you are the beloved wife of one who has made Honor and reputation the ruling motive in every action of his life."*

Children: He and Dorothy had one son.

Interesting Highlights: One of 56 men to sign the *Declaration of Independence*. Hancock was the *only* one to sign on July 4, 1776. Another 49 signed on August 2. Six signed at a later date – they were Richard Henry Lee, Gerry, McKean, Thorton, Wolcott and Wythe.

Orphaned as a child and brought up by an uncle.

An avid patriot, he was designated as secretary to the Second Provincial Congress convened in July of 1775.

Wounded during Siege of Savannah (November and December of 1778) when struck by a bullet in his thigh.

Captured by the British and incarcerated in their notorious Sunbury, Georgia, prison. Beaten, starved and otherwise treated inhumanely.

Delegate to Georgia's Constitutional Convention in 1788.

Governor of Georgia under the new *Constitution* in 1789 and 1790.

Quotable Quote: He is credited with writing this declaration, passed by the Continental Congress on July 6, 1775: *"With a humble confidence in the mercies of the Supreme and impartial God and ruler of the universe, we most humble implore His divine goodness to protect us happily through this great conflict, and to dispose of our adversaries to reconciliation on reasonable terms, and thereby to relieve the empire from the calamities of war."*

Heroic Deed: Signing the *Declaration*. George Walton knew that should the struggle for independence fail, an ignominious death by hanging would most certainly be his punishment.

Refused an offer of amnesty from British Governor Gage in June 1775.

Little Known Fact: Colonel in the Georgia militia

Price Paid for Signing: All the Signers, including Walton, suffered monetary losses because of their connection with the cause. Some were brought to the brink of financial ruin, or even worse, abject poverty.

Christmas Bread --
Lewis Family's Favorite

9 cups flour	Flour to suit
1 tbls shortening	5 cups raisins
½ handful salt	¼ cup candied citron
½ cup brown sugar	1 tsp cinnamon
2 medium-size potatoes	1 tsp mace
1-1/2 cups yeast	1 tsp allspice
¼ cup sugar	½ handful caraway seeds
¼ cup maple syrup	¼ cup honey

Blend flour, shortening, salt and brown sugar in large pan. Set on back of stove to warm. Now boil potatoes. When soft, strain into large wooden mixing bowl and allow to cool. After strained potatoes have become lukewarm, add yeast, sugar and enough flour to make sponge. Cover with heavy towel or cloth and set in warm place to rise. While sponge is rising, add raisins, citron, spices and caraway seeds to flour in pan.

When the sponge is ready, (after it has risen), pour warm ingredients from pan into bowl. Add maple syrup or honey along with sufficient lukewarm water to make nice dough. Cover dough with heavy towel or cloth and set aside to rise overnight. In the morning, simply break dough and form pieces into individual loaves. Place loaves in greased bread pans. Cover again and set aside to rise once more. Then bake in slow oven (300 degrees) for 35 to 50 minutes or until done. Test for doneness by sticking toothpick in center of each loaf. Toothpick will come out clean if bread is done.

Francis Lewis (1713 – 1803)

Heritage: Welsh. Born in Llandaff, Glamoganshire, Wales. Orphaned when about 5-years old. Brought up by maiden aunt. Immigrated to America from Wales sometime around 1734 when he was 21-years old.

Religion: Devout Christian. Only child of an Episcopal minister. Mother was a minister's daughter. See quote below.

Education: Portion of his education was obtained in Scotland while living there with a relative. Became proficient in his native tongue (the ancient Briton) as well as in the Gaelic language, then mostly used in Scotland. His uncle, Dean of St. Paul's in London, eventually sent him to prestigious Westminister to obtain a well-rounded education.

Marriage: Wed Elizabeth Annesely in 1745, a New York girl who was the sister of his business partner.

Children: Three. – two sons, Frances and Morgan; one daughter, Ann. Some sources say they actually had seven children.

Interesting Highlights: One of 56 men to sign the *Declaration of Independence.* Hancock was the *only* one to sign on July 4, 1776. Another 49 signed on August 2. Six signed at a later date – they were Richard Henry Lee, Gerry, McKean, Thorton, Wolcott and Wythe.

Only Signer of the *Declaration* to have been born in Wales.

Inherited some money when 21. Most was invested in a great deal of merchandise. Only 21 at this time, he sailed with his merchandise to America. A highly successful business partnership was then set up in New York.

Quotable Quote: *"I agree, without reservation, with my colleague, Hamilton, who said: 'I have carefully examined the evidences of the Christian religion, and if I was sitting as a juror upon its authenticity I would unhesitatingly give my verdict in its favor. I can prove its truth as clearly as any proposition ever submitted to the mind of man.' "*

Heroic Deed: Signing the *Declaration.* Francis Lewis knew that should the struggle for independence fail, an ignominious death by hanging would most certainly be his punishment.

Refused an offer of amnesty from British Governor Gage in June 1775.

Little Known Fact: Unselfishly used much of his fortune to support the American Revolution.

Seldom spoke during the debates in the Continental Congress.

Price Paid for Signing: British thugs were sent out "to seize the lady and devastate the property." They burned everything found in the house and kidnapped his wife, Elizabeth. She was beaten often and severely. Tossed in a New York prison and forced to sleep on the floor. Her early death is attributed to the inhuman treatment she received from her British captors.

5

Corn Bread Baking
as Done for Our Forefathers

Corn Cake Recipe –
Hannah Thornton's Breakfast Treat

2 cups corn meal	1 tsp salt
¾ cup flour	½ cup yeast
4 cups milk	2 eggs, well beaten
2 tsp butter (melted)	½ tsp baking soda

Start at night before going to bed. Put corn meal in large wooden mixing bowl. Add flour and blend well. Pour milk in saucepan and scald. Then gradually pour hot milk over corn meal-flour combination. Stir until batter is smooth and lump free. Set aside to cool. When cool, add butter, salt and yeast. Mix thoroughly. Cover bowl with folded towel or piece of heavy table linen. Set aside in warm place until the next morning. Upon rising, thoroughly beat eggs. Dissolve baking soda in teaspoon of warm water. And both to batter and harshly beat entire mixture again.

Pour batter into deep, well-buttered earthen baking dishes. Cover again with towel or cloth. Let stand in warm place for 15 minutes to again rise. Then put in rather quick oven (400 to 425 degrees). Bake for 20 to 30 minutes. Test for doneness by sticking toothpick in center of each loaf. Toothpick will come out clean if bread is done. Serve with plenty of butter and eat while hot.

Matthew Thornton (1714 – 1803)

Heritage: Irish. Born in Ireland. Brought to America as a child (three to four years old) by his Scots-Irish parents around 1718. Family first settled in Wiscasset, Maine, and subsequently Worcester, Massachusetts.

Religion: Christian. See quote below.

Education: Little formal education. He got a basic, well-rounded education through tutoring at home and attending local common schools. A brilliant youngster, he undertook a serious study of medicine under the tutorship of a prominent local doctor.

Marriage: Wed Hannah Jack in 1760. He was 46 and she was but an 18-year old girl. Both were Scots-Irish. He outlived her by about 17-years.

Children: This union produced five children. One died as an infant.

Interesting Highlights: One of 56 men to sign the *Declaration of Independence*. Hancock was *only* one to sign on July 4, 1776. Another 49 signed on August 2. Six signed at a later date – they were Thornton, Gerry, Richard Henry Lee, McKean, Wolcott and Wythe.

One of three Signers of the *Declaration of Independence* who were born in Ireland. The others were Smith and Taylor.

Took seat in Continental Congress in November of 1776. Then requested permission to add his name to the *Declaration of Independence*.

Became last man to affix his signature to the document.

One of four Signers of the *Declaration of Independence* who were physicians. The others were Bartlett, Hall and Rush.

Held offices of both President of the Provincial Assembly and the Constitutional Convention in 1775 and 1776.

Spent his last years operating a ferry across the Merrimack River as well as a great deal of farming.

Quotable Quote: An 1848 textbook reported: *"Dr. Thornton was greatly beloved by all who knew him, and to the close of his long life he was a consistent and zealous Christian."*

Heroic Deed: Signing the *Declaration*. Matthew Thornton knew that should the struggle for independence fail, an ignominious death by hanging would most certainly be his punishment.

Refused an offer of amnesty from British Governor Gage in June 1775.

Little Known Fact: One of eight Signers of the *Declaration of Independence* who were foreign born. The others were Gwinnett, Lewis, Robert Morris, Smith, Taylor, Wilson and Witherspoon.

Price Paid for Signing: All the Signers, including Thornton, suffered monetary losses because of their connection with the cause. Some were brought to the brink of financial ruin, or even worse, abject poverty.

Ultra Rich Corn Bread --
Mary Middleton's Special

4 cups cream   ½ tsp salt
¾ cup powdered sugar   Yellow corn meal to suit
¼ cup butter   3 eggs
                    ¾ cup yeast

Pour cream into large wooden mixing bowl. Add powdered sugar and blend well. Cut butter in tiny pieces. Put butter and the salt in mixing bowl. Blend ingredients thoroughly. Pour mixture into cast iron skillet. Cover with lid and set on stove. Heat until scalding.

Now sift yellow corn meal. Take skillet from stove and pour in as much sifted corn meal as is required to make batter the consistency of thick boiled mush. Beat very  hard for a minimum of 15 minutes. Then set aside to cool. While batter is cooling, beat eggs until light. Stir into the batter when about as warm as new milk. Add yeast and harshly beat whole mixture for at least another 15 minutes. Much of this bread's essential goodness depends on its being long and well beaten.

Get round baking mold or earthen baking dish with a pipe in the center (to diffuse heat through middle of corn bread). Baking dish or pan must be well-buttered as corn meal tends to stick badly. Pour in batter mixture. Cover with thick towel or cloth. Set in warm place to rise. It should be raised in about 4 hours. When ready, place in moderately slow oven (325 degrees). Allow it to bake for 2 full hours or until done. Test for doneness by sticking toothpick in center of each loaf. Toothpick will come out clean if bread is done.

When corn bread is done baking, turn out of the pan with top facing down on plate. Should be served hot and whole. Cut in slices and eat with plenty of butter. **NOTE:** *This will be found to be an excellent corn bread. If wanted for breakfast, mix and set aside to rise the night before. If properly made, standing overnight will not harm it in any way.*

Arthur Middleton (1743 – 1788)

Heritage: English descent. Born at Middleton Place, South Carolina. His grandfather had emigrated from England to America in the mid to late 1600s. The family settled in South Carolina.

Religion: Devout Christian. See quote below.

Education: Sent to England in 1755 when about 12 for his education. Attended only the best private schools. Finally matriculated at the University of Cambridge. Graduated with distinguished honors when 22.

Marriage: Wed young and beautiful Mary Izard in 1764. Left her a widow on his plantation in 1788. Mary died 26-years later in 1814.

Children: Had nine children – three sons and six daughters.

Interesting Highlights: Served heroically and with a great deal of distinction in the South Carolina militia.

Delegate to the Continental Congress in 1776 and voted in favor of the *Declaration of Independence* on July 4, 1776.

One of 56 men to sign the *Declaration of Independence*. Hancock was the *only* one to sign on July 4, 1776. Another 49 signed on August 2. Six signed at a later date – they were Richard Henry Lee, Gerry, McKean, Thorton, Wolcott and Wythe.

Reelected to the Continental Congress in 1779 and 1780, but failed to bother attending any of the sessions.

One of the many influential Colonists who were taken prisoner in 1780 when Charleston fell to the British.

He and fellow Signers of the *Declaration of Independence,* Heyward and Rutledge, were incarcerated in the Crown Stockade in St. Augustine, Florida. Released in a prisoner exchange about a year later.

Middleton and his father were both sympathetic to the patriot cause. They saw the dark storm clouds of revolution gathering. They believed that no one in the Colonies could be neutral in the coming confrontation.

Quotable Quote: *"I believe that eternal salvation comes only through the blood of Jesus Christ, our most blessed Lord and Saviour."*

Heroic Deed: Signing the *Declaration*. Arthur Middleton knew that should the struggle for independence fail, an ignominious death by hanging would most certainly be his punishment.

Refused an offer of amnesty from British Governor Gage in June 1775.

Little Known Fact: Severely beaten, starved and made to suffer many indignities while a British prisoner in the Crown Stockade.

Price Paid for Signing: All the Signers, including Middleton, suffered monetary losses because of their connection with the cause. Some were brought to the brink of financial ruin, or even worse, abject poverty.

:

Sour Milk Corn Bread –
Annis Stockton's Best Receipt

¾ cup corn meal   ½ tsp baking soda
1 cup flour   ½ tsp salt
¼ cup sugar   1 egg, well beaten
2 tsp baking powder   1 cup sour milk
3 tbls butter, melted

Sift together in wooden mixing bowl the corn meal, flour, sugar, baking powder, baking soda and salt. Stir in well beaten egg, sour milk and melted butter. Beat all ingredients thoroughly. Grease shallow baking pan. Pour batter into this and bake in a quick oven (425 degrees) for 20 minutes or more until done. Test for doneness by sticking toothpick in center of each loaf. Toothpick will come out clean if bread is done.

Richard Stockton (1730 – 1781)

Heritage: English ancestors. Born on October 1 at Morven, the family estate in Princeton, New Jersey. Great grandfather immigrated to America from England sometime between 1660 and 1680. Some say it was in 1678.

Religion: Devout Christian. Quaker. See quote below.

Education: Pre-college schooling at prestigious West Nottingham Academy. Entered the College of New Jersey (now Princeton) two years later. Graduated in 1748. Studied law under prominent local attorney.

Marriage: Wed 27-year old poetess, Annis Boudinet, when he was 30. Annis was of French Huguenot ancestry, intellectual, and extremely wealthy. Her fiery patriotism was matched only by that of her husband.

Children: Six children – two sons and four daughters. Julia, their oldest daughter, married Dr. Benjamin Rush of Philadelphia, fellow Signer of the *Declaration of Independence.*

Interesting Highlights: Member of Continental Congress in 1776.

One of 56 men to sign the *Declaration of Independence*. Hancock was the *only* one to sign on July 4, 1776. Another 49 signed on August 2. Six signed at a later date – they were Richard Henry Lee, Gerry, McKean, Thorton, Wolcott and Wythe.

This unsung American hero became an invalid as a result of his brutal treatment at the hands of his vengeful British captors. Finally freed in a prisoner exchange. Died soon afterwards.

In 1774, he was fearful regarding the possibility of war with England. Yet, when elected to the Continental Congress two short years later, he gave his unqualified vote of approval for the *Declaration* on July 2, 1776.

Quotable Quote: *"I think it proper here, not only to subscribe to the entire belief ... of the Christian religion ... remember, that the fear of the Lord is the beginning of wisdom."*

Heroic Deed: Signing the *Declaration*. Richard Stockton knew that should the struggle for independence fail, an ignominious death by hanging would most certainly be his punishment.

Refused an offer of amnesty from British Governor Gage in June 1775.

Little Known Fact: Had the honor of being on the Committee that drafted the *Articles of Confederation.* But he did not sign this document.

Price Paid for Signing: Captured by the British and held in prison. Severely beaten and starved in an attempt to force him to betray his country and his friends. His estate was pillaged, plundered and burned. Crops were wantonly destroyed, cattle and horses either stolen or killed. He ended up a destitute man, a beggar

Cracklin' Corn Bread – Holiday Favorite of Richard Henry Lee

2 tbls flour	3 tsp baking powder
1-1/2 cups corn meal	1 egg, well beaten
2 tsp sugar	1-1/4 cups milk
½ tsp salt	2 cups cracklins

In wooden mixing bowl, blend together flour, corn meal, sugar, salt, baking powder, beaten egg and milk. Blend everything well and then stir in cracklins. Grease shallow baking pan. Pour batter into pan and bake in very quick oven (450 degrees) for about 20 minutes or until golden brown. Test for doneness by sticking toothpick in center of each loaf. Toothpick will come out clean if bread is done. **NOTE:** *Cracklins are the crisp pieces of browned roasted pork skin. They are the crisp pieces left over after the hod fat has been rendered after the lard has been fried out of the hog's fat.*

Richard Henry Lee (1732 – 1794)

Heritage: English. Direct descendant of early settlers un the Virginia Colony who had emigrated from England to America in the early 1600s.

Religion: A man of strong Christian convictions. Was known as a sincere practicing Christian. His character was above reproach.

Education: Father sent him to England as a young boy to get his education. Had the finest tutors and attended the most prestigious private schools. Returned to Virginia a polished scholar when nearly 19-years of age.

Marriage: Twice married. First married Anne Aylett in 1757. Her father was a close friend and advisor to General George Washington. Her mother and Martha Washington were first cousins. She died in 1767 at the age of 35 years. He remarried in 1769, this time to Anne Pincard.

Children: Had 4 children – 2 boys and 2 girls in his first marriage. His second wife bore him 5 more children – 3 girls and 2 more sons.

Interesting Highlights: First man in Virginia to publicly denounce the British Stamp Act.

One of 56 men to sign the *Declaration of Independence*. Hancock was the *only* one to sign on July 4, 1776. Another 49 signed on August 2. Six signed at a later date – they were Richard Henry Lee, Gerry, McKean, Thorton, Wolcott and Wythe.

His younger brother, Francis Lightfoot Lee, was also a signer of the *Declaration of Independence*.

He and fellow patriot, Patrick Henry, were the closest of friends

Lee and Henry, young America's greatest orator, opposed ratifying the *Constitution* unless specific Amendments were added.

Ludwell, one of Lee's sons, was on the staff of General Lafayette.

Lee became Virginia's first Senator under the new *Constitution*.

Quotable Quote: Regarding guns, he said: *"To preserve liberty, it is essential that the whole body of the people always possess arms, and be taught alike, especially when young, how to use them."*

Heroic Deed: Signing the *Declaration*. Richard Henry Lee knew that should the struggle for independence fail, an ignominious death by hanging would most certainly be his punishment.

Refused an offer of amnesty from British Governor Gage in June 1775.

Little Known Fact: He was the daring Colonial patriot who bravely introduced the first *Resolution for Independence* before the Continental Congress in July 2, 1776. John Adams immediately seconded it.

Price Paid for Signing: All the Signers, including Lee, suffered monetary losses because of their connection with the cause. Some were brought to the brink of financial ruin, or even worse, abject poverty.

Apple Corn Bread –
Dickinson's Christmas Favorite

2 cups yellow corn meal   2 tbls butter, melted
¼ cup honey   2 eggs, well beaten
1-1/2 tsp salt   1 tsp baking soda
2 cups sour milk   2 cups apples, chopped fine

Place yellow corn meal, honey, salt, sour milk and butter in upper part of double boiler. Stir well and allow to cook 12 minutes. Set aside to cool. Then stir in beaten eggs. Dissolve baking soda in tablespoonful of warm water. Add this to pot. Lastly, stir in finely chopped apple pieces. Blend everything thoroughly. Grease a 9 x 9 inch baking pan. Pour batter into this. Bake in quick oven (425 degrees) for 35 to 40 minutes or until done. Test for doneness by sticking toothpick in center of each loaf. Toothpick will come out clean if bread is done. Serve hot with plenty of butter.

John Dickinson (1732 – 1808)

Heritage: English. Father was prosperous farmer who immigrated to America from England sometime between the late 1600s and early 1700s.

Religion: Devout Christian. See quote below.

Education: Private tutors most of his childhood and as a young adult. Studied law in 1750 under prominent attorney, John Moland in Philadelphia. Sailed to England in 1753 to continue studies at London's Middle Temple.

Marriage: Married Mary Morris in 1770. She was the daughter of an extremely wealthy businessman. Little more is known about their married life.

Children: One daughter.

Interesting Highlights: Delegate to the First Continental Congress that convened on September 5, 1774, at Carpenter's Hall in Philadelphia.

Delegate to the Second Continental Congress that convened on May 10, 1775, at the State House in Philadelphia. While in attendance he wrote **"The Causes of Taking Up Arms."**

Met with other delegates to the Second Continental Congress less than two months before the vote for the *Declaration of Independence*. He suggested that all delegates be required to repeat the oath quoted below before they would be allowed to be seated and take part in the congressional sessions.

One of 39 signers of the *Constitution.*

One of five men who signed both the *Constitution* and the *Articles of Confederation*. Others were Daniel Carroll, Gouverneur and Robert Morris, and Roger Sherman.

One of the first patriots in the Colonies to advocate using force against England in order to gain independence.

Quotable Quote: *"I do profess faith in God the Father, and in Jesus Christ his Eternal Son the true God, and in the Holy Spirit, one God blessed for ever more; and I do acknowledge the Holy Scriptures of the Old and New Testaments to be given by Divine Inspiration."*

Heroic Deed: Enthusiastically supporting the *Declaration*. John Dickinson knew that should the struggle for independence fail, an ignominious death by hanging would most certainly be his punishment.

Refused an offer of amnesty from British Governor Gage in June 1775.

Little Known Fact: Only man to not personally affix his name to the Constitution. Illness prevented him from being there at the time. He thereby authorized another delegate and close friend, George Read, to sign his name on the grand document.

Price Paid for Signing: All the Signers, including Dickinson, suffered monetary losses because of their connection with the cause. Some were brought to the brink of financial ruin, or even worse, abject poverty.

Sugarless Custard Corn Bread – Prepared by Martha Jefferson

1 cup corn meal	3 cups heavy cream
1 cup flour	or
2 tsp baking powder	3 cups milk
½ tsp salt	2 tbls butter, melted
2 egg yolks, beaten	2 egg whites, beaten stiff

Sift corn meal, flour, baking powder and salt into large wooden mixing bowl. Beat egg yolks in smaller bowl. Add 2 cups cream or milk to beaten eggs. Then stir in melted butter. When everything has been blended well, add to flour mixture in larger

bowl. Stir until everything is perfectly blended. Now beat egg whites to stiff froth. Carefully fold them into other ingredients. Butter square baking pan. Pour in batter. It should be about 2 inches thick. Lastly, while holding other cup of cream or milk about 6 to 10 inches above batter, slowly pour back and forth over top. *Do not stir!* Very gently place baking pan in moderate oven (350 degrees) and bake 50 minutes or until done. Test for doneness by sticking toothpick in center of each loaf. Toothpick will come out clean if bread is done. When done, carefully turn out corn bread on large plate. Cut into squares and serve while piping hot with lots of butter. **NOTE:** *A nice line of delicious custard will be found throughout this corn bread. Makes enough to serve 6 to 8 people.*

Thomas Jefferson (1743 – 1826)

Heritage: Born in Virginia. Family was among the early immigrants to the Colonies. Ancestors were from Wales. Mother was of Scottish descent.

Religion: Christian (See quote below).

Education: Privately tutored in the classics as a young man. Attended William and Mary College. Graduated after only two years. Tutored in law by eminent attorney, George Wythe, who was a fellow Signer of the *Declaration*.

Marriage: Was 29 when he married independently wealthy widow, Martha Skelton. She was the 23-year old daughter of George Wales, an eminent Virginia lawyer. They were wed on January 1, 1772.

Children: Martha had one child that died as an infant during her first marriage to Bathhurst Skelton. She and Thomas had five more, the last born in November of 1779.

Interesting Highlights: One of 49 men to sign the *Declaration of Independence* on August 2, 1776. Hancock was *only* man to sign on July 4. Six others signed at a later date – they were Gerry, Richard Henry Lee, McKean, Thornton, Wolcott and Wythe.

An accomplished scholar, he read several languages with ease.

Lacked the charisma enjoyed by so many of the other political leaders.

Founded the University of Virginia and actually designed the buildings.

Died exactly 50 years after the adoption of the *Declaration of Independence* on July 4, 1826, as did fellow signer, John Adams.

Those who knew him best said he *never ever* lost his temper.

First man to propose laws in the Virginia legislature prohibiting the importation of slaves.

Quotable Quote: *"I am a real Christian, ... a disciple of the doctrines of Jesus. ... I am a Christian in the only sense in which He wished anyone to be, sincerely attached to His doctrine in preference to all others."*

Heroic Deed: Signing the *Declaration of Independence*. Thomas Jefferson knew that should the struggle for independence fail, an ignominious death by hanging would most certainly be his punishment.

Refused an offer of amnesty from British Governor Gage in June 1775.

Little Known Fact: Was a skillful performer on a violin.

First President to serve meringue on pies for White House State dinners.

Last words: *"I resign myself to my God, and my child to my country."*

Price Paid for Signing: All the Signers, including Jefferson, suffered monetary losses because of their connection with the cause. Some were brought to the brink of financial ruin, or even worse, abject poverty. Sadly enough, Jefferson was so desperately in need of money before he died that he had to sell his magnificent library to the government for a mere $30,000.

Rye and Corn Bread – Catherine Few's Receipt

> 5 cups rye flour   2 tsp salt
> 6 cups corn meal   ¾ cup yeast
> ½ cup molasses   1 tsp baking soda

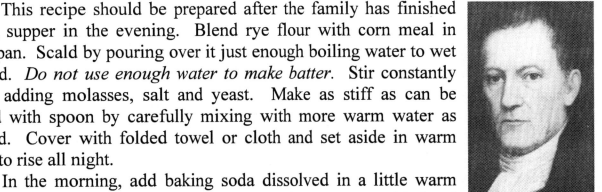

This recipe should be prepared after the family has finished eating supper in the evening. Blend rye flour with corn meal in large pan. Scald by pouring over it just enough boiling water to wet it good. *Do not use enough water to make batter.* Stir constantly while adding molasses, salt and yeast. Make as stiff as can be stirred with spoon by carefully mixing with more warm water as needed. Cover with folded towel or cloth and set aside in warm place to rise all night.

In the morning, add baking soda dissolved in a little warm water. Put into large baking pan. Smooth over top with hand dipped in cold water. Cover and again set aside to rise for 30 minutes to an hour. Then put in slow oven (300 degrees). Bake 5 to 6 hours or until done. Test for doneness by sticking toothpick in the center of the corn bread. Toothpick will come out clean if corn bread is done. **NOTE:** *This old recipe is similar to the "Rye and Injun" (Indian meal or corn meal) that was popular in the late 1700s. When Mrs. Few prepared it for her family, she would place mixture in kettle and allow to rise. She then covered kettle and placed it on the hearth before a fire. Live coals were heaped over the lid and it was left to slowly bake all night. This lady sometimes substituted graham flour for rye flour in order to get a nice taste variation.*

William Few (1748 – 1828)

Heritage: English. Born on a farm near Baltimore, Maryland. Descendant of Quaker farmers who had immigrated to America from England sometime during the 1680s. First settled in Pennsylvania.

Religion: Devout Christian. Methodist. See quote below regarding the words he and Hall chose when helping write the *Constitution* of Georgia.

Education: Farming left little time for formal schooling. Briefly attended local school run by a traveling teacher in 1760. This provided a rudimentary education. Had a lifelong love of reading and was primarily self-educated this way. Also found time to study law and become an attorney.

Marriage: Wed Catherine Nicholson on an unknown date.

Children: Three daughters.

Interesting Highlights: Delegate to the Constitutional Convention held in Philadelphia from May 25 to September 17, 1787.

Missed majority of the sessions during the Convention.

Was never known to make a speech or enter into any debates during sessions of the Convention..

Absent during July and August because of his duties as one of his State's first Senators.

One of 39 men who signed the *Constitution*.

Delegate to the Continental Congress from 1780 to 1788.

Commanded a company in the Georgia militia.

Frequently skirmished with British units and eventually forced the enemy to withdraw and abandon Augusta, Georgia.

Quotable Quote: *"We, the people of Georgia, relying upon the protection and guidance of Almighty God, do ordain and establish this Constitution."*

Heroic Deed: Refused an offer of amnesty from British Governor Gage in June 1775.

Little Known Fact: Few, along with his brothers and father joined the *"regulators"* in 1771. This was a group that vigorously opposed the Royal Governor. His brother was captured by the British forces and unceremoniously hanged from the closest tree. As a result, the rest of the family fled to Georgia.

Price Paid for Signing: Family was forced to flee when the vengeful British totally destroyed their farm. Everything was taken from the house, piled in front, and burned. Then the pillaged house was totally destroyed, farm animals killed and crops laid waste.

All Signers, including William Few, suffered monetary losses because of their connection with the cause. Some were brought to the brink of financial ruin, or even worse, abject poverty.

Johnnie Cake --
Made by Deborah Franklin for Benjamin

4 cups corn meal   2 cups warm water

Sift corn meal into large wooden mixing bowl or a pan. Make a hole in middle. Pour in warm water and stir in salt. Using good-size wooden spoon, beat meal and water mixture into soft dough. Then stir very briskly 15 minutes more, until it becomes

light and spongy. When ready, spread dough smoothly and evenly on a flat board (a piece of the head of a flour barrel served this purpose in the olden days). Place board nearly upright before open fire (you may use your oven for this, or fireplace if you have one). Place old flat iron against back of board for support. Bake until nicely browned. When done, cut into small squares. Split and butter each piece and eat while hot. **NOTE:** *This type corn cake was extremely popular in its day for serving at teas and special dinners.*

Benjamin Franklin (1706 – 1790)

Heritage: English. Born in Boston. Father immigrated in 1682 to America from England and settled in Massachusetts.

Religion: Christian. A Puritan. Franklin said this on the eve of the American War for Independence in 1774: *"We think it is incumbent upon this people to humble themselves before God on account of their sins. ... so God may be pleased to continue to us the blessings we enjoy, and remove the tokens of His displeasure."*

Education: Could never afford private tutoring or prestigious schools. Read and studied on his own extensively. Taught himself five languages.

Marriage: Took a common law wife in September of 1730. She was Deborah Read, a 25-year old Philadelphia widow. Franklin was 24 at the time. Some sources say they were formally married, others dispute this.

Children: They had two children out of wedlock. Sarah was born in 1774. Their son died as an infant.

Interesting Highlights: The oldest Signer of the *Declaration of Independence* at 70, and of the *Constitution* at 83.

Founder of the University of Pennsylvania.

Developed the first streetlights in Philadelphia.

Organized the first postal system in America and was Deputy Postmaster General of the Colonies (1737-1752).

Organized the first volunteer fire department in America.

Was the fifteenth of seventeen children in his family.

Made a motion that Congress be opened each day with a prayer.

Last official act was making a recommendation to Congress that they formally abolish slavery.

Quotable Quote: *"In the beginning of the Contest with Great Britain, when we were sensible of the danger we had daily prayer ... for the Divine protection. Our prayers ... were heard, and they were graciously answered."*

Heroic Deed: Signing the *Declaration*. Benjamin Franklin knew that should the struggle for independence fail, an ignominious death by hanging would most certainly be his punishment.

Refused an offer of amnesty from British Governor Gage in June 1775.

Little Known Fact: Sickly and frail when he signed the *Constitution*, he had to be carried in a chair from his home to the sessions of the Constitutional Convention. Prisoners incarcerated in the city jail were recruited to undertake this task.

Price Paid for Signing: All the Signers, including Franklin, suffered monetary losses because of their connection with the cause. Some were brought to the brink of financial ruin, or even worse, abject poverty.

Corn Bread Favorite --
Enjoyed by the Rush Family

2 cups corn ,meal	¼ cup molasses
½ cup flour	or
2 cups sour milk	½ cup sugar
2 tbls butter, melted	2 eggs, well beaten
1 tsps salt	1 tsp baking soda

Sift corn meal in large wooden mixing bowl. Then mix this with the flour. Smoothly and gradually blend in sour milk. Now add melted butter, salt and molasses or sugar. Beat mixture hard. Then stir in beaten eggs. Lastly dissolve baking soda in little warm water. Beat everything thoroughly. Take a little butter and grease some moderately deep baking pans. Pour in corn bread batter. Place in rather quick oven (400 to 425 degrees). Bake for nearly an hour or until golden brown. Test for doneness by sticking toothpick in center of each loaf. Toothpick will come out clean if bread is done. Serve hot with plenty of butter.

Benjamin Rush (1745 – 1813)

Heritage: English. Born at Berberry, about 12 miles northeast of Philadelphia. His father, an officer in Cromwell's army, immigrated to America from England during the late 1600s or early 1700s.

Religion: Christian. He explained it in this manner: *"I have alternately been called an Aristocrat and a Democrat. I am neither, I am a Christocrat."* Cofounder of the ***Philadelphia Bible Society***, a group that strongly advocated using the *Bible* and *Scripture* in all public schools. Also see quote below.

Education: Attended prestigious West Nottingham Academy in Rising Sun, Maryland. Graduated with honors from the College of New Jersey (now Princeton) in 1760 when just 15-years old. Then returned to Philadelphia and began an apprenticeship with a prominent physician.

Marriage: Married Julie Stockton on January 11, 1776. She was oldest daughter of another zealous patriot, Richard Stockton. Her father later became a Signer of the *Declaration of Independence*.

Children: They had 13 children, all of whom survived him. Some sources say only six sons and three daughters survived him.

Interesting Highlights: One of 56 men to sign the *Declaration of Independence*. Hancock was the *only* one to sign on July 4, 1776. Another 49 signed on August 2. Six signed at a later date – they were Richard Henry Lee, Gerry, McKean, Thorton, Wolcott and Wythe.

One of *the* youngest Signers of the *Declaration of Independence* at 30 years of age.

Served his country as Surgeon General in the Continental Army. Resigned after a disagreement with General Washington.

Helped found the ***Pennsylvania Society for Promoting the Abolition of Slavery*** in 1787. Later served as the organization's President.

Quotable Quote: His last words before dying: *"... blessed Jesus, wash away all my impurities, and receive me into Thy everlasting kingdom."*

Heroic Deed: Signing the *Declaration*. Benjamin Rush knew that should the struggle for independence fail, an ignominious death by hanging would most certainly be his punishment.

Refused an offer of amnesty from British Governor Gage in June 1775.

Little Known Fact: In 1776, he suggested to Thomas Paine that he should write his famous book, **COMMON SENSE**. He even gave Paine the title and helped finance its publication.

Died during a typhus epidemic in 1813 at the age of 67.

Price Paid for Signing: All the Signers, including Rush, suffered monetary losses because of their connection with the cause. Some were brought to the brink of financial ruin, or even worse, abject poverty.

6

Sweet Rolls and Coffecakes
Early American Style

Nutty Cinnamon Rolls –
Made by Martha for Thomas Jefferson

1-1/4 cups milk, scalding	Flour to suit
3 egg whites, well beaten	½ cup butter, melted
Sugar to suit	Butter to suit, soft
1 tsp salt	Cinnamon to suit
2 yeast cake	Walnuts to suit, chopped

Put scalding hot milk in large wooden mixing bowl and set aside until it becomes lukewarm. Beat in frothy beaten egg whites, ½ cup sugar and salt. Crumble yeast cakes and dissolve in little warm water. Stir this into the mixture. Add 3 cups flour and melted butter. Blend everything well and then work in enough flour to make soft, pliable dough. Put dough in large buttered bowl and cover with heavy towel or cloth. Set aside in warm place to rise until doubled in size.

When ready, turn dough out of bowl onto lightly floured board (or countertop). Roll dough out into ½ inch sheet. Using knife, spread soft butter over entire sheet of dough. Sprinkle generously with cinnamon, sugar and finely chopped walnuts. Carefully roll sheet up like a scroll. Cut into ½ inch thick slices. Lay each slice in shallow, well-buttered baking pan. Baste with more melted butter. Sprinkle tops with cinnamon, sugar and finely chopped walnuts (other kinds of nuts can be substituted if desired). Set aside to again rise. When double in size, bake in moderate oven (350 degrees) for about 25 minutes or until done. . Test for doneness by sticking toothpick in center of a roll. Toothpick will come out clean if rolls are done. The rolls should be nicely browned.

Thomas Jefferson (1743 – 1826)

Heritage: Born in Virginia. Family was among the early immigrants to the Colonies. Ancestors were from Wales. Mother was of Scottish descent.

Religion: Christian (See quote below).

Education: Privately tutored in the classics as a young man. Attended William and Mary College. Graduated after only two years. Tutored in law by eminent attorney, George Wythe, who was a fellow Signer of the *Declaration.*

Marriage: Was 29 when he married independently wealthy widow, Martha Skelton. She was the 23-year old daughter of George Wales, an eminent Virginia lawyer. They were wed on January 1, 1772.

Children: Martha had one child that died as an infant during her first marriage to Bathhurst Skelton. She and Thomas had five more, the last born in November of 1779.

Interesting Highlights: One of 49 men to sign the *Declaration of Independence* on August 2, 1776. Hancock was *only* man to sign on July 4. Six others signed at a later date – they were Gerry, Richard Henry Lee, McKean, Thornton, Wolcott and Wythe.

An accomplished scholar, he read several languages with ease.

Founded the University of Virginia and actually designed the buildings.

Died exactly 50 years after the adoption of the *Declaration of Independence* on July 4, 1826, as did fellow signer, John Adams.

Those who knew him best said he *never ever* lost his temper.

First man to propose laws in the Virginia legislature prohibiting the importation of slaves.

Lacked the charisma enjoyed by so many of the other political leaders.

Quotable Quote: *"I am a real Christian, ... a disciple of the doctrines of Jesus. ... I am a Christian in the only sense in which He wished anyone to be, sincerely attached to His doctrine in preference to all others."*

Heroic Deed: Signing the *Declaration of Independence.* Thomas Jefferson knew that should the struggle for independence fail, an ignominious death by hanging would most certainly be his punishment.

Refused an offer of amnesty from British Governor Gage in June 1775

Little Known Fact: Was a skillful performer on a violin.

Last words: *"I resign myself to my God, and my child to my country."*

First President to serve meringue pies for White House State dinners.

Price Paid for Signing: All the Signers, including Jefferson, suffered monetary losses because of their connection with the cause. Some were brought to the brink of financial ruin, or even worse, abject poverty. Sadly enough, Jefferson was so desperately in need of money before he died that he had to sell his magnificent library to the government for a mere $30,000.

Apple-Maple Coffeecake –
Mary Spaight's Special Treat

1-1/2 cups dried apples chopped fine	2 eggs
	½ cup sour milk
1 cup maple syrup	or
or	½ cup coffee, strong
1 cup molasses	1 tsp baking soda
or	1 tsp cloves
1 cup honey	1 tsp cinnamon
1 cup sugar	1 tsp allspice
½ cup butter, soft	Flour to suit

Put dried apples in saucepan with a little water and let stew for 10 minutes. Add maple syrup, molasses or honey. Stir well. Let this mixture simmer for 1 full hour. When done, set aside to cool.

Meanwhile, take large wooden mixing bowl and cream the sugar and butter. Beat in eggs , sour milk or coffee, baking soda and spices. When apple mixture in saucepan has cooled to lukewarm, stir it while adding ingredients from mixing bowl. Lastly, work in enough flour to make stiff batter. Pour into a well-buttered and shallow baking pan. Bake in moderately quick oven (375 degrees) 30 to 40 minutes, or until done. Test for doneness by sticking toothpick in center of coffeecake. Toothpick will come out clean if coffeecake is done.

Richard Dobbs Spaight, Sr. (1758 – 1802)

Heritage: Irish-English. Born to a prominent Irish-English family in New Bern, North Carolina. Family immigrated to America from England sometime between the late 1600s and early 1700s.

Religion: Dedicated Christian. See quote below regarding what he, Blount and Williamson wrote in North Carolina's *Constitution*.

Education: Following death of parents, his guardian sent him to Ireland *"to get a proper education."* After much tutoring, he attended the University of Glascow in Scotland and graduated.

Marriage: Wed Mary Leach sometime in 1795.

Children: Five.

Interesting Highlights: One of 39 men who signed the *Constitution*.

One of the three youngest Signers of the *Constitution*. The others were Jonathan Dayton and Charles Pinckney.

Helped organize and mobilize of the North Carolina Militia in 1778 and again in 1779. Was an aide to the State militia commander.

Commanded an artillery regiment as a Lieutenant Colonel.

Saw battlefield action in the Revolutionary War during the Battle of Camden, South Carolina, in 1780.

Faithfully attended every session of the Continental Congress and spoke several times during the debates.

Fought ferociously for ratification of the *United States Constitution* in North Carolina where it was exceptionally difficult.

Killed in a senseless duel with a political opponent, federalist John Stanley. His final words could well have been as those muttered by Alexander Hamilton: *"I have lived like a man, but I die as a fool."* He died in his late forties while in the prime of life.

Quotable Quote: *"No person who should deny the being of God or the truth of the religion [Christian], or the divine authority of either the Old or New Testaments, or who should hold religious principles incompatible with the freedom and safety of the state, shall be capable of holding any office, or place of trust ...within this state."*

Heroic Deed: Refused an offer of amnesty from British Governor Gage in June 1775.

Little Known Fact: One of 12 Signers of the *Constitution* who owned slaves. Others were Bassett, Blair, Blount, Butler, Daniel Carroll, Jenifer, Madison, the two Pinckneys, Rutledge and Washington.

Price Paid for Signing: All the Signers, including Spaight, suffered monetary losses because of their connection with the cause. Some were brought to the brink of financial ruin, or even worse, abject poverty.

Apple Coffeecake –
Favorite of Nicholas Gilman

½ cup milk   ½ cup sugar
¼ cup butter. Melted   2 tbls baking powder
2 eggs, well beaten   ½ tsp salt
1-1/2 cups flour   1 tsp cinnamon
2 cups apples, finely chopped

Blend milk, butter and frothy beaten eggs in large wooden mixing bowl. In a separate bowl, sift together flour, sugar, baking powder, salt and cinnamon. Repeat sifting 3 times. Then add these dry ingredients to those in first mixing bowl. Beat everything hard. Lastly, blend in finely chopped apples

Pour batter into well-buttered, square baking pan. Set aside while preparing following mixture:

1 tbls butter, soft   2 tbls flour
¼ cup sugar   1 tsp cinnamon
1 tsp nuts, finely chopped   Pinch of nutmeg

Blend all above ingredients in small wooden mixing bowl. Work them together until it results in a good crumbly mixture. Sprinkle over batter in baking pan. Put in quick oven (400 degrees) for about 30 minutes. Test for doneness by sticking toothpick in center of coffeecake. Toothpick will come out clean if coffeecake is done. When coffeecake is finished baking, take it from the oven and set on wire rack to cool (about 15 minutes). Then, carefully take cake from baking pan and put it on a large dish to finish cooling.

Nicholas Gilman (1755 – 1814)

Heritage: English. Born in Exter, New Hampshire. Second son in family of eight. Parents immigrated to America from England in the late 1600s or early 1700s.

Religion: Christian. See quote below.

Education: attended various local schools. Mother tutored (home schooled) him as a child and young adult. Voracious reader. Never had either the time or the money to attend college. Had to work as a clerk for his father.

Marriage: Never married. Was lifelong bachelor.

Children: Didn't father any children as he was never married.

Interesting Highlights: One of 39 men who signed the *Constitution*.

Had no experience in public speaking or debating.

Never made a speech or entered into a debate during sessions of the Constitutional Convention due to his inherent shyness.

Played important role and spent much time to obtain ratification of the new *United States Constitution* in New Hampshire.

One of three Signers of the *Constitution* who were bachelors. The others were Abraham Baldwin and Daniel of St. Thomas Jenifer. Only two bachelors signed the *Declaration of Independence* – Joseph Hewes and Caesar Rodney.

Served as a delegate to the Continental Congress (1785-1787) but didn't bother attending any sessions.

President of the Continental Congress from June 1786 to January 1787.

Served in House of Representatives under the new *Constitution* from 1789 to 1797.

Played minor role in developing the *Constitution*, but a major role in shepherding it through the Continental Congress.

Quotable Quote: Gilman assisted John Langdon in writing New Hampshire's *Constitution*. Here is how he chose to word part of the document: *"Every individual has a natural and inalienable right to worship God according to the dictates of his own conscience, and reason. ... every denomination of Christians ... shall be equally under the protection of the laws. ... And no subordination of any one sect or denomination to another, shall ever be established by law."*

Heroic Deed: Refused an offer of amnesty from British Governor Gage in June 1775.

Little Known Fact: Served throughout the Revolutionary War as a Captain in the Continental Army.

Price Paid for Signing: All the Signers, including Gilman, suffered monetary losses because of their connection with the cause. Some were brought to the brink of financial ruin, or even worse, abject poverty.

Unique Layer Coffeecake –
Enjoyed by the Harrison Family

3 cups flour	½ tsp cinnamon
3 tsp baking powder	¼ nutmeg
¾ cup sugar	¼ cup butter, soft
1 tsp salt	3 eggs

1 cup milk

Blend flour, baking powder, sugar, salt and spices. Then sift these ingredients into large mixing bowl. Stir in unbeaten eggs and milk. Continue stirring until batter is lump free and smooth. Put mixture into a well-buttered, round baking pan. Set aside and prepare the topping:

¾ cup brown sugar	1 tsp cinnamon
¼ cup butter, soft	1 tsp nutmeg
3 tbls flour	1 cup walnuts,
¼ tsp salt	chopped fine

1 cup heavy cream

Put brown sugar, soft butter, flour, salt, cinnamon and nutmeg into large wooden mixing bowl. Beat together until it becomes a light and creamy. Spread this over mixture in baking pan. Sprinkle with chopped nuts. Bake in moderately hot oven (375 degrees) for about 25 minutes. Test for doneness by sticking toothpick in center of coffeecake. Toothpick will come out clean if coffeecake is done. When coffeecake is ready, take from oven and set pan on a wire rack to cool for 10 minutes or more. Then remove coffeecake from pan and set aside to cool completely. When cold, split into 2 layers. Whip the cream until stiff. Spread whipped cream between layers. Cut in pieces as you would a pie and serve.

Benjamin Harrison (1726 – 1791)

Heritage: English. Born at Berkeley, his father's huge estate in Charles County, Virginia. Family was one of the most prominent planters in the South. His ancestors immigrated to America from England in 1640. They were among early settlers in the Virginia Colony.

Religion: Devout Christian. He once said: *"I believe in Jesus Christ for He will surely pardon all of my sins."*

Education: Tutored at home as child and young adult. Went to William an Mary College. Quit in 1775 due to serious disagreement with a professor. And was forced to run the family business when his father died.

Marriage: Married beautiful Elizabeth Bassett who was born in 1741 or 1742. Her correct birth date and the date of their marriage are unknown. She was daughter of Colonel William Bassett and niece of Martha Washington.

Children: Numerous offspring but only seven survived past infancy – four daughters and three sons.

Interesting Highlights: One of 56 men to sign the *Declaration of Independence*. Hancock was the *only* one to sign on July 4, 1776. Another 49 signed on August 2. Six signed at a later date – they were Richard Henry Lee, Gerry, McKean, Thorton, Wolcott and Wythe.

One son, William Henry Harrison, went on to become ninth President of the United States in 1841 and died in the White House.

Wouldn't support Patrick Henry's 1765 resolution urging widespread civil disobedience.

Father was one of the wealthiest men and largest landholders in Virginia.

Quotable Quote: At the adoption of the *Declaration of Independence* on July 4, 1776, Hancock declared: *"We must all hang [stick] together."* Franklin smilingly responded with: *"Yes, we must all hang together, or most assuredly, we shall hang separately."* It was at this point that the very large Benjamin Harrison, with a twinkle in his eyes, looked over at smallish Elbridge Gerry and said: *"With me it will be over in a minute, but you, you will be dancing on air an hour after I am gone."*

Heroic Deed: Signing the *Declaration*. Benjamin Harrison knew that should the struggle for independence fail, an ignominious death by hanging would most certainly be his punishment.

Refused an offer of amnesty from British Governor Gage in June 1775.

Little Known Fact: His colleague and close relative, Peyton Randolph, was elected to serve as President of the Continental Congress.

Price Paid for Signing: All the Signers, including Harrison, suffered monetary losses because of their connection with the cause. Some were brought to the brink of financial ruin, or even worse, abject poverty.

7

Biscuit Baking
as Done in Colonial Kitchens

Plain but Tasty Soda Biscuits
Gouverneur Morris Often Ate These

4 cups flour	Pinch of salt
3 tsp baking powder	3 tbls shortening
	2 cups milk

Blend flour and baking powder. Sift together in a large wooden mixing bowl. Stir in salt and rub in shortening quickly and lightly. Slowly pour milk in last and stir until smoothly mixed. Knead dough with as few strokes as possible. Too much handling will ruin the biscuit. Dough should be *very* soft and pliable. If flour stiffens it too much, simply add little more milk. When ready, turn dough out on lightly floured board (or countertop). Roll dough out lightly into ¼ to ½ inch thick sheet. Cut into small 2 inch round biscuits using floured biscuit cutter or upside down drinking glass of appropriate size. Place each biscuit on shallow, floured baking pan. Bake in quick oven (425 degrees) for about 12 to 15 minutes. **NOTE:** *Split biscuits when ready to eat them and they are still warm. Spread with butter or favorite jams or jellies, honey or molasses. Makes two dozen biscuits.*

Gouverneur Morris (1752 – 1816)

Heritage: French-English ancestors. Born at the Morrisania Estate in Westchester County (now the Bronx), New York. Family emigrated from England to America sometime in the late 1600s or early 1700s.

Religion: Devout Christian. Said just before dying: *"Descend towards the grave full of gratitude to the Giver of all good."* Also see quote below.

Education: Brilliant, highly educated man. Taught all of his youth by the best of tutors. Attended a prestigious Huguenot school in New Rochelle. Later attended Kings College (presently Columbia University in New York City). Graduated in 1768 when just 16-years old. Studied law on his own.

Marriage: Wed rather late in life. Married Anne Cary Randolph in 1809 when he was 57-years old. She was from a prominent Virginia family.

Children: One son.

Interesting Highlights: One of 39 men who signed the *Constitution.*

One of five men who signed both the *Constitution* and the *Articles of Confederation.* The others who also signed were Carroll, Dickinson, Robert Morris and Sherman.

Very close friend of George Washington.

Appointed by President Washington to replace Thomas Jefferson as Minister to France (1792-1794).

He, along with Robert Livingston and John Jay, were the three men most responsible for the development of New York's first *Constitution.*

Served in the Pennsylvania militia in 1776.

One of the wittiest and most brilliant members of the Constitutional Convention. Spoke often and humorously,

Responsible for coming up with the idea of using the dollar as the basis for American money.

Wrote the final draft of the *Constitution.*

Originator of the phrase: *"We the People of the United States."*

Older half-brother, Lewis, had the distinction of being one of the Signers of the *Declaration of Independence.*

Quotable Quote: *"Religion is the only solid basis of good morals; therefore education should teach the precepts of religion, and the duties of man toward God."*

Heroic Deed: Refused an offer of amnesty from British Governor Gage in June 1775.

Little Known Fact: Lost one leg in a childhood carriage accident.

Price Paid for Signing: All the Signers, including Morris, suffered monetary losses because of their connection with the cause. Some were brought to the brink of financial ruin, or even worse, abject poverty.

Rich Cream Biscuits –
Mrs. Sherman's Christmas Best

2 cups flour   ½ tsp salt
3 tbls baking powder   4 tbls butter
          ¾ cup heavy cream

Sift together in wooden mixing bowl flour, baking powder and salt. Cut in butter with fork or finger tips. Mixture should resemble coarse corn meal. Lastly stir in cream, again using fork. Turn dough out onto lightly floured board. Knead for about 30 seconds. Longer kneading will ruin biscuits. Then roll out to ½ inch thick sheet. Cut with floured biscuit cutter or appropriate size upside down drinking glass. Place each biscuit on shallow, ungreased baking pan. Bake in very quick oven (450 degrees) for 12 to 15 minutes. Yield is 12 to 16 biscuits.

Roger Sherman (1721 – 1793)

Heritage: English descent. Born in Newton, Massachusetts. Parents immigrated to the Colonies from England in the late 1600s or early 1700s.

Religion: Devout Christian. John Adams described Sherman as *"...an old Puritan, as honest as an angel and as firm in the cause of American Independence as Mount Atlas."* Also see quote below.

Education: Early formal education extremely limited. Avid reader. Self-taught in mathematics, astronomy and numerous other subjects.
Always kept book open on the workbench while repairing shoes. Studied law by reading books borrowed from local attorneys.

Marriage: Twice married. Wed first wife, Elizabeth Hartwell, in 1749. He was 28. Little is known about Elizabeth other than she was a fine Christian young woman. She died 11 years later in 1760. Remarried, this time to Rebecca Prescott. She was 20 and he was 42 at this time.

Children: Seven children born to first union. Eight more born to Roger and his second wife. All but one lived to maturity. Rebecca raised her own eight children as well as the seven born to Roger and Elizabeth.

Interesting Highlights: One of 56 men to sign the *Declaration of Independence*. Hancock was the *only* one to sign on July 4, 1776. Another 49 signed on August 2. Six signed at a later date – they were Richard Henry Lee, Gerry, McKean, Thorton, Wolcott and Wythe.

One of 6 Signers who also affixed his signature to the *Constitution*. The others were Clymer, Franklin, Robert Morris, Read and Wilson.

Seconded Benjamin Franklin's motion that congress be opened each day with a prayer.

Made an astounding 128 speeches at the Constitutional Convention.

Quotable Quote: *"I believe there is one only living and true God, existing in three persons, the Father, the Son, and the Holy Ghost ... that the Scriptures of the old and new testaments are a revelation from God, and a complete rule to direct us as how we may glorify and enjoy him."*

`Heroic Deed: Signing the *Declaration*. Roger Sherman knew that should the struggle for independence fail, an ignominious death by hanging would most certainly be his punishment.

Refused an offer of amnesty from British Governor Gage in June 1775.

Little Known Fact: Only man to sign all four of the main founding documents: *Articles of Association* (1774); *Declaration of Independence* (1776); *Articles of Confederation* (1777); and *Constitution* (1787).

Price Paid for Signing: All the Signers, including Sherman, suffered monetary losses because of their connection with the cause. Some were brought to the brink of financial ruin, or even worse, abject poverty.

Unique Potato Biscuits --
Charles Cotesworth Pinckney Favorite

8 medium size potatoes   2 tbls sugar
2 cups milk   Flour to suit
1 cup yeast   4 tbls butter, melted
Pinch of salt

Boil potatoes until soft. Finely mash in large wooden mixing bowl. Warm milk ever so slightly and add along with the yeast and sugar. Blend ingredients with sufficient flour to make a thin batter. Cover bowl with heavy towel or cloth. Set aside in warm place to rise for 4 to 5 hours.

After batter has risen nicely and become light, add melted butter and salt to mixture. Blend in enough flour to make soft, pliable dough. Cover with heavy towel or cloth. Set aside to rise another 4 hours. When risen, turn dough out on lightly floured board (or countertop). Roll dough out to ¾ inch thick sheet. Cut into round biscuits using floured biscuit cutter or appropriate size upside down drinking glass. Place in rows on floured shallow baking pan. Again cover and let biscuits rise for 1 more hour. Bake immediately in quick oven (between 425 degrees) for 10 to 15 minutes.

Charles Cotesworth Pinckney (1746 – 1825)

Heritage: English. Born in Charleston, South Carolina. Ancestors immigrated to America from England in the mid or early or mid-1600s.

Religion: Devout Christian. Never allowed to go to sleep at night until after having prayer with either his mother or father. First President of the Charleston *Bible* Society. Also see quote below.

Education: Taken to England by his father when seven in order *"to get a proper education."* Tutored in London and attended the finest British prep schools. Attended Christ Church College in Oxford. Taught by Sir William Blackstone, the foremost legal authority of his day. Then studied for a military career at the prestigious Royal Military Academy of France.

Marriage: Twice married. Wed first wife, Sarah Middleton, in 1773. After Sarah died, he remarried Mary Stead in 1786. Both wives came from wealthy Charleston families of the highest social standing.

Children: None with first wife, Sarah. Three daughters with second wife, Mary. Survived by these daughters.

Interesting Highlights: Washington's trusted aide-de-camp during the War for Independence.

Saw much military action. Participated in the battles fought at Charleston, Brandywine, Germantown and during the Siege of Savannah.

Captured by the British when Charleston fell in 1780. Remained their prisoner until 1782.

Delegate to the Constitutional Convention held in Philadelphia for a four months between May 25 to September 17, 1787.

One of 39 men who signed the *Constitution*.

Younger second cousin, Charles, also signed the *Constitution*.

One of the Constitutional Convention's outstanding leaders.

Quotable Quote: *"Blasphemy against the Almighty is denying his being or providence, or uttering contumelious reproaches on our Savior Christ. It is punished, at common law by fine and imprisonment, for Christianity is part of the laws of the land."*

Heroic Deed: Refused an offer of amnesty from British Governor Gage in June 1775.

Little Known Fact: Charles Cotesworth was one of 12 Signers of the *Constitution* who owned slaves. Others were Bassett, Blair, Blount, Butler, Daniel Carroll, Jenifer, Madison, the other Pinckney, John Rutledge, Spaight and Washington.

Price Paid for Signing: All the Signers, including Pinckney, suffered monetary losses because of their connection with the cause. Some were brought to the brink of financial ruin, or even worse, abject poverty.

Dolly Madison's Baking Powder Biscuits – Made Them for Her Husband, James

2 cups flour   ½ tsp salt
2-1/2 tsp baking powder   ¼ cup butter, melted
¾ cup milk (about)

Sift together in wooden mixing bowl the flour, baking powder and salt. Pour cooled melted butter into this. Stir until mixture becomes grainy and resembles coarse corn meal. Make well in the center and add milk. Stir lightly until everything is nicely blended. Mixture should be soft but not sticky. Dump onto lightly floured board. Knead about 10 to 15 strokes. Pat or roll out to ¼ inch thick for thin crispy biscuits or ½ inch thick for soft biscuits. Cut dough with floured biscuit cutter or appropriate size upside down drinking glass. Place biscuits on shallow ungreased baking pan. Bake in very quick oven (450 degrees) for 12 to 15 minutes or until golden brown. Makes about 16 biscuits.

James Madison (1751 – 1836)

Heritage: English. Born to a planter aristocracy in Port Conway, King George County, Virginia. Descendants immigrated to America from England sometime in the 1600s. May also have Scottish and Welsh relatives.

Religion: Christian. First considered becoming a minister and did postgraduate study in theology. Also see quote below.

Education: Home schooled by his mother and tutored by a variety of the best teachers. Also attended a number of prestigious private schools. Graduated from the College of New Jersey (now Princeton).

Marriage: Married Dolly Payne Todd in 1749. She was a widow and 16 years younger than James.

Children: No children of their own, but lovely and vivacious Dolly brought a son to their marriage.

Interesting Highlights: The oldest of 10 children in his family.

A slave owner all of his life, he was an active member of the *American Colonization Society*, a group dedicated to sending all slaves back to Africa.

One of the most influential members of the *Constitutional Convention*. Rarely absent, he almost totally dominated the proceedings.

Deservedly known today *as "The Father of the Constitution."*

His most important contribution as one of our Founding Fathers was his work on the writing of our *Constitution*.

One of 39 men who signed the *Constitution*.

He outlived all other Signers of the *Constitution*.

Collaborated with John Jay and fellow Signer of the *Constitution,* Alexander Hamilton, in writing a series of essays. They were published in newspapers in 1787 and 1788. These writings were later published as a book titled *The Federalist Papers*.

Quotable Quote: *"We have all been encouraged to feel in the guardianship of that Almighty Being, whose power regulates the destiny of nations."*

Heroic Deed: When the *Constitution* came up for ratification in Virginia, he had to defend the document against such great patriot orators as Patrick Henry, Richard Henry Lee and George Mason.

Refused an offer of amnesty from British Governor Gage in June 1775.

Little Known Fact: Madison was one of 12 signers of the *Constitution* who owned slaves. The others were Bassett, Blair, Blount, Butler, Daniel Carroll, Jenifer, both Pinckneys, Rutledge, Spaight and Washington.

Price Paid for Signing: All the Signers, including Madison, suffered monetary losses because of their connection with the cause. Some were brought to the brink of financial ruin, or even worse, abject poverty.

Whole Wheat Biscuits –
Baked for the Fitzsimons' Family

1 cup flour	1 cup whole wheat flour
1 tsp salt	6 tbls butter, soft
3 tsp baking powder	½ cup milk

Sift together flour, salt and baking powder in large wooden mixing bowl. Stir in whole wheat flour and blend well. Cream in soft butter. Lastly, add milk. Work the mixture into soft dough. Turn dough out on lightly floured board. Knead 5 minutes. Then roll dough out into ¾ inch thick sheet. Cut into 3-inch round biscuits using floured biscuit cutter or upside down drinking glass of appropriate size. Place biscuits close together on shallow, buttered baking pan. Bake in a very quick oven (450 degrees) from 15 to 18 minutes.

Thomas Fitzsimons (1741 -- 1811)

Heritage: Irish. Born in Ireland. Immigrated to America from Ireland in 1760 when only 19-years old.

Religion: Devout Christian. Roman Catholic. See quote below.

Education: All that is known is that an adequate education was provided for him before his father died in America. Mostly tutoring by the best available teachers.

Marriage: Wed Catherine Meade in 1761. She was daughter of a wealthy and prominent Philadelphia businessman. As a result of this union, he soon after went into business with one of Catherine's brothers.

Children: Not known.

Interesting Highlights: Attended the Constitutional Convention religiously and seldom missed a session.

Apparently made no significant contributions during the Constitutional Convention insofar as in the development of the document.

One of 39 men who signed the *Constitution*.

Called the Constitution he helped devise *"a treasure to posterity."*

One of two Roman Catholics who signed the *Constitution*. The other Catholic signer was Daniel Carroll of Maryland.

One of four Signers of the *Constitution* who was born in Ireland. The others were Butler, McHenry and Paterson.

Commanded a Pennsylvania militia group in 1776 and 1777.

Fought against the British during the Revolutionary War at the Battle of Trenton, and later in defense of Philadelphia.

His integrity impressed James Madison.

Donated a large part of his fortune to help the independence movement.

Helped Robert Morris organize the banking facilities used to support the Continental Army and Navy in the final years of the Revolutionary war

Quotable Quote: One of the men who developed the *Constitution* of Pennsylvania. Fitzsimons insisted on this wording for what legislators must say before being seated: *"I do believe in one God, the Creator and Governor of the universe, the rewarder of the good and the punisher of the wicked."*

Heroic Deed: Refused an offer of amnesty from British Governor Gage in June 1775.

Little Known Fact: As a result of his marriage, he soon after went into business with a brother of his wife, George Mead (the grandfather of the famous Civil War General).

Price Paid for Signing: All the Signers, including Fitzsimmons, suffered monetary losses because of their connection with the cause. Some were brought to the brink of financial ruin, or even worse, abject poverty.

Tantalizing Tea Biscuits –
Delight of the Gerry Family

4 cups milk	¾ cup yeast
¾ cup shortening	2 tbls sugar
or	1 tsp salt
¾ cup butter	Flour to suit

Warm milk slightly and melt shortening or butter in it. Stir in yeast, sugar, salt and enough flour to make thin sponge batter. Cover bowl with thick towel or cloth. Allow to sit in warm place to rise for about 5 hours. Then work more flour into the sponge until it forms a rather stiff dough. Cover again and set aside to rise for 5 more hours. When ready, turn dough out on lightly floured board. Roll dough out into ¼ inch thick sheet. Cut into small round biscuits using floured biscuit cutter or an upside down drinking glass of the appropriate size. Set biscuits close together in shallow, floured baking pan. Cover and set aside in warm place to rise for about 20 more  minutes. When ready, bake in rather quick oven (at 425 to 450 degrees) for 20 minutes. **NOTE:** *This kind of biscuit was considered to be one of the best for snacks and teas.*

Elbridge Gerry (1744 -- 1814)

Heritage: English descent. Born in Marblehead, Massachusetts, on July 17, the third of 12 children.

Religion: Devout Christian. Attended church regularly. Brought up in a home where prayers were always said before meals and before going to bed. The *Bible* was read nightly.

Education: Father resolved to making certain his son got the best possible education. Taught at home by mother and best available tutors money could buy. Attended only the finest of prep schools. Attended Harvard and graduated in 1762 when just 18-years old.

Marriage: Wed a beautiful Irish girl, Ann Thompson, of New York while a member of the Continental Congress. Ann was born in 1763. Graduate of University of Edinburg in Scotland. She was a high society favorite.

Children: Nine children – six daughters and three sons.

Interesting Highlights: One of 56 men to sign the *Declaration of Independence*. Hancock was the *only* one to sign on July 4, 1776. Another 49 signed on August 2. Six signed at a later date – they were Gerry, Richard Henry Lee, McKean, Thorton, Wolcott and Wythe.

Not a shy man, he spoke a total of 119 times while a delegate to the Continental Congress.

One of the most vocal members of the 1787 Constitutional Convention. Said another delegate: *"He objected to everything he did not propose."*

Quotable Quote: At the adoption of the *Declaration of Independence* on July 4, 1776, Hancock declared: *"We must all hang [stick] together."* Franklin smilingly responded with: *"Yes, we must all hang together, or most assuredly, we shall hang separately."* It was at this point that the very large Benjamin Harrison with a tinkle in his eyes looked over at smallish Elbridge Gerry and said: *"With me it will be over in a minute, but you, you will be dancing on air an hour after I am gone.."*

Heroic Deed: Signing the *Declaration*. Elbridge Gerry knew that should the struggle for independence fail, an ignominious death by hanging would most certainly be his punishment.

Refused an offer of amnesty from British Governor Gage in June 1775.

Little Known Fact: His wife, Ann, died in 1849 at age 86. She was the last surviving wife of a Signer of the *Declaration of Independence*.

Although an invalid, Ann supervised the children's religious schooling and their basic education.

Price Paid for Signing: All the Signers, including Gerry, suffered monetary losses because of their connection with the cause. Some were brought to the brink of financial ruin, or even worse, abject poverty.

Blueberry Biscuits –
Mrs. Baldwin's Breakfast Special

1 cup whole wheat flour	1 egg
1-1/2 tbls butter	1 cup blueberries
1 tsp salt	2 tsp baking powder
2 tbls sugar	1 cup milk

Flour to suit

Sift whole-wheat flour into large wooden mixing bowl. Rub in butter, salt and sugar. Add egg and lightly stir until everything is well blended. Dredge blueberries in little regular flour and stir into mixture. Lastly stir in baking powder and milk. Add sufficient flour to make soft, easily handled dough. Turn dough out on lightly floured board (or countertop). *Do not knead!* Roll dough out into ½ inch thick sheet. Cut into small round cakes with floured biscuit cutter or appropriate size upside down drinking glass. Place biscuits in rows on well-buttered shallow baking pan. Bake for about 20 minutes in quick oven (425 degrees), or until golden brown on top. When done baking, quickly turn biscuits out of pan. Lay them on soft cloth and cover with towel until ready to serve.

NOTE: *Mrs. Baldwin considered this recipe to be one of her best.*

Abraham Baldwin (1754 – 1807)

Heritage: English and Scots. Born at Guilford, Connecticut. Family immigrated to America sometime in the late 1600s or early 1700s. The second son of a blacksmith who had 13 children by two wives.

Religion: Devout Christian. Chaplain in the Continental Army during the Revolutionary War. Became a tutor and minister at Yale (1775 to 1779). Also see quote below.

Education: Getting his son a proper education was of the utmost importance to his blacksmith father, who went heavily in debt to pay for this.

Attended nearby village school. Also taught by the best private tutors. A brilliant scholar, he graduated with honors from Yale in 1772. Later studied law and admitted to the bar in 1783.

Marriage: None. Was a bachelor.

Children: None.

Interesting Highlights: Coming from a rather humble background, he was highly successful as a clergyman, lawyer, teacher and politician.

One of 39 men who signed the *Constitution*.

One of three Signers of the *Constitution* who was a lifelong bachelor. The others were Gilman and Jenifer. Two bachelors signed the *Declaration of Independence*. They were Hewes and Rodney.

Turned down the offer to be the Professor of Divinity at Yale in 1781.

Founded Franklin College in 1798, a school that would later become the University of Georgia. Served as its first President.

Baldwin's half-brother, Henry, became a Justice on the United States Supreme Court.

Quotable Quote: Believed it to be in the country's best interest *"to support the principles or religion and morality."*

Heroic Deed: In June of 1775, British Governor Gage made a desperate attempt to stem the tide of the blossoming independence movement. Amnesty was offered to every Colonist – with the exception of Samuel Adams and John Hancock – who would lay down their arms and swear loyalty to the Crown. To their credit, not one patriot, including Baldwin, turncoated and accepted the pardon.

Little Known Fact: Went on to serve for 18 years in the House of Representatives (1789 to 1799) and the Senate (1799 to 1807). Bitterly fought against the policies of Alexander Hamilton and was an ally of Jefferson and Madison.

Price Paid for Signing: All the Signers, including Baldwin, suffered monetary losses because of their connection with the cause. Some were brought to the brink of financial ruin, or even worse, abject poverty.

Tiny Tea Biscuits –
Lovingly Prepared by Mrs. Butler

Flour to suit   1 tsp salt
1-1/2 tbls shortening   2 tsp baking powder

1 cup milk or cream

Start by sifting 1 cup flour into large wooden mixing bowl. Run shortening and salt into flour. Stir in baking powder and milk. Beat lightly until batter is free of lumps. Add sufficient flour to make soft, easily handled dough. Turn dough out on lightly floured board. The dough must not be stirred or kneaded too much or it will ruin the biscuits. Roll dough out to ½ inch sheet. Cut into round cakes about 1-inch in diameter using a floured biscuit cutter or upside down drinking glass of appropriate size. Place biscuits on shallow, well-buttered baking pan. Immediately put in a quick oven (425 degrees). Bake for about 20 minutes or until golden brown on top. Turn out of baking pan on soft cloth and cover with napkin until ready to serve. **NOTE:** *These biscuits are extremely good when made with sour milk in place of sweet milk. And even better when made with heavy cream instead of milk. When sour milk is used, substitute baking soda for baking powder called for above. Makes 2 dozen delightful little tea biscuits.*

Pierce Butler (1744 – 1822)

Heritage: Irish. Born in Ireland. Family immigrated to America from Ireland sometime in the late 1600s or early 1700s.

Religion: Devout Christian. Learned to read using a *Bible* in the home. Active member of Christ's Church. See quote below.

Education: As a member of the British hereditary aristocracy, much of his early education was obtained at home with the finest available tutors. Also attended prestigious private schools.

Marriage: Wed Mary Middleton in 1771. She was the daughter of a wealthy South Carolina planter and prominent Colonial leader.

Children: One daughter who grew up and married a doctor.

Interesting Highlights: Played a major role at the Constitutional Convention.
One of the Constitutional Convention's most aristocratic members.
One of 39 men who signed the *Constitution*.
One of four Signers of the *Constitution* who was born in Ireland. The others were Fitzsimmons, McHenry and Paterson.
Personally contributed money and supplies to help the Continental Army under General Washington.
Father-in-law was President of the First Continental Congress that convened on September 5, 1774, at Carpenter's Hall in Philadelphia.
Brother-in-law, Arthur Middleton, was a delegate to the Second Continental Congress that convened on May 10, 1775, at the State House in Philadelphia. Middleton also signed the *Declaration of Independence*.
Owned 10,000+-acre plantation in coastal region of South Carolina.
Owned fleet of coastal ships for use in his prosperous export business.
Ranking officer of 29th Regiment of Foot, his unit in the British Royal Army. A detachment of his unit fired *"the shots heard 'round the world,"* in 1770 at what became famous as ***"The Boston Massacre."***

Quotable Quote: *"All men are absolutely dependent upon their Father in Heaven for everything. Each man must find it necessary, in every manner, to conform to the absolute will of his Maker."*

Heroic Deed: Refused an offer of amnesty from British Governor Gage in June 1775

Little Known Fact: One of 12 Signers of the *Constitution* who owned slaves. The others were Bassett, Blair, Blount, Daniel Carroll, Jenifer, Madison, both Pinckneys, Rutledge, Spaight and Washington.

Price Paid for Signing: All the Signers, including Butler, suffered monetary losses because of their connection with the cause. Some were brought to the brink of financial ruin, or even worse, abject poverty

8

Homemade Crackers
as Made for Our Founders

Beaten Crackers --
Anne Chase Baked These for Samuel

4 cups flour   ½ tsp baking soda
3 tbls butter   Pinch of salt
         2 cups milk

Put flour in wooden mixing bowl. Rub butter into flour. Dissolve baking soda in little hot water. Add this along with salt and milk. Blend thoroughly and then work into ball of dough. Lay dough on well- floured board. Beat hard with rolling pin for at least 30 minutes. Turn and shift the dough mass often while beating. Then roll out into even sheet about ¼ inch thick or less. Prick deeply all over surface with a fork. Bake entire sheet in moderate oven (350 degrees) until hard. When finished baking, break sheet into chunks and hang pieces up in muslin bag. Leave for 2 days to dry. Crackers will then be ready to eat.

Samuel Chase (1722 – 1811)

Heritage: English. Born in Somerset County, Maryland. Family immigrated to America from England in the late 1600s or early 1700s.

Religion: Devout Christian. Son of an Anglican clergyman, a minister of the Protestant Episcopal Church. Also see quote below.

Education: Avid reader of everything he could get his hands on as a child and young adult. Father provided him with a basic education in the classics. Studied at home with the best of private tutors. Studied law under the auspices of Messrs. Hammond and Hall, the most prestigious law firm in the Annapolis area.

Marriage: Twice married. Wed first to Anne Baldwin in 1762. She died right after the Revolutionary War started. Second marriage was to Hannah Kilty Giles in 1783. She was a lovely young woman he met while on a business trip to London.

Children: Samuel and Anne had six children – two sons and four daughters. Second wife, Hannah, bore him two daughters.

Interesting Highlights: Voted for acceptance of the *Declaration of Independence* on July 2, 1776.

One of 56 men to sign the *Declaration of Independence*. Hancock was the *only* one to sign on July 4, 1776. Another 49 signed on August 2. Six signed at a later date – they were Richard Henry Lee, Gerry, McKean, Thorton, Wolcott and Wythe.

Had law practice with William Paca, later also to be a delegate to the Continental Congress and fellow Signer of the *Declaration of Independence*.

Chairman of special congressional committee formed to punish Americans who were known to have given "aid and comfort to the enemy."

Quotable Quote: An 1848 textbook described him this way: *"Judge Chase was a man of great benevolence of feeling and in all his walks, he exemplified the beauties of Christianity, of which he was a sincere professor."*

Heroic Deed: Signing the *Declaration*. Samuel Chase knew that should the struggle for independence fail, an ignominious death by hanging would most certainly be his punishment.

Refused an offer of amnesty from British Governor Gage in June 1775.

Little Known Fact: Samuel Chase said this: *"By our form of government, the Christian religion is the established religion; and all sects and denominations of Christians are placed upon the same equal footing, and are equally entitled to protection in their religious liberty."*

Price Paid for Signing: All the Signers, including Chase, suffered monetary losses because of their connection with the cause. Some were brought to the brink of financial ruin, or even worse, abject poverty.

Delicate Wafer Thins
Elizabeth Ingersoll's Secret Receipt

4 cups flour   Pinch of salt
2 tbls butter   Milk to suit

Put flour into wooden mixing bowl. Rub butter into flour. Then add salt and enough milk to make very stiff dough. Lay dough on well-floured board and roll out *extremely* thin. Cut sheet of dough into small round or square segments. Then again roll these as thin as can possibly be handled. Using a spatula, lift each cracker carefully and lay on floured (not buttered) shallow baking pan. Immediately bake in quick oven (425 degrees) until crackers are hard. **NOTE:** *These wafers are especially good for invalids. They should be hardly thicker than writing paper.*

Jared Ingersoll (1749 – 1822)

Heritage: English. Born in New Haven, Connecticut. Father was a British official in the Colonies and later a prominent loyalist. Family immigrated to America from England in the late 1600s or early 1700s.

Religion: Devout Christian. Brought up in a Christian home where *Bible* readings were commonplace. Regularly attended the Presbyterian Church in Philadelphia. Also see quote below.

Education: Privately tutored as a child and young adult. Graduated from Yale in 1766. Sent to England in 1773 to study law in London's Middle Temple. Completed studies at London's Middle Temple in 1776 and then toured Europe for two more years in order to avoid serving in the Revolutionary War.

Marriage: Married Elizabeth Pettit in 1781. No more is known about this union.

Children: Three. Little or nothing is known about any of them.

Interesting Highlights: Elected to be delegate to the Continental Congress (1780-1781).

Religiously attended every session of the Constitutional Convention held in Philadelphia for about four months from May 25 to September 17, 1787.

Although a lawyer who was known to be a good debater, Ingersoll rarely spoke during the proceedings.

One of 39 men who signed the *Constitution*.

Believed that the election of Thomas Jefferson as President in 1780 to be a terrible blow for the new nation and he called it a "great subversion."

Unsuccessfully ran for Vice-President in 1812 on the Federalist ticket.

Quotable Quote: One of the men who developed the *Constitution* of Pennsylvania. It clearly spells out what each member of the legislature must say before being seated: *"I do believe in one God, the Creator and Governor of the universe, the rewarder of the good and the punisher of the wicked."*

Heroic Deed: In June of 1775, British Governor Gage made a desperate attempt to stem the tide of the blossoming independence movement in the Colonies. Amnesty was offered to *every* Colonist with the exception of Samuel Adams and John Hancock, who would lay down his arms and swear their unwavering loyalty to the Crown. To their credit, not one patriot, including Jared Ingersoll, turncoated and accepted the pardon.

Little Known Fact: Was attorney who represented William Blount when he was impeached in 1779.

Price Paid for Signing: All the Signers, including Ingersoll, suffered monetary losses because of their connection with the cause. Some were brought to the brink of financial ruin, or even worse, abject poverty.

Crispy Cracknels –
Mary Bartlett Concocted Them

2 cups milk   ½ cup yeast
4 tbls butter   1 tsp salt
          Flour to suit

Put milk and butter in saucepan. Warm enough to melt butter. Then blend in yeast and salt. Pour this into large wooden mixing bowl. Work in enough flour to make light, elastic dough. Cover with heavy towel or cloth and set in warm place to rise. When nicely risen and light, put dough on floured board. Knead hard at least 30 minutes. Then roll dough out until *very* thin. Cut into long 3-inch wide strips. Prick all over surface with fork. Bake strips in slow oven (300 degrees) until hard. **NOTE:** *These are much like soda crackers in appearance. They are to be broken onto chunks after they are finished baking and cooled. Hang pieces up in a muslin bag and leave for at least 2 days to dry sufficiently. They are then ready for eating.*

Josiah Bartlett (1729 – 1795)

Heritage: English. Born in Amesbury, Massachusetts. Ancestors originally from Normandy and had moved to Great Britain. Family sailed to America from England in the late 1600s. Settled in Beverly, Massachusetts.

Religion: Devout Christian. See quote below.

Education: Very little formal education. Tutored in Greek and Latin by a Doctor Webster. Began study of medicine when only 16-years old.. Five years later, in 1750, he opened his own medical practice.

Marriage: Like fellow signer, Whipple, he married a cousin, Mary Bartlett, in 1754. He was 24-years old. Little is known about Mary in her youth except for the fact that she was well educated and an avid patriot.

Children: Mary bore him 12 children. Four died as infants.

Interesting Highlights: Delegate to the First Continental Congress that convened on September 5, 1774, in Carpenter's Hall, Philadelphia.

First man to cast his vote in favor of adopting the *Declaration.*

Delegate to the Second Continental Congress that convened on May10, 1775, in Philadelphia's State House.

One of 56 men to sign the *Declaration of Independence.* Hancock was the *only* one to sign on July 4, 1776. Dr. Bartlett was one of the 49 men to sign on August 2. Six signed at a later date – they were Richard Henry Lee, Gerry, McKean, Thorton, Wolcott and Wythe.

First man to affix his signature to the *Declaration of Independence* on August 2, 1776, when most other members of the Second Continental Congress added their signatures to the historic document.

First man to vote for the *Articles of Confederation* in 1781.

First man to sign the State *Constitution* of New Hampshire when it was ratified in 1788.

First Governor of New Hampshire under the new *Constitution* in 1793.

Founder of the *New Hampshire Medical Society.*

Quotable Quote: *"There should be absolutely no governmental power over religion. This I believe, is clearly supported by the Constitution."*

Heroic Deed: Signing the *Declaration.* Dr. Josiah Bartlett knew that should the struggle for independence fail, an ignominious death by hanging would most certainly be his punishment.

Refused an offer of amnesty from British Governor Gage in June 1775.

Little Known Fact: Awarded honorary degree as a Doctor of Divinity from Dartmouth in 1790.

Price Paid for Signing: All the Signers, including Bartlett, suffered monetary losses because of their connection with the cause. Some were brought to the brink of financial ruin, or even worse, abject poverty.

Anne Johnson's Plain Crackers –
Her Husband Dearly Loved Them

8 cups flour   1-1/2 tbls shortening,
¼ tbls salt   melted
4 cups water, warm

Blend above ingredients in large wooden mixing bowl. Gradually stir in warm water. Keep dough as tight as can be worked. Lay dough on floured board. Beat with rolling pin for at least 30 minutes. Turn and shift dough mass often while beating. Then roll dough out to ¼ inch thick sheet (the thinner the better). Cut in round or square shapes. Using spatula, place crackers on shallow, floured baking pan. Bake in moderate oven (350 degrees) until hard. **NOTE:** *These crackers must have time to slowly dry out well during baking. If not sufficiently dry after baking, hang pieces up in a muslin bag and leave until they are completely dry and ready to eat.*

William Samuel Johnson (1727 – 1819)

Heritage: English-Scottish. Born in Stratford, Connecticut. Family immigrated to America from England sometime late in 1600s or early 1700s.

Religion: Devout Christian. Father was a highly regarded and well-known Anglican minister. See quote below showing a few of the words selected by Johnson for inclusion in the *Constitution* of Connecticut.

Education: Privately tutored as child and young adult. Graduated from Yale when just 17-years of age. Masters Degree in 1747. Later awarded honorary Masters Degree by Harvard as well as Oxford University in 1765 and his Doctorate in 1766. Studied law on his own.

Marriage: Twice married. Wed Anne Beach in 1749. This union added immensely to his wealth. Retired in 1800, a short time after Anne died. Soon thereafter remarried, this time to Mary Brewster Beach, a relative of his first wife, Anne.

Children: Samuel and Anne had six sons and five daughters. Most died as infants or young children. No children were born to the second union.

Interesting Highlights: One of 39 men who signed the *Constitution*.

Delegate to the First Continental Congress that convened on September 5, 1774, at Carpenter's Hall in Philadelphia.

Initially refused to take an active part in any of the proceedings.

Found it impossible to take sides regarding the *Declaration* and the oncoming war because of his many friends residing in England.

Delegate to the Constitutional Convention that met for a four month period in Philadelphia from May 25 to September 17, 1787.

Arrived at the Constitutional Convention on June 2, 1787, and never missed a session.

An officer in the Connecticut militia during the 1750s.

One of the most highly educated signers of the *Constitution*.

Sent to mediate with General Gage in an effort to stop the fighting and bloodshed. The mission failed because of the General's obstinacy.

Quotable Quote: *"The people of this State ... by the Providence of God hath the sole and exclusive right of governing themselves as a free, sovereign, and independent State."*

Heroic Deed: Refused an offer of amnesty from British Governor Gage in June 1775.

Little Known Fact: Son of the first President of King's College, Samuel Johnson (presently Columbia University in New York City).

Price Paid for Signing: All the signers, including Johnson, suffered monetary losses because of their connection with the cause. Some were brought to the brink of financial ruin, or even worse, abject poverty.

Katherine Whipple's Cracker Treat -- She Made These for William

8 cups flour   1 cup shortening
1-3/4 cups sugar   ½ tbls ammonia

Blend all ingredients in large wooden mixing bowl. Add water as needed to make very stiff dough. Lay dough on floured board. Beat with rolling pin for at least 30 minutes. Turn and shift dough mass often while beating. Then roll the dough out to ¼ inch thick sheet (or even thinner is better). Cut into round or square shapes of any desired size. Using spatula, lay unbaked crackers on shallow, floured baking pan. They should be close together, but not quite touching. Bake in moderate oven (350 degrees) until nicely browned.

William Whipple (1730 – 1785)

Heritage: English. Born in Kittery, New Hampshire (now what we know as the State of Maine) Parents emigrated from England to America sometime during the 1730s.

Religion: Devout Christian. One of his colleagues said: *"Not a single moral stain marked his long and useful life."* Also see quote below.

Education: Consisted of going to the local common (public) school. Had no private tutoring as did so many of the other Signers. Did not have an opportunity to attend college. An avid reader and brilliant minded, most of what he learned was self-taught.

Marriage: Like his fellow Signer, Dr. Josiah Bartlett, William married his first cousin, Katherine Moffat. Little is known about their marriage. She was held in especially high esteem because of her breeding, family ties and high social standing. Her family was one of the wealthiest in New Hampshire.

Children: One child, a daughter, died during infancy. Later adopted a niece, Mary Tufton Moffat, in the early 1760s.

Interesting Highlights: Chosen to be a delegate to the Continental Congress in 1776.

Voted to adopt the *Declaration of Independence* on July 2, 1776.

One of 56 men to sign the *Declaration of Independence*. Hancock was the *only* one to sign on July 4, 1776. Whipple was one of 49 men who signed on August 2. Six signed at a later date – they were Richard Henry Lee, Gerry, McKean, Thorton, Wolcott and Wythe.

Had task of escorting British prisoners to a camp near Boston. There they were confined while awaiting British ships to return them to England.

Advocated using strong military aggression in the Revolutionary War rather than a pussyfooting kind of diplomacy.

Quotable Quote: *"Almighty God, I will always indulge in my sacred duty as a Christian. Should you give me forgiveness, I greatly rejoice. Should you be angry with me, I will bear any of your punishment. The Book [Bible] has been written. Life's die has been cast."*

Heroic Deed: Signing the *Declaration*. William Whipple knew that should the struggle for independence fail, an ignominious death by hanging would most certainly be his punishment.

Refused an offer of amnesty from British Governor Gage in June 1775.

Little Known Fact: Left the Continental Congress in 1777 to serve as a Brigadier General in the New Hampshire militia.

Price Paid for Signing: All the Signers, including Whipple, suffered monetary losses because of their connection with the cause. Some were brought to the brink of financial ruin, or even worse, abject poverty.

9

Roll Baking
as Done by Colonial Women

Vienna Yeast Rolls –
Favorite of the Morton Family

4 cups water, warm	1 tsp salt
2 tbls sugar	1 yeast cake, crumbled

Flour to suit, sifted

Put warm water into large wooden mixing bowl. Blend in sugar, salt and crumbled yeast. When yeast is dissolved, work in enough sifted flour to make medium soft dough. Knead well in bowl to assure all the ingredients are well blended. Cover bowl with heavy towel or cloth and set aside in warm place to rise.

When it risen to about double in size, turn dough out on floured board. Break into large chunks and shape into small, tapered loaves (about 6-inches long and 2-inches around). Knead lightly. Place each loaf on shallow, nicely buttered baking pan. Allow a little space between loaves. Cover again and set aside to rise. When light (risen), gash the tops diagonally from 3 to 5 times. Bake in moderate oven (350 degrees) for about 25 minutes or until lightly browned. **NOTE:** *For a delightful change, Anne, John Morton's wife, sometimes didn't gash loaves. She simply brushed them with beaten egg and sprinkled the tops with caraway seeds, ground peanuts or almonds.*

John Morton (1725 – 1777)

Heritage: Swedish. Descendant of ancestors who immigrated to America from Sweden in the early Seventeenth Century (1600s).

Religion: Devout Quaker and *Bible* believing Christian.

Education: Highly educated stepfather tutored him to make certain he had a good basic education. Taught him all subjects and especially stressed mathematics and surveying. Morton never attended college.

Marriage: Married Anne Justice in 1745 or 1746. Both were Swedes. Families farmed in Chester County (now Delaware County), Pennsylvania.

Children: Eight – five daughters and three sons. One son became a major in the Continental Army.

Interesting Highlights: Politically active for many years before becoming a delegate to the First Continental Congress.

Elected to the Stamp Act Congress in 1765.

Delegate to the First Continental Congress that convened on September 5, 1774, at Carpenter's Hall in Philadelphia.

Delegate to he Second Continental Congress that convened on May 10, 1775, at the State House in Philadelphia

One of 56 men to sign the *Declaration of Independence*. Hancock was the *only* one to sign on July 4, 1776. Another 49 signed on August 2. Six signed at a later date – they were Richard Henry Lee, Gerry, McKean, Thorton, Wolcott and Wythe.

Became sick in the Spring of 1777. Died at age of 51, less than a year after having signed the *Declaration*. Holds the distinction of being the first Signer to die.

Quotable Quote: This *Bible* believing Christian was rejected and shunned by both Quaker friends and family for signing the historic *Declaration of Independence*. His final words before dying were: *"Tell them that they will live to see the hour when they shall acknowledge it [the signing] to have been the most glorious service that I ever rendered to my country."*

Heroic Deed: Signing the *Declaration*. John Morton knew that should the struggle for independence fail, an ignominious death by hanging would most certainly be his punishment.

Refused an offer of amnesty from British Governor Gage in June 1775.

Little Known Fact: Broke tie by casting the decisive ballot that swung Pennsylvania over to the "yes" vote for Independence.

Close friend of Benjamin Franklin.

Price Paid for Signing: All the Signers, including Morton, suffered monetary losses because of their connection with the cause. Some were brought to the brink of financial ruin, or even worse, abject poverty.

Tea Rolls
Made by Abigail Adams for John

1 cup milk, scalded   ¼ cup sugar
1 yeast cake   1 tsp salt
3-1/2 cups flour   Pinch of nutmeg
¼ cup butter, melted   2 eggs, well beaten

Put scalded milk into large wooden mixing bowl. Crumble yeast cake in ¼ cup warm water and let dissolve completely. When milk is lukewarm, add 2 cups of flour. Beat thoroughly and add yeast mixture to this. Cover bowl with heavy towel or cloth and set in warm place to rise for a couple of hours. When light (risen), stir in melted butter, sugar, salt, nutmeg and frothy beaten eggs. Lastly, add the rest of the flour and mix until it forms smooth soft dough.

Turn dough out on floured board and knead hard for 15 minutes. Put dough back in mixing bowl and cover with towel or cloth. Set aside to again rise until double in size. When the dough has risen, take from the bowl and break into small egg-size chunks. Form into small rolls. Place rolls close together in shallow buttered baking pan. Cover once again and let rise until light. Bake in quick oven (425 degrees) for 15 minutes or until lightly browned on top.

John Adams (1735 – 1826)

Heritage: English. Born in Braintree (now Quincy), Massachusetts. Direct descendant of John Alden who came to America on the Mayflower

Religion: Christian. Considered going into the ministry. He said this: *"The Ten Commandments and the Sermon on the Mount contain my religion"*

Education: Graduated from Harvard College in 1775. Later studied law under a local lawyer.

Marriage: Married Abigail Smith on October 26, 1764, when she was 20. From a Christian family, both her father and grandfather were clergymen.

Children: Four children – three sons and a daughter.

Interesting Highlights: Delegate to the Continental Congress from 1774 to 1778.

He and his cousin, Samuel Adams, were two of the 49 men who signed the *Declaration of Independence* on August 2, 1776. Six others signed the *Declaration* at a later date. They were Gerry, Richard Henry Lee, McKean, Thornton, Wolcott and Wythe. John Hancock was *only* man to sign on July 4.

He and Abigail's life together was one of history's everlasting love affairs. They were completely devoted to each other throughout their blissful marriage of 54 years.

A major force behind getting the various states to ratify the *Constitution*.

John Adams and Jefferson (1743-1826) were two of the last three Signers of the *Declaration of Independence* to die. Charles Carroll (1737-1832) was the last signer to pass away.

America's second President (1797-1801) following George Washington.

Was the man most influential in getting George Washington appointed as Commander-in-Chief of the Continental Army.

Quotable Quote: Regarding the day the Continental Congress approved the *Declaration,* he said this: *"It ought to be commemorated, as a Day of deliverance, by solemn acts of devotion to God Almighty."*

Heroic Deed: Signing the *Declaration.* John Adams knew that should the struggle for independence fail, an ignominious death by hanging would most certainly be his punishment.

Refused an offer of amnesty from British Governor Gage in June 1775.

Little Known Fact: Worked with Franklin and Jefferson on a special committee to develop the *Declaration of Independence.*

Price Paid for Signing: Especially high price put on his head. He eluded capture, even though the British hunted him down like an animal. All the Signers, including Adams, suffered monetary losses because of their connection with the cause. Some were brought to the brink of financial ruin, or even worse, abject poverty.

Pocketbook Rolls --
David Brearly's Favorite

1 cup water, boiling	½ yeast cake
2 tbls butter, melted	½ cup water, lukewarm
1 tsp salt	3-1/2 cups flour
¼ cup sugar	1 egg, well beaten

Put boiling water into large wooden mixing bowl. Stir in butter, salt and sugar. Blend everything thoroughly. Meanwhile crumble yeast cake in lukewarm water and let dissolve. Stir this into mixture in bowl. Sift flour into mixture and blend with other ingredients. When done, cover with thick towel or cloth. Set in warm place to rise.

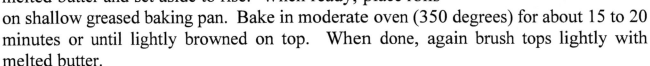

When double in bulk, stir in well-beaten egg. Dump dough on floured board (or countertop). Knead lightly. Take rolling pin and roll dough out until ½ inch thick. Using upside drinking glass of appropriate size, cut rolls about 3-inches in diameter. Crease each roll in center with dull knife. Brush liberally with melted butter. Fold over. Pinch dough at sides to make pocketbook. Brush tops with melted butter and set aside to rise. When ready, place rolls on shallow greased baking pan. Bake in moderate oven (350 degrees) for about 15 to 20 minutes or until lightly browned on top. When done, again brush tops lightly with melted butter.

David Brearly (1745 – 1790)

Heritage: English.   Born in Spring Grove, New Jersey, near Trenton. Descendant of a Yorkshire, England, family.   They emigrated from England to the Colonies around 1680.

Religion: Devout Christian.   Compiler of the **PROTESTANT EPISCOPAL PRAYER BOOK.** Also see quote below.

Education: Private tutors handled most schooling.   Attended the College of New Jersey (presently Princeton).   Another of our Founding Fathers who studied under the highly influential Reverend John Witherspoon.

Marriage: Twice married.   Wed Elizabeth Mullen around 1767, a young woman from a prominent, well-to-do family.   She died and left him a remorseful widower.   He remarried in 1783, this time to the lovely and quite wealthy Elizabeth Higbee.

Children: Unknown.

Interesting Highlights: Was 42-years old when chosen to be a delegate to the Constitutional Convention held in Philadelphia for a four month period between May 25 to September 17, 1787.

One of 39 men who signed the *Constitution*.

Although not a leading figure during the Constitutional Convention, he religiously attended every session.

Once arrested by the British and charged with "high treason," because of his outspokenness regarding the cause of liberty and independence

When the *Constitution* was ratified by New Jersey in 1788, he was the man who presided over that State Convention.

Served as a Presidential Elector in 1789.

Rewarded by President Washington for his loyalty in 1789. Appointed to his last government position before he died – that of Federal District Judge.

Quotable Quote: Brearly, Dayton, William Livingston and Paterson are credited with the New Jersey *Constitution*. Here is what they wrote: *"We the people ... grateful to Almighty God for the civil and religious liberty which He hath so long permitted us to enjoy, and looking to Him for a blessing upon our endeavors to secure and transmit the same unimpaired to succeeding generations, do ordain and establish this Constitution."*

Heroic Deed: Refused an offer of amnesty from British Governor Gage in June 1775.

Little Known Fact: Fought courageously under General George Washington as a Colonel in the Continental Army.

Price Paid for Signing: All the Signers, including Brearly, suffered monetary losses because of their connection with the cause. Some were brought to the brink of financial ruin, or even worse, abject poverty.

Quick Yeast Rolls –
Favorite of Sarah Paine's Husband

1-1/2 cups milk, scalded ¼ cup sugar
¾ cup shortening 2 tsp salt
1 cup potatoes, mashed Flour to suit
2 cups yeast 2 tbls butter, melted

Stir scalded milk and shortening with mashed potatoes in wooden mixing bowl. Blend thoroughly. Let stand until it becomes lukewarm. Then add yeast, sugar and salt. Mix well. Gradually stir in enough flour to make smooth and easily handled dough. Dump dough onto lightly floured board. Knead until dough is extremely elastic.

Take rolling pin and roll dough out to ¼-inch thick sheet. Using upside drinking glass of the appropriate size, cut rolls about 2 to 3-inches in diameter. Take dull knife and make crease near the center of each roll. Brush liberally with melted butter. Fold over so top slightly overlaps the under edge. Pinch dough together on edges of crease. Lightly brush tops with melted butter. Set aside to rise until doubled in size. When ready, place rolls on shallow , well-buttered baking pan. Bake in moderate oven (350 degrees) for about 15 minutes or until lightly browned on top. When done, again brush tops with melted butter.

Robert Treat Paine (1731 – 1814)

Heritage: English. Born in Boston, Massachusetts. Father and mother immigrated to America from England in the late 1600s or early 1700s.

Religion: Raised in Christian family. Father a clergyman, mother the daughter of a minister. Eventually broke away from his Calvinist upbringing. Became a Unitarian. Also see quote below.

Education: Highly educated. Much private tutoring. Brilliant scholar. Head of his class at the prestigious Boston Latin School. Entered Harvard when only 14. Graduated with honors at 18.

Marriage: Wed young Sarah Cobb in 1770 when he was 39 years of age. Sarah came from a prominent Massachusetts family. Her brother, Daniel, served in the Continental Army all through the Revolutionary War as an aide on General Washington's staff.

Children: Eight. Four sons and four daughters.

Interesting Highlights: One of 56 men to sign the *Declaration of Independence*. Hancock was the *only* one to sign on July 4, 1776. Another 49 signed on August 2. Six signed at a later date – they were Richard Henry Lee, Gerry, McKean, Thorton, Wolcott and Wythe.

One of the prosecuting attorneys in the 1770 ***Boston Massacre*** trial. Became well known throughout the Colonies as a result.

Delegate to the Second Continental Congress that convened on May 10, 1775, at the State House in Philadelphia.

Privately tutored by Mr. Lovell, the same teacher who tutored John Hancock and John Adams, both of whom became close friends of Paine.

Quotable Quote: The Provincial Congress of Massachusetts met in Boston. Using words penned by Paine, the Congress addressed the citizens of Massachusetts Bay in this manner: *"Resistance to tyranny becomes the Christian and social duty of each individual. ... Continue steadfast, and with a proper sense of your dependence on God, nobly defend those rights which heaven gave and no man ought to take from us."*

Heroic Deed: Signing the *Declaration of Independence*. Robert Treat Paine knew that should the struggle for independence fail, an ignominious death by hanging would most certainly be his punishment.

Refused an offer of amnesty from British Governor Gage in June 1775.

Little Known Fact: One of four Signers of the *Declaration of Independence* who was trained for the ministry. The others were Hall, Hooper and Witherspoon.

Price Paid for Signing: All the Signers, including Paine. suffered monetary losses because of their connection with the cause. Some were brought to the brink of financial ruin, or even worse, abject poverty.

Fancy Yeast Rolls –
Mrs. Bassett Loved Making These

1 cup milk	1 tbls sugar
2 tbls butter	Pinch of salt
4 cups flour	¾ cup yeast

3 tbls butter, melted

Put milk in saucepan and bring to boil. Add butter and stir until melted. Let mixture get cold and then pour into large wooden mixing bowl. Gradually stir in 2 cups of flour along with the sugar, salt and yeast. Beat all ingredients together. Cover bowl with heavy towel or cloth. Set aside in warm place to rise. When the dough has risen to twice its original quantity, add baking powder and the other 2 cups flour. Blend everything thoroughly. Now place dough on floured board. Take rolling pin and roll out until sheet is about ½-thick. Rub entire top of sheet with melted butter. Using drinking glass of appropriate size, cut dough into small 2-inch round cakes. Fold cakes, not quite in the center, like turnovers. Pinch dough together on edges. Or just leave them as small round cakes. Set in rows on shallow, well-buttered baking pan. Bake in hot oven (425 degrees) for 10 to 15 minutes or until lightly browned on top. **NOTE:** *These rolls are delicious and relatively easy to prepare. For 6 o'clock supper, begin at 2:00 o'clock in the afternoon.*

Richard Bassett (1745 – 1815)

Heritage: English. Born in Cecil County, Maryland. Family immigrated to America from England in the late 1600s or early 1700s.

Religion: Devout Christian. Became a Methodist while serving as a Captain in the Continental Army. Held many church services in his home, Bohemian Manor. Always supported his church financially. See quote below.

Education: Wealthy foster father made certain he received a decent education. Had only the best tutors while being home schooled during his youth. No record of attending college. Studied law in Philadelphia

Marriage: Twice wed. First wife was Ann Ennals, his second a woman named Bruff. Little is known about either of these women.

Children: Fathered an unknown number of children.

Interesting Highlights: Another great man in America's historic past who is often shamefully forgotten with the passage of time.

Delegate to the Constitutional Convention.

Served on no committees and made no speeches during the debates in the Constitutional Convention.

Of the One of 39 men who signed the *Constitution*.

Raised by relative, Peter Lawson, after father abandoned the family.

Led the battle to get his State to ratify the *United States Constitution*. Efforts paid off on December 7, 1787. Delaware became the first to do so.

Raised a 10,000-man militia unit. This was to provide General Washington with assistance should it be needed to hold New York City

Captain in the cavalry militia of Dover, Delaware.

Quotable Quote: Major William Pierce of Georgia wrote character sketches of various delegates to the Constitutional Convention. Here's how he described Bassett: *"A religious enthusiast, lately turned Methodist, who serves his country because it is the will of the people that he should do so. He is a man of plain sense, and has modesty enough to hold his tongue. He is a gentlemanly man, and is in high estimation among Methodists."*

Heroic Deed: Refused an offer of amnesty from British Governor Gage in June 1775.

Little Known Fact: One of 12 Signers of the *Constitution* who owned slaves. The others were Blair, Blount, Butler, Carroll, Jenifer, Madison, Charles and Charles Cotesworth Pinckney, Rutledge, Spaight and Washington.

Advocated unrestricted slave trade while attending the Constitutional Convention held in Philadelphia from May 25 to September 17, 1787.

Price Paid for Signing: All the Signers, including Bassett,. suffered monetary losses because of their connection with the cause. Some were brought to the brink of financial ruin, or even worse, abject poverty.

Crispy Crescent Rolls –
Favorite of the Langdon Family

These delicious early American crescent rolls are relatively easy to make. Use ordinary bread dough after kneading the final time. Just add a little sugar and enough flour to make it a little stiffer than dough to be used to make bread. Then roll out into 1/8-inch thick sheet. Cut into 6-inch wide strips. Cut I each strip into sharp triangular  shapes. Roll up each triangle, starting at the base (the widest end). The point of the triangle will be in the center of the roll.. Then merely bend end points toward each other to form a crescent. Place each roll on shallow, well-buttered baking pan. Cover with heavy towel or cloth. Set aside in warm place to rise for 30 about minutes. When light (risen), brush top of each roll with water and place pan in the oven. Bake in moderate oven (350 degrees) for 10 to 15 minutes, or until tops of rolls are lightly browned.

John Langdon (1741 – 1819)

Heritage: English. Born in or near Portsmouth, New Hampshire. Descendant of a family that immigrated to America from England prior to 1660. They were among the first to settle at the mouth of the Piscataqua River (today better known as Portsmouth, a major New England seaport).

Religion: Devout Christian. Founder and first President of the **New Hampshire** *Bible* **Society**. His goal was to make certain that every home in New Hampshire had a *Bible*. See quote below.

Education: Primarily educated at a local school. Some tutoring at home by his mother. Private tutors hired as necessary. Never attended college.

Marriage: Wed Elizabeth Sherburne in 1777. Nothing is known about their marriage.

Children: One daughter. May have had more, but this is unknown.

Interesting Highlights: Paid own way as well as Gilmans in order that they could attend the Constitutional Convention as official delegates. New Hampshire couldn't or wouldn't pay the expenses of their delegates.

Known to have spoken at least 20 times during the debates.

One of 39 men who signed the *Constitution*.

Heroically fought during the Revolutionary War as a Colonel in the New Hampshire militia.

Generously and unselfishly donated money and supplied guns as well as other arms to the Continental Army.

Built privateers (ships) to operate against the British fleet.

In command of a militia unit at Saratoga, New York, when British General John Burgoyne surrendered.

Quotable Quote: In a Thanksgiving proclamation made on October 12, 1785, Governor Langdon said this: *"It ... becomes our indispensable Duty ... to ... acknowledge ... our dependence on the Supreme Ruler of the Universe, but as a people particularly favoured, to testify our Gratitude to the Author of all our Mercies, in the most solemn and public manner."*

Heroic Deeds: Refused an offer of amnesty from British Governor Gage in June 1775.

Key figure when a number of patriots boldly confiscated munitions from the fort in Portsmouth, New Hampshire.

Little Known Fact: Used his own money in 1777 to organize and underwrite the cost of a military expedition led by General John Stark from New Hampshire to join the fight against British General John Burgoyne.

Price Paid for Signing: All the Signers, including Langdon, suffered monetary losses because of their connection with the cause. Some were brought to the brink of financial ruin, or even worse, abject poverty.

Plain Yeast Rolls --
Made by Dorothy Hancock for John

4 cups milk, warm   2 tbls butter, melted
¼ cup yeast   1 tsp salt
5 cups flour   1 tbls sugar
1 egg, well beaten   ½ tsp baking soda

Flour to suit

Make sponge by blending milk, yeast and flour in large wooden mixing bowl. Cover bowl with thick towel or cloth. Set aside in warm place to rise. When light (risen), stir in beaten egg, melted butter, salt and sugar. Dissolve baking soda in a little hot water and add while stirring. Put in sufficient flour to make soft, pliable dough. Cover as before and set in warm place to rise for about 4 or 5 hours.

When ready, tear off small chunks of dough. Roll these out to about ½-inch cakes. Fold cakes, not quite in center, like turnovers. Or simply shape with hands into balls. Set cakes or balls close together on shallow, buttered baking pan. Cover once again and set aside in warm place. Let the dough rise a third time for about 1 hour.

When risen, cut deeply across top of each roll with sharp knife. Put into quick oven (425 degrees). Bake about 30 minutes or until tops of rolls are lightly browned.

John Hancock (1737 – 1793)

Heritage: Born near Quincy, Massachusetts. Descendant of an English family who immigrated to America sometime in the late 1600s or early 1700s.

Religion: Devout Christian. Father and grandfather were Congregational ministers of note in Massachusetts. See quote below.

Education: Had only the finest tutors. Studied at the prestigious Boston Latin School. Graduated from Harvard College when 17 in 1754

Marriage: Married beautiful Dorothy Quincy on August 23, 1775. She was a relative of John and Samuel Adams. He was 38, she 28.

Children: Two. Daughter died as an infant and a son, John George Washington Hancock, died when 9 years old.

Interesting Highlights: Delegate to the First Continental Congress that convened on September 5, 1774, at Carpenter's Hall in Philadelphia.

President of the Second Continental Congress that convened on May 10, 1775, at the State House in Philadelphia.

His wife, Dorothy, also an ardent patriot, matched the enthusiasm of her husband when it concerned freedom and independence.

Dorothy's father, Judge Quincy, also a fearless patriot, strongly supported his son-in-laws fight for American independence.

The *only* man to actually affix his signature on the *Declaration of Independence,* July 4, 1776. There were 49 others who signed on August 2, 1776. Six signed at a later date – Gerry, Richard Henry Lee, McKean, Thornton, Wolcott and Wythe.

Boldly stepped forward, picked up the quill, and placed his name on the Declaration in large letters. Stepping back, he spoke those immortal words: *"There! His Majesty can now read my name without spectacles, and can now double his reward of 500 pounds on my head. That is my defiance."*

Quotable Quote: *"We think it is incumbent upon this people to humble themselves before God on account of their sins. … so God may be pleased to continue to us the blessings we enjoy, and remove the tokens of His displeasure."* Spoken on the eve of the Revolution (October 1774).

Heroic Deed: Signing the *Declaration.* John Hancock knew that should the struggle for independence fail, an ignominious death by hanging would most certainly be his punishment.

Refused an offer of amnesty from British Governor Gage in June 1775.

Little Known Fact: As a Major General in the Massachusetts militia, he led an expeditionary force to oust the British from Rhode Island.

Price Paid for Signing: All the Signers, including Hancock, suffered monetary losses because of their connection with the cause. Some were brought to the brink of financial ruin, or even worse, abject poverty.

10

Muffin Baking
from Kitchens in the Colonies

Eggy Egg Muffins –
Favorite of the Rutledge Family

3 egg whites	3 cups milk
3 egg yolks	Pinch of salt
4 cups flour	

Beat egg whites until light and fluffy. Beat egg yolks until heavy and custard-like. Put both in large wooden mixing bowl and lightly blend. Stir in milk, salt and flour. Thoroughly beat batter until you cannot beat any longer. Whip harshly, for the secret of this muffin is in the mixing procedure. Immediately pour batter into well-buttered muffin pan. Bake in quick oven (425 degrees) for about 20 minutes *Note*: Test for doneness by sticking toothpick in center of one or more muffins. They are done if the toothpick comes out clean. Send to dinner table as soon as taken from oven. **NOTE:** *Try recipe with heavy cream in place of milk and whole wheat flour in place regular flour as called for above.*

John Rutledge (1739 – 1800)

Heritage: Irish. Born near Charleston, South Carolina. Father immigrated to America from Ireland in 1735. Settled in Charleston.

Religion: Devout Christian. Episcopal. Also see quote below.

Education: Sent to London for his education. Had only the best private tutors and attended the most prestigious prep schools. Studied law at London's Middle Temple. Admitted to the English bar in 1760.

Marriage: Wed Elizabeth Grimke sometime in 1763. Nothing more is known about this woman or their marriage.

Children: 10 children. How many lived past childhood isn't known.

Interesting Highlights: Delegate to the First Continental Congress that convened on September 5, 1774, at Carpenter's Hall in Philadelphia.

Delegate to the Second Continental Congress that convened on May 10, 1775, at the State House in Philadelphia.

One of the most influential delegates at the Constitutional Convention held in Philadelphia from May 25 and September 17, 1787.

Religiously attended every session of the Convention.

One of the 39 Signers of the *Constitution*.

Younger brother, Edward, was one of the 56 Signers of the *Declaration of Independence*. Hancock was the *only* one to sign the *Declaration* on July 4, 1776. Another 49 signed on August 2. Six signed at a later date – they were Richard Henry Lee, Gerry, McKean, Thorton, Wolcott and Wythe.

Quotable Quote: Helped Charles Pinckney and Charles Cotesworth Pinckney write the *Constitution* of South Carolina. Here is one of the articles: *"All persons and religious societies who acknowledge that there is one God, and a future state of rewards and punishments, and that God is publicly to be worshipped, shall be freely tolerated. ... all denominations of Christian[s] ... shall enjoy equal religious and civil privileges."*

Heroic Deed: Vigorously supported the Signing the *Declaration*. John Rutledge knew that should the struggle for independence fail, an ignominious death by hanging would most certainly be his punishment.

Refused an offer of amnesty from British Governor Gage in June 1775.

Little Known Fact: One of 12 Signers of the *Constitution* who owned slaves. The others were Bassett, Blair, Blount, Butler, Carroll, Jenifer, Madison, both Pinckneys, Spaight and Washington

Advocated unrestricted slave trade while attending the Constitutional Convention held in Philadelphia from May 25 to September 17, 1787.

Price Paid for Signing: All the Signers, including Rutledge, suffered monetary losses because of their connection with the cause. Some were brought to the brink of financial ruin, or even worse, abject poverty.

Apple Muffins –
Specialty of Mrs. Gertrude Read

1 egg, well beaten	2-tsp baking powder
1 cup milk	1 tsp salt
½ cup shortening, melted	4 tbls sugar
4 cups flour	½ tsp cinnamon

¾ cup apple, grated

Put beaten egg, milk and melted shortening in wooden mixing bowl. Beat until thoroughly blended. Sift together in separate bowl the flour, baking powder, salt, sugar and cinnamon. Add dry ingredients to those in first bowl. Stir only until everything is nicely moistened. Lastly, add grated apple and blend well. Pour batter into well-greased muffin pans. Bake in rather quick oven (400 to 425 degrees) for about 25 minutes. Test for doneness by sticking toothpick in the center of one or more muffins.  They are done if toothpick comes out clean. **NOTE** *These muffins should be sent to the dinner table as soon as they are taken from the oven.*

George Read (1733 – 1798)

Heritage: Irish-Welsh. Born in Maryland. Father immigrated to America from Dublin, Ireland, about 1726. Grandfather was wealthy Dublin businessman. Mother was daughter of wealthy Welsh planter.

Religion: Dedicated Christian. Father-in-law, the Reverend George Ross, was pastor for 50 years of the Immanuel Church in New Castle. See quote below regarding what he and McKean wrote in Delaware's *Constitution*.

Education: Much early education came from private tutors. Attended school in Chester, Pennsylvania. Later was able to study under the renown Reverend Francis Alison's most prestigious academy in London, Pennsylvania. Studied law when 15 under the auspices of a prominent Philadelphia attorney.

Marriage: Wed the Gertrude Ross, in 1763. She was the widowed sister of George Ross, fellow Signer of the *Declaration of Independence.*

Children: Six. One daughter. Five sons. Their firstborn died at birth.

Interesting Highlights: Delegate to the Second Continental Congress that convened on May 10, 1775, at the State House in Philadelphia.

One of 56 men to sign the *Declaration of Independence.* Hancock was the *only* one to sign on July 4, 1776. Another 49 signed on August 2. Six signed at a later date – they were Richard Henry Lee, Gerry, McKean, Thorton, Wolcott and Wythe.

One of six men to sign both the *Declaration of Independence* and the *Constitution*. Others were Clymer, Franklin, Morris, Sherman and Wilson.

President of Delaware's Constitutional Convention held in 1776.

Quotable Quote: *"Everyone appointed to public office must say: 'I do profess faith in God the Father, and in Jesus Christ His only Son, and the Holy Ghost one God and blessed forevermore. And I do acknowledge the Holy Scriptures of the Old and New Testament to be given by divine inspiration'."*

Heroic Deed: Signing the *Declaration*. George Read knew that should the struggle for independence fail, an ignominious death by hanging would most certainly be his punishment.

Refused an offer of amnesty from British Governor Gage in June 1775.

Little Known Fact: Was known to have, on numerous occasions, taken up his musket and marched with the militia to help repel British invaders.

Price Paid for Signing: Wife was forced to flee from their home with the children in tow. Bore many hardships due to the close proximity of the vindictive British Army.

All the Signers, including Read, suffered monetary losses because of their connection with the cause. Some were brought to the brink of financial ruin, or even worse, abject poverty.

Raisin-Wine Egg Muffins – Dolly Madison Served These to James

2 cups butter	8 egg yolks
2 cups sugar	2 tbls rose water
4 cups flour	2 tbls white wine
3 cups raisins	½ tsp mace

Cream butter and sugar in wooden mixing bowl. Add flour and blend thoroughly. Work in raisins. In separate bowl, beat together egg yolks, rose water, white wine and mace. Pour into first mixture. Blend well. Cover with heavy towel or cloth. Set aside in warm place for 1 hour. Meanwhile, butter muffin tin. When ready, fill openings 2/3 full. Bake in moderately slow oven (325 degrees) for about 30 minutes. Test for doneness by sticking toothpick in center of one or more muffins. They are done if the toothpick comes out clean. **NOTE:** *Send to the dinner table as soon as taken from oven.*

James Madison (1751 – 1836)

Heritage: English. Born to a planter aristocracy in Port Conway, King George County, Virginia. Descendants immigrated to America from England sometime in the 1600s. May also have Scottish and Welsh relatives.

Religion: Christian. First considered becoming a minister and did postgraduate study in theology. See quote below.

Education: Home schooled by his mother and tutored by a variety of the best teachers. Also attended a number of prestigious private schools. Graduated from the College of New Jersey (now Princeton).

Marriage: Married Dolly Payne Todd in 1749. She was a widow and was 16 years younger than James.

Children: No children of their own, but lovely, vivacious Dolly brought a son to their marriage.

Interesting Highlights: The oldest of 10 children in his family.

A slave owner all of his life, he was an active member of the *American Colonization Society*, a group dedicated to sending all slaves back to Africa.

One of the most influential members of the *Constitutional Convention*. Rarely absent, he almost totally dominated the proceedings.

Deservedly known today as *"The Father of the Constitution."*

His most important contribution as one of our Founding Fathers was his work on the writing of our *Constitution*.

One of 39 men who signed the *Constitution*.

He outlived all other Signers of the *Constitution*.

Collaborated with John Jay and fellow Signer of the *Constitution*, Alexander Hamilton, in writing a series of essays. They were published in newspapers in 1787 and 1788. These writings were later published as a book titled *The Federalist Papers*.

Quotable Quote: *"We have all been encouraged to feel in the guardianship of that Almighty Being, whose power regulates the destiny of nations."*

Heroic Deed: When the *Constitution* came up for ratification in Virginia, he had to defend the document against such great patriot orators as Patrick Henry, Richard Henry Lee and George Mason.

Refused an offer of amnesty from British Governor Gage in June 1775.

Little Known Fact: Madison was one of 12 Signers of the *Constitution* who owned slaves. The others were Bassett, Blair, Blount, Butler, Daniel Carroll, Jenifer, both Pinckneys, Rutledge, Spaight and Washington.

Price Paid for Signing: All the Signers, including Madison, suffered monetary losses because of their connection with the cause. Some were brought to the brink of financial ruin, or even worse, abject poverty.

Easy-To-Make Cream Muffins –
Elizabeth Clymer's Very Best

3 cups heavy cream
½ cup yeast
½ tsp salt

Flour to suit
2 tbls butter
½ tsp baking powder

Blend milk, yeast and salt in large wooden mixing bowl. Add sufficient flour to make good batter. Cover with heavy towel or cloth and set aside to rise in warm place. When risen, melt butter and blend with *very little* flour. This will prevent butter from thinning too much. Then beat into the batter. When finished, harshly whip in baking powder. Immediately pour batter into buttered muffin rings until each is 2/3 full. Cover with heavy towel or cloth. Let stand near heat for 15 minutes before baking. Put baking pan in quick oven (425 degrees). Let bake for about 20 minutes. Test for doneness by sticking toothpick in the center of one or more muffins. They are done if toothpick comes out clean. **NOTE:** *Muffins should be sent to dinner table as soon as taken from oven.*

George Clymer (1739 – 1813)

Heritage: English. Born in Philadelphia. Father immigrated to America from Bristol, England, sometime early in the 1700s.

Religion: Devout Christian. See quote below.

Education: Received excellent education through private tutors as a child and young man. Attended the College of Philadelphia (presently the University of Pennsylvania).

Marriage: Was 26 when he wed Elizabeth Meredith in March of 1765. Said to be a "handsome woman" from a prominent Philadelphia family. She was the daughter of his business partner.

Children: Eight. Three died during childhood. Those who lived were Henry, George, Meredith, Margaret and Nancy.

Interesting Highlights: He and George Ross were appointed to be delegates to the Continental Congress in 1776. They were sent to take the place of two Pennsylvania delegates who declined to cast their vote in favor of the *Declaration of Independence*.

One of 56 men to sign the *Declaration of Independence*. Hancock was the *only* one to sign on July 4, 1776. Another 49 signed on August 2. Six signed at a later date – they were Richard Henry Lee, Gerry, McKean, Thorton, Wolcott and Wythe.

Quotable Quote: One of the men who developed the Pennsylvania *Constitution*. Clymer spelled out what each member of the legislature must repeat say being seated: *"I do believe in one God, the Creator and Governor of the universe, the rewarder of the good and the punisher of the wicked."*

Heroic Deed: Signing the *Declaration*. George Clymer knew that should the struggle for independence fail, an ignominious death by hanging would most certainly be his punishment.

Refused an offer of amnesty from British Governor Gage in 1775.

Little Known Fact: Given command of a large volunteer militia group in 1774 when it appeared to be inevitable that military action would be necessary to gain independence from England.

Orphaned in 1740 when only one year old. Raised by wealthy uncle who left him a sizable amount of land and money.

Price Paid for Signing: Most of his property was destroyed. Home sacked and pillaged. Everything movable was either stolen or burned in the front yard as his family watched. Horses, cattle and other animals were either confiscated to feed the soldiers, or killed on the spot.

All the Signers, including Clymer, suffered great monetary losses because of their connection with the cause. Some were brought to the brink of financial ruin, or even worse, abject poverty.

Risen Corn Meal Muffins –
Baked by Mrs. Rachel Broom

4 cups corn meal	2 tbls yeast
4 cups milk	½ tsp salt
2 tbls sugar	3 tbls shortening

Put corn meal in large wooden mixing bowl. Bring milk to a boil and pour over the corn meal. Let stand until lukewarm. Then stir sugar, yeast and salt into mixture. Cover with heavy towel or cloth. Set aside in warm place to rise for about 5 hours. After batter has risen sufficiently, melt shortening and stir in lightly. Beat entire mixture well. Immediately pour batter into buttered muffin rings until each is 2/3 full. Again cover with heavy towel or cloth and set beside heat for 15 minutes before baking. Then put in quick oven (425 degrees) for about 30 minutes and bake. Test for doneness by sticking toothpick in center of one or more muffins. They are done if toothpick comes out clean. **NOTE:** *Send to dinner table as soon as taken from the oven.*

No
Picture
Available

Jacob Broom (1752 – 1810)

Heritage: Swedish. Born in Wilmington, Delaware. Father immigrated to America from Sweden sometime in the mid-1700s.

Religion: Devout Christian. Lay leader at the Old Swedes Church. See quote below.

Education: Primarily tutored at home by his mother. Attended the local Old Academy. Studied surveying on his own. An avid reader.

Marriage: Wed Rachel Pierce in 1773 when he was 21-years of age. Very little is known about her.

Children: Eight.

Interesting Highlights: Delegate to the Constitutional Convention in Philadelphia, convened from May 25 to September 17, 1787.

One of 39 men who signed the *Constitution*.

Wasn't a prominent patriot as were so many of the other Signers.

Never absent from any session of the Constitutional Convention.

Offered his opinion in some debates, but overall had little to say.

Said to be an extremely shy man. Appeared to be uncomfortable in the presence of the other wealthier, better-educated delegates.

Apparently made no significant contributions during the Convention.

Worked diligently to get the Continental Congress to approve this new instrument of government.

Participated in the effort to get the *Constitution* ratified in Delaware.

Became first Postmaster in Wilmington, Delaware from 1790 to 1792.

Little is known about this successful businessman. But he was in the import-export trade, owned a cotton mill and ran a machine shop.

One of the more obscure Signers of the *Constitution*, and possibly the most obscure of all.

Quotable Quote: Brave immigrants from Sweden settled in America and started the first Lutheran Colony. According to Broom, *"the founding of the Colony was based on their belief, and my personal belief as well, in: 'Jesus Christ the Savior of the World'."*

Heroic Deed: Refused an offer of amnesty from British Governor Gage in June 1775.

Little Known Fact: No pictures have been found of this Signer of the *United States Constitution.*

His claim to fame, other than for signing the *Constitution*, was to draw maps for General Washington prior to the Battle of Brandywine.

Price Paid for Signing: All the Signers, including Broom, suffered monetary losses because of their connection with the cause. Some were brought to the brink of financial ruin, or even worse, abject poverty.

After Supper Walnut Muffins – Favorite of Thomas Lynch

2 cups milk   1 tbls butter
½ cup yeast   Flour to suit
1 tsp salt   1 egg
      ½ cup walnut pieces

Recipe must be started in evening after supper. Blend milk, yeast and salt in large wooden mixing bowl. Melt butter and add. Then stir in enough flour to make rather stiff batter. Cover with heavy towel or cloth. Set aside in warm place to rise overnight. In the morning, beat egg slightly. Stir beaten egg and walnut pieces into batter. Pour into buttered muffin rings until each is 2/3 full. Put in quick oven (425 degrees). Bake about 20 minutes. Test for doneness by sticking toothpick in center of one or more muffins. They are done if toothpick comes out clean. **NOTE:** *Send to dinner table as soon as taken from oven.*

Thomas Lynch, Jr. 1749 – 1779)

Heritage: Irish-Austrian. Born in Prince George's Parish, on the North Santee River, in South Carolina. Descendant of old line Austrian family, some of who moved to Ireland. Great grandfather immigrated to America from Ireland. Settled in South Carolina, sometime in the late 1600s or early 1700s.

Religion: Dedicated Christian. Little more is known. See quote below.

Education: Tutored by only the finest teachers until he reached 13 years of age. Sent to England to further his education. Stayed eight years. Graduated from the University of Cambridge and then returned to the Colonies.

Marriage: Married Elizabeth Shubrick in 1773. She was the lovely daughter of an old and prominent Colonial family. Thomas and Elizabeth had been childhood sweethearts.

Children: None.

Interesting Highlights: Delegate to the *Stamp Act Congress*.

Delegate to the First Continental Congress convened on September 5, 1774, at Carpenter's Hall in Philadelphia.

Took his father's place in the Continental Congress in 1776 when he resigned his seat due to paralysis resulting from a stroke.

One of 56 men to sign the *Declaration of Independence*. Hancock was the *only* one to sign on July 4, 1776. Another 49 signed on August 2. Six signed at a later date – they were Richard Henry Lee, Gerry, McKean, Thorton, Wolcott and Wythe.

An extremely handsome man at 27, he was the second youngest Signer of the *Declaration of Independence*.

Played important role in establishing the Continental Army.

Became a Captain in the South Carolina Regiment of Continentals,

Died at sea in 1779 while sailing to the West Indies with his wife. The ship sunk. Lynch was only 30-years old at the time of the disaster.

Quotable Quote: *"The Sacred Book, the Bible, gives us a system of the purest morals and morality. Our Saviour, Jesus Christ, was placed before us to clearly illustrate this purest of pure systems."*

Heroic Deed: Signing the *Declaration*. Thomas Lynch knew that should the struggle for independence fail, an ignominious death by hanging would most certainly be his punishment.

Refused an offer of amnesty from British Governor Gage in June 1775.

Little Known Fact: Active as a patriot in the Colonies as soon as he returned from schooling in England.

Price Paid for Signing: All Signers, including Lynch, suffered monetary losses because of their connection with the cause. Some were brought to the brink of financial ruin, or even worse, abject poverty.

Blueberry Muffins --
Ann Hooper Made These for William

4 cups milk	1 tsp salt
¾ cup yeast	1 tbls butter
2 tbls sugar	Flour to suit
2 eggs, well beaten	1 cup blueberries

Blend milk, yeast, sugar and salt in large wooden mixing bowl. Melt butter and stir into mixture. Add enough flour to make good batter. Cover with thick towel or cloth and set in warm place to rise overnight. In the morning, beat eggs until light. Stir beaten eggs into risen batter. Lastly, add blueberries and stir until nicely blended. Pour into buttered muffin rings until each is 2/3 full. Bake for about 20 minutes in quick oven (425 degrees). Test for doneness by sticking toothpick in center of one or  more muffins. They are done if toothpick comes out clean. **NOTE**: *Send muffins to dinner table as soon as taken from oven.*

William Hooper (1742 – 1790)

Heritage: Scottish. Born in Boston in June. Father a Scotsman who graduated from University of Edinburgh. Immigrated from Scotland to America sometime in mid-1600s to early 1700s.

Religion: Devout Christian. Father a clergyman. See quote below.

Education: Attended finest prep schools as a youth. Admitted to prestigious Harvard College as a sophomore. Graduated with honors at 18-years. Rejected the ministry for which he had been carefully groomed. Studied law under James Otis, a radical attorney in the Colonies.

Marriage: Married the beautiful and cultured Anne Clark. Her father was a General in the Continental Army.

Children: They had 2 sons and 1 daughter.

Interesting Highlights: One of 56 men to sign the *Declaration of Independence*. Hancock was the *only* one to sign on July 4, 1776. Hooper was one of the 49 who carefully affixed his signature on the document on August 2. Six signed at a later date – they were Richard Henry Lee, Gerry, McKean, Thorton, Wolcott and Wythe.

One of four Signers of the Declaration of Independence who were trained for the ministry. The others were Hall, Paine and Witherspoon.

Although younger than most of the other delegates to the Continental Congress, he was placed on many of the most important committees.

Quotable Quote: Had a hand in the writing of the *Constitution* for his home state of North Carolina. Here is how some of it is worded: *"... no person who shall deny the being of God, or the truth of the ... divine authority of the Old or New Testaments ... shall be capable of holding any office or place of trust or profit ... within this State."*

Heroic Deed: Signing the *Declaration*. William Hooper knew that should the struggle for independence fail, an ignominous death by hanging would most certainly be his punishment.

Refused an offer of amnesty from British Governor Gage in June 1775.

Little Known Facts: A brilliant but frail young lawyer, he gave up his practice in 1778 when only 36 due to failing health.

Initially loyal to the Crown. Because of this, many patriots involved in the independence movement for a time viewed him with suspicion.

Price Paid for Signing: Hunted down like an animal. Forced to hide out with friends and depend on them for food. The British made shambles of his Finian estate. It was left in total ruin.

All Signers, including Hooper, suffered monetary losses because of their connection with the cause. Some were brought to the brink of financial ruin, or even worse, abject poverty.

Rye Muffins as Made for Oliver – Laura Wolcott's Finest

2 cups rye flour	2 tsp baking powder
2 cups wheat flour	1 egg, well beaten
1 tsp salt	1 tbls sugar

1 cup milk or cream

Sift together in large wooden mixing bowl the rye flour, wheat flour, salt and baking powder. Blend well and make well (indentation) in the middle of flour mixture. Add beaten egg and sugar. Lastly stir in milk or cream. Whip batter until thoroughly blended. Pour into well-buttered muffin pans. Fill each ring 2/3 full of batter. Bake in quick oven (425 degrees) for about 20 minutes. Test for doneness by sticking toothpick in center of one or more muffins. They are done if toothpick comes out clean. **NOTE:** *Send muffins to dinner table as soon taken from oven.*

Oliver Wolcott (1726 – 1797)

Heritage: English. Born in Windsor, Connecticut, on November 20. An English ancestor had immigrated to America from England in 1630. Settled in Dorchester, Massachusetts. Moved to Connecticut and started new settlement there in 1736.

Religion: Devout Christian. See quote below.

Education: Had only the finest of tutors as a child and young adult. Entered Yale at 17 years of age. Graduated in 1747 at the head of his class.

Marriage: Wed Laura Collins in 1759. She was from a well-to-do, high society Connecticut family. Oliver was 33 and Laura 23 at the time of their marriage.

Children: Five. Three sons and two daughters. One child died as an infant, which was not at all unusual in those days. One son followed in his father's footsteps and became Governor of Connecticut.

Interesting Highlights: : One of 56 men to sign the *Declaration of Independence*. Hancock was the *only* one to sign on July 4, 1776. Another 49 signed on August 2. Six signed at a later date. Wolcott signed sometime during October of 1776. The other five who later signed were Gerry, Richard Henry Lee, McKean, Thorton and Wythe.

Wife, Laura, was also an avid patriot. She managed their farm and tutored the children. She made it possible for Oliver to devote all of his time and energy to the cause of freedom and independence.

Family donated blankets and other supplies to the Continental Army.

Pushed hard for ratification of the *United States Constitution* during the 1778 Connecticut State Convention.

Quotable Quote: An 1848 textbook had this to say about Wolcott: *"As a patriot and statesman, a Christian and a man, Governor Wolcott presented a bright example; for inflexibility, virtue, piety, and integrity, were his prominent characteristics."*

Heroic Deed: Signing the *Declaration of Independence*. Oliver Wolcott knew that should the struggle for independence fail, an ignominious death by hanging would most certainly be his punishment.

Refused an offer of amnesty from British Governor Gage in June 1775

Little Known Fact: Shortly after signing the *Declaration of Independence*, in October, 1776, he was given command of large detachment (14 regiments) of the Connecticut militia. They were to assist in defending New York from British attack.

Price Paid for Signing: All the Signers, including Wolcott, suffered monetary losses because of their connection with the cause. Some were brought to the brink of financial ruin, or even worse, abject poverty.

Sweet Apple-Peanut Muffins -- Sarah Mifflin's Unique Treat

1 cup corn meal   1 egg, well beaten
1 cup flour   ¼ cup sugar
½ tsp salt   2 tbls butter, melted
3 tsp baking powder   1 cup milk
1 cup apples, diced

Sift together in large wooden mixing bowl the corn meal, flour, salt and baking powder. In separate bowl, blend frothy egg, sugar and melted butter. Then add milk or cream and blend nicely. Lowly stir this liquid into dry ingredients in first bowl. Add diced apple pieces. Stir everything lightly and pour into well-buttered muffin pans until each ring is 2/3 full. Bake in quick oven (425 degrees) for about 20 minutes. Test for doneness by sticking toothpick in center of one or more muffins. They are done if toothpick comes out clean.

NOTE: *Muffins should be sent to dinner table as soon taken from the oven.*

Thomas Mifflin (1744 -- 1780)

Heritage: English. Born in Philadelphia, Pennsylvania, the "Cradle of Liberty". Family immigrated to America from England during the early 1600s.

Religion: Devout Christian. Quaker. See quote below.

Education: Attended a Quaker school and was privately tutored as a child and a young man. Later attended the College of Philadelphia (presently University of Pennsylvania. Graduated when only 16-years old.

Marriage: Wed Sarah Morris in 1767. Little more is known about the marriage, except that she wholeheartedly supported her husband's involvement in the independence movement.

Children: Unknown.

Interesting Highlights: Delegate to the Constitutional Convention in 1787 and never missed a session.

Made no significant contributions while at the Convention.

One of 39 men who signed the *Constitution.*

One of the wealthier Signers of the *Constitution.* Others of the wealthy elite included Carroll and Jenifer. The richest men of all were probably Robert Morris and George Washington.

Delegate to the First Continental Congress that convened on September 5, 1774, at Carpenter's Hall in Philadelphia.

Delegate to the Second Continental Congress that convened on May 10, 1775, at the State House in Philadelphia.

Became close friends with Washington after successfully recruiting troops for the Continental Army.

Had strong pacifist beliefs.

Saw combat in the battles of Princeton and Trenton, New Jersey, as well as on Long Island, New York.

Quotable Quote: One of the men who developed the *Constitution* of Pennsylvania. It clearly spells out what each member of the legislature must say before being seated: *"I do believe in one God, the Creator and Governor of the universe, the rewarder of the good and the punisher of the wicked."*

Heroic Deed: Refused an offer of amnesty from British Governor Gage in June 1775.

Little Known Fact: Expelled from Quaker faith in May of 1775, for joining Continental Army. Was an aide-de-camp to General Washington.

Price Paid for Signing: Lived an affluent life, but was broke when he died at the age of 56. There wasn't even enough money to pay his burial expenses. All of the Signers suffered monetary losses because of their connection with the cause. Some of the others were also brought to the brink of financial ruin, or even worse, abject poverty as was the case with Mifflin.

Creamy Christmas Muffins --
Enjoyed by the Nelson Family

6 egg whites	Pinch of salt
6 egg yolks	1 tbls butter
2 cups milk	1 tbls shortening
2 cups heavy cream	4 cups flour

Beat egg whites until light and fluffy. Beat egg yolks until they are the consistency of custard. Put both in large wooden mixing bowl. Stir in milk or cream and salt. Melt butter and shortening together and add to bowl ingredients. Lastly, slowly stir in enough flour to make smooth batter. Pour into muffin tin until each ring is 2/3 full of batter. The oven should be hot (425 degrees). Bake for 12 to 15 minutes. Test for doneness by sticking toothpick in  center of one or more muffins. They are done if toothpick comes out clean. **NOTE:** *Muffins should be sent to dinner table as soon as taken from oven.*

Thomas Nelson, Jr. (1738 – 1789)

Heritage: English. Born in Yorktown, Virginia. Oldest of five sons. His father, William, emigrated to America from England sometime in the early 1600s. Considered to be among the *First Families* of Virginia,

Religion: Devout Christian. See quote below.

Education: Thoroughly home schooled as a child. Sent to England in 1752, when 14 years of age to further his studies at prestigious Hackney School and Cambridge University. Privately tutored by Dr. Proteus, who later became Bishop of London. Returned to Virginia in 1761.

Marriage: Wed Lucy Grimes on August 29, 1762, when both were 24 years of age. She was the daughter of a wealthy planter. Through her mother, Lucy was closely related to many of Virginia's most notable families.

Children: Union produced 11 offspring – six boys and five girls.

Interesting Highlights: Proposed forming a militia in Virginia during the Continental Congress. Many others at the Congress were alarmed because they felt such activity would constitute *"treason against the Crown."*

One of 56 men to sign the *Declaration of Independence*. Hancock was the *only* one to sign on July 4, 1776. Another 49 signed on August 2. Six signed at a later date – they were Richard Henry Lee, Gerry, McKean, Thorton, Wolcott and Wythe.

Fearless Commander-in-Chief of the 3,000 member Virginia militia.

In General Washington's official account of the Siege of Yorktown, he made special note of Nelson's invaluable service with his Virginia militia.

Led Virginia Militia against Cornwallis during the Siege of Yorktown.

Quotable Quote: *"I call to God to witness that if any British troops are landed in the county of York ... I will wait no orders, but I will summon the militia and drive the invaders into the sea."*

Heroic Deed: Signing the *Declaration*. Thomas Nelson, Jr. knew that should the struggle for independence fail, an ignominious death by hanging would most certainly be his punishment.

Refused an offer of amnesty from British Governor Gage in June 1775.

Little Known Fact: At one time he owned 400 slaves.

Price Paid for Signing: Gave all of his horses to the Continental Army for use in hauling ammunition. His immense grain stores were given to General Washington's starving soldiers. All of his wealth went to tirelessly and unselfishly supporting the War for Independence.

All the Signers, including Nelson, suffered monetary losses because of their connection with the cause. Some were brought to the brink of financial ruin, or even worse, abject poverty. Nelson died without a dime left. He was broke and living in poverty.

11

Bun Baking Secrets
of Signer's Wives and Mothers

Sweet Potato Buns –
A Specialty of Nancy Taylor

3 large sweet potatoes   3 cups flour
2 cups heavy cream   Pinch of salt
1-1/2 tsp baking powder

Boil sweet potatoes until soft. Rub through colander while still hot. Mix in cream. Then stir in flour, salt and baking powder. Blend everything to smooth dough. Break dough into egg-size chunks. Using hands, mold each piece of dough into round ball. Neatly lay balls in rows on shallow buttered baking sheet. Bake in hot oven (425 degrees) for about 15 to 20 minutes. Test for doneness by sticking toothpick in center of one or more buns. They are done if toothpick comes out clean. **NOTE:** *Send to dinner table as soon as taken from oven.*

George Taylor (1716 – 1781)

Heritage: Irish. Born in Ireland. Emigrated to America from Ireland in 1773. Settled in Pennsylvania.

Religion: Devout Christian. Son of a clergyman. It isn't known if he was Protestant or Roman Catholic. See quote below.

Education: Primarily self-taught through extensive reading. Some home schooling by various tutors. An extremely bright young man, he taught himself fluent Latin as well as numerous subjects on running a business.

Marriage: Married a widow, Nancy Savage, in 1742. Nancy died in 1768. George never remarried. Had long-standing affair with housekeeper. Why they didn't marry is unknown.

Children: He and Nancy had three children – two sons and a daughter. Taylor and his housekeeper had five children out of wedlock.

Interesting Highlights: One of 56 men to sign the *Declaration of Independence*. Hancock was the *only* one to sign on July 4, 1776. Another 49 signed on August 2. Six signed at a later date – they were Richard Henry Lee, Gerry, McKean, Thorton, Wolcott and Wythe.

One three signers of the *Declaration of Independence* to be born in Ireland. The other two were Smith and Thornton.

One of eight signers of the Declaration of Independence who were foreign born. The others were: Gwinnett, Lewis, Robert Morris, Smith, Thornton, Wilson and Witherspoon.

In 1776, his Durham Iron Works made cannons and cannon balls for the Continental Army.

Elected to the Colonial Assembly in 1764 and was a member when the British imposed the notorious ***Stamp Act*** in March of 1765.

Quotable Quote: *"I do not believe the Bible can have a value placed upon it. God's Holy Book is worth more to me than all other books that have ever been published throughout the world."*

Heroic Deed: Signing the *Declaration of Independence*. George Taylor knew that should the struggle for independence fail, an ignominious death by hanging would most certainly be his punishment.

Refused an offer of amnesty from British Governor Gage in June 1775.

Little Known Fact: Only *Signer of the Declaration* of Independence to have run away from home and came to America as a "redemptioner" or what is more commonly known as an indentured servant.

Price Paid for Signing: All the Signers, including Taylor, suffered monetary losses because of their connection with the cause. Some were brought to the brink of financial ruin, or even worse, abject poverty.

Yeast Buns Made by Jane Bedford –
Her Famous Husband Loved Them

        1 cup milk   ¾ cup sugar
        3 tbls yeast   1 tsp salt
        3 eggs, well beaten   Flour to suit

Warm milk and pour it in large wooden mixing bowl. Stir in yeast. Add beaten eggs, sugar and salt. Beat thoroughly. Add enough flour to make soft, rather light dough. Cover bowl with heavy towel or cloth and set in warm place to rise. Allow to stand until very light (raised). After dough has sufficiently risen, break into small egg-sized pieces. Knead each chunk individually. Place pieces in neat rows on well-buttered baking tins. Cover and set aside to rise once again. Let rise until the buns have almost doubled in size. Pierce top of each bun. Glaze with mixture of sugar and milk, or with the white of an egg. Put pan in quick oven (425 degrees). Bake for 15 to 20 minutes, or until lightly tanned on top. Test for doneness by sticking a toothpick in center of one or more buns. They are done if toothpick comes out clean. Send to dinner table as soon taken from oven. **NOTE:** *Mrs. Bedford sometimes added raisins to her biscuits for variety.*

Gunning Bedford (1747 – 1812)

Heritage: English. Born in Philadelphia, Pennsylvania. Family emigrated to America from England sometime in the late 1600s or early 1700s. Originally settled in Jamestown, Virginia.

Religion: Devout Christian. See quote below.

Education: Had only the best private tutors as a child and young adult. Graduated with honors from the College of New Jersey (presently Princeton). Studied law under Joseph Read, a prominent Philadelphia attorney.

Marriage: Wed Jane B. Parker while attending Princeton.

Children: At least one child – a daughter.

Interesting Highlights: Delegate to the Constitutional Convention that convened in Philadelphia from May 25 to September 17, 1787

One of the best speakers and debaters at the Convention.

One of the most active members of the Constitutional Convention. Seldom missed a session.

One of 39 men who signed the *Constitution*.

Close friend of fellow Signer of the *Constitution,* and future President of the United States, James Madison.

Madison was Bedford's roommate while attending the College of New Jersey (presently Princeton).

Bore arms during the War for Independence. Served in Continental Army as an aide to General Washington.

Delegate to the Continental Congress from 1783 to 1785.

Delegate to Annapolis Convention in 1785, but failed to attend and sessions. Was busy with other responsibilities.

Attended the Delaware Constitutional Convention where the *United States Constitution* was ratified.

President Washington appointed him to be a Federal District Judge for Maryland. Held this position until he died.

Quotable Quote: Bedford said he believed the Bible was *"given by divine inspiration."* Openly professed his faith *"in God the Father, and in Jesus Christ, His only Son."*

Heroic Deed: Refused an offer of amnesty from British Governor Gage in June 1775.

Little Known Fact: One of numerous Founding Fathers who studied under John Witherspoon, Signer of the *Declaration of Independence,* and leading scholar and theologian of the period.

Price Paid for Signing: All the Signers, including Bedford, suffered monetary losses because of their connection with the cause. Some were brought to the brink of financial ruin, or even worse, abject poverty.

Cinnamon Buns –
Baked by Mary King for Rufus

1 cup sugar   2 cups raised bread dough
¼ cup butter   Sugar to suit
2 eggs, well beaten   Cinnamon to suit

Cream butter and sugar in large wooden mixing bowl. Blend it and beaten eggs with bread dough. Add sufficient flour to make a very stiff dough. Cover with heavy towel or cloth and set in warm place to rise. When dough mixture is light (risen), break into egg-sized chunks. Using hands, mold each piece of dough into round ball. Neatly lay balls in rows on a shallow buttered baking sheet. Cover again and let rise once more before baking. When buns have doubled in size, mix together some dampened sugar and cinnamon. Rub mixture across the top of each bun. Place in rather quick oven (400 to 425 degrees) for about 20 minutes or until slightly browned on top. Test for doneness by sticking toothpick in the center of one or more buns. They are done if toothpick comes out clean. **NOTE:** *Send to dinner table as soon taken from oven.*

Rufus King (1755 – 1827)

Heritage: English. Born in Scarboro, Massachusetts. Family emigrated to America from England sometime in the late 1600s or early 1700s. Son of prosperous farmer-merchant.

Religion: Devout Christian. See quote below for the kind of wording he and Gorham used in drafting the *Constitution* of Massachusetts.

Education: Educated in local schools until he was 12. Privately tutored from then to adulthood. Attended highly regarded Drummer Academy in South Bayfield, Massachusetts. Graduated from Harvard in 1777.

Marriage: Wed Mary Alsop in 1786. She was the daughter of an extremely wealthy new York businessman.

Children: Several offspring, but actual number is unknown.

Interesting Highlights: One of the youngest men elected to be a delegate to the Constitutional Convention (age 32) that convened in Philadelphia for four month period from May 25 to September 17, 1787

One of the 39 signers of the *Constitution.*

Early opponent of slavery in the Colonies, along with his friend from Rhode Island, William Ellery, Signer of the *Declaration of Independence.*

Tried to have slavery abolished in 1785 with the assistance of Ellery.

Served during Revolutionary War as aide to unknown general.

Ran for President in 1816. Was soundly defeated by James Madison, fellow Signer of the *Constitution.*

Quotable Quote: Any person elected to the Legislature or a State office must believe in and make this declaration: *"I _____, do declare, that I believe the Christian religion, and have firm persuasion of its truth."* In Part 1, Article 11: *"It is the right, as well as the duty, of all men ... to worship the Supreme Being, the Great Creator and Preserver of the Universe. And no subject shall be hurt, molested, or restrained ... for worshipping God in the manner ... most agreeable to the dictates of his own conscience."*

Heroic Deed: Strongly supporting the *Declaration.* Rufus King knew that should the struggle for independence fail, an ignominious death by hanging would most certainly be his punishment.

Refused an offer of amnesty from British Governor Gage in June 1775.

Little Known Fact: King strongly objected to setting a date for Congress to meet each year. He felt this wasn't necessary and possibly even dangerous. His exact words were: *"A great vice in our system is that of legislating too much."* Were not his words prophetic?

Price Paid for Signing: All the Signers, including King, suffered monetary losses because of their connection with the cause. Some were brought to the brink of financial ruin, or even worse, abject poverty.

149

Unfermented Sweet Buns –
Mrs. Gwinnett's Secret Receipt

3 cups flour   2 tbls butter
3 tsp baking powder   3 eggs, well beaten
1 tsp salt   ½ nutmeg, grated
3 tbls sugar   1 tsp cinnamon
            1-1/4 cups milk

Sift together flour, baking powder, salt and sugar into large wooden mixing bowl. Carefully rub in butter. Add well beaten eggs, spices and milk. Stir thoroughly until dough is soft and pliable. Break off pieces of dough about as big as an egg. Using hands, roll each chunk of dough into round ball. Lay rolls of dough on shallow buttered baking tin. Rub top of each bun with a mixture of sugar and water. Sprinkle dry sugar on them. Bake in moderately quick oven (375 degrees) for 10 to 15 minutes or until slightly browned on top. Test for doneness by sticking toothpick in center of one or more buns. They are done if toothpick comes out clean. **NOTE:** *Send hot buns to the dinner table as soon as taken from oven.*

Button Gwinnett (1732 – 1777)

Heritage: Welsh-English. Born in Gloucestershire, England. Family emigrated to America from Bristol, England in 1770. Settled in Charleston, South Carolina. Father was from Wales, mother had English ties.

Religion: Devout Christian. Brought up in strict Christian home. Son of a Welsh Anglican Vicar. See quote below.

Education: Good education but details are mostly unknown. Much private tutoring at home. Avid reader. Highly motivated, brilliant mind as well as numerous superior talents. Apprenticed to a grocer in Bristol, England.

Marriage: Wed his grocer employer's beautiful daughter. Little more is known about his wife, not even her name.

Children: Three – all girls, Each daughter was born in England.

Interesting Highlights: Delegate to the Second Continental Congress that convened on May 10, 1775, at the State House in Philadelphia.

Never popular with his peers because of his inexhaustible ego.

One of 56 men to sign the *Declaration of Independence*. Hancock was the *only* one to sign on July 4, 1776. Another 49 signed on August 2. Six signed at a later date – they were Richard Henry Lee, Gerry, McKean, Thorton, Wolcott and Wythe.

One of the most obscure signers of the *Declaration of Independence*. Very little is known about the man or his family.

Shot in a duel and had his hip shattered. Gangrene set in. He suffered for 12 long days before dying at the age of only 45 years. He could well have repeated the words that Alexander Hamilton spoke after being fatally wounded in a duel with Aaron Burr: *"I have lived like a man, but I die as a fool."*

One of eight Signers of the *Declaration of Independence* who were foreign born. The others were Lewis, Robert Morris, Smith, Taylor, Thornton, Wilson and Witherspoon.

Quotable Quote: While lying on his deathbed, he told his family: *"I have tirelessly tried to conform to the Sacred Volume as near as I possibly could. I rest my hope on the Bible for my eternal salvation."*

Heroic Deed: Signing the *Declaration*. Button Gwinnett knew that should the struggle for independence fail, an ignominious death by hanging would most certainly be his punishment.

Refused an offer of amnesty from British Governor Gage in June 1775.

Little Known Fact: One of two Signers of the *Declaration of Independence* who were born in England. The other was Robert Morris.

Price Paid for Signing: All the Signers, including Gwinnett, suffered monetary losses because of their connection with the cause. Some were brought to the brink of financial ruin, or even worse, abject poverty.

English Rusks –
Mrs. Penn's Fabled Concoction

2 cups warm milk	½ cup butter
1 cake yeast	2 eggs, well beaten
Flour to suit	1 tsp salt
½ cup sugar	1 cup raisins

Cinnamon and sugar to suit

Put warm milk into large wooden mixing bowl. Crumble yeast cake and dissolve in warm milk. Add sufficient flour to make thick batter. Cover bowl with thick towel or cloth. Set in warm place to rise until light (risen). Beat sugar and butter to a cream in separate bowl. Blend in frothy beaten eggs. Add to risen batter in first bowl. Stir in salt, raisins and enough flour to form soft, pliable dough. Break off pieces of dough about as big as a large egg. Using hands, roll each chunk of dough into round ball. Lay balls of dough close together on shallow buttered baking tin. Cover again and let them rise to double in size. Then uncover and brush tops with beaten egg white. Sprinkle generously with cinnamon and sugar. Bake in quick oven (425 degrees) for 30 minutes. Test for doneness by sticking toothpick in center of one or more buns. They are done if toothpick comes out clean. **NOTE:** *Send buns to the dinner table as soon as taken from oven.*

John Penn (1741 – 1778)

Heritage: English. Born in Carolina County, Virginia. Ancestors emigrated to America from England in the late 1600s or early 1700s.

Religion: Christian. See quote below.

Education: Basic education took place in a county (public) school. Father had ample money, but cared little about educating his son. The young man was given no tutoring and attended no private schools. Most of his education was a result of avid reading. Eventually taught himself law by studying books borrowed from the law library of a relative, Edmund Pendleton.

Marriage: Wed Susan Lyme who was born in 1741 or 1742. They were married in 1763. Susan outlived her husband by quite a number of years.

Children: Three children. Two died at birth or during infancy. Lucy, the surviving child, married John Taylor, a Colonel in the Virginia cavalry.

Interesting Highlights: Voted in favor of adopting the *Declaration* on July 2, 1776.

Delegate to the Second Continental Congress that convened on May 10, 1775, at the State House in Philadelphia. Took his seat in October.

One of 56 men to sign the *Declaration of Independence*. Hancock was the *only* one to sign on July 4, 1776. Another 49 signed on August 2. Six signed at a later date – they were Richard Henry Lee, Gerry, McKean, Thorton, Wolcott and Wythe.

Remained in the Continental Congress for three successive years and faithfully discharged his duties.

Shy and rather introverted. Took little part in any of the debates during the Continental Congress. Seldom challenged other delegates as they spoke.

Quotable Quote: *"Jesus Christ and the Holy Bible give the only spiritual light we have in this world. Through Christ alone can we find forgiveness of sin. Through Christ alone can we gain redemption."*

Heroic Deed: Signing the *Declaration*. John Penn knew that should the struggle for independence fail, an ignominious death by hanging would most certainly be his punishment.

Refused an offer of amnesty from British Governor Gage in June 1775.

Little Known Fact: Challenged to a duel by the President of the Continental Congress, Harry Laurens. Penn used his good sense of humor and easy-going manner to change the mind of his adversary. The confrontation was called off on the way to the dueling site. They decided to bury their differences rather than themselves.

Price Paid for Signing: All the Signers, including Penn, suffered monetary losses because of their connection with the cause. Some were brought to the brink of financial ruin, or even worse, abject poverty.

12

Layer Cakes
as Eaten by the Signers

Tips on Making Good Cakes – Mrs. Livingston's Pointers

Use only the best ingredients for baking cakes. If you cannot afford good flour and the best materials, make up your mind to go without your cake.

Be accurate in measurements of ingredients. There is no short road to good cake-making. What is worth doing at all is worth doing well.

Do not cut any more at one time than you can use as cake isn't very good when dry.

Do not leave oven door open, or change cake from one oven to another.

Unskillful mixing causes streaks in cake. Too rapid or unequal baking heat will also cause this. A sudden decrease in heat before the cake is quite done will streak it.

Test whether or not cake is fully done by running clean broom straw into thickest part. Straw should come out clean

Sweet milk makes a spongy cake. Sour milk makes a cake, that has a closer grain or texture.

Always stir butter and sugar to a cream. Cakes often fail because this important rule is not carefully followed.

Beat egg yolks in cool stone bowl until they cease to froth. They will thicken to custard-like consistency as if mixed with flour.

Beat egg whites in large and shallow dish until you can cut froth with a knife. It should leave clear and distinct incision as with a solid substance.

If egg whites are cold, they will beat much quicker and lighter.

It is quite difficult to beat egg whites in warm room.

After beating has been initiated, it should not be stopped until egg whites are beaten to desired stiffness. Never stop and start over again.

Don't delude yourself, and maltreat those who are to eat your cake, by trying to make baking soda do the duty of eggs. Others have tried this before with unfortunate results.

Do not use fresh and sour milk in same cake. It acts as disastrously as a piece of new cloth on an old garment.

There is no disgrace in not having time to mix and bake a cake properly. If all rules are followed and you still come up with a failure, what then? Try again. You may not satisfy yourself in a dozen tries. You certainly will not, if you never make another attempt.

William Livingston (1723 – 1790)

Heritage: Scottish-Dutch. Born in Albany, New York, to one of the wealthiest and most politically powerful families in the Colonies. Descendants emigrated to America from Rotterdam, Holland, sometime during the 1600s.

Religion: Christian. Descendant of a Scots minister. Spent one year as missionary when 14-years old. Also see quote below.

Education: Tutored (home schooled) by his maternal grandmother until 14-years of age. Went on to Yale, as did older brother, Philip. Graduated at age 18 in 1741. Studied law in office of a prominent attorney.

Marriage: Wed to a lovely young girl named Susanna French in 1745 before completing his study of law. She was the daughter of a wealthy New Jersey land owner.

Children: Had 13 children, but it isn't known how many survived beyond infancy.

Interesting Highlights: One of 39 men who signed the *Constitution*.

Delegate to the First Continental Congress that convened on September 5, 1774, in Philadelphia at Carpenter's Hall.

Delegate to the Second Continental Congress that convened on May 10, 1775, in the Philadelphia State House.

Served as a delegate to the Constitutional Convention from May 25 to September 17, 1787.

Instrumental in getting New Jersey to quickly ratify the new *United States Constitution*.

Became the first Governor of New Jersey under the new *Constitution*.

Published the controversial weekly, *The Independent Reflector*.

Quotable Quote: Livingston, Dayton, Paterson and Brearly are credited with the New Jersey *Constitution*. Here is what they wrote: *"We the people ... grateful to Almighty God for the civil and religious liberty which He hath so long permitted us to enjoy, and looking to Him for a blessing upon our endeavors to secure and transmit the same unimpaired to succeeding generations, do ordain and establish this Constitution."*

Heroic Deed: Dropped out of the Second Continental Congress in 1776 to take command of the New Jersey militia as a Brigadier General. Led his troops during the first days of the Revolutionary War.

Refused an offer of amnesty from British Governor Gage in June 1775.

Little Known Fact: His older brother, Philip, was a Signer of the *Declaration of Independence*.

Price Paid for Signing: All the Signers, including Livingston, suffered monetary losses because of their connection with the cause. Some were brought to the brink of financial ruin, or even worse, abject poverty.

Jelly Layer Cake –
Made by Caesar Rodney's Mother

Butter the size of an egg 1 tsp baking soda
1 cup sugar 1 tbls warm milk
3 egg whites, beaten 1 tsp cream of tartar
3 egg yolks, beaten 1 cup flour

Cream butter and sugar in large wooden mixing bowl. Stir in stiffly beaten egg whites and custard-like beaten egg yolks. Then stir in baking soda dissolved in warm milk. Sift together cream of tartar and flour. Add this last. When well blended, pour batter in large, shallow buttered baking pan. Bake in moderate oven (350 degrees) for about 20 minutes or until done. Test for doneness by sticking toothpick in center of cake. It is done if toothpick comes out clean. Spread when cold, between layers and on top, with any kind of fruit jelly or jam. **NOTE**: *This cake seldom fails to come out right. It will taste even better when filled with orange icing and frosted with lemon meringue.*

Caesar Rodney (1728 – 1784)

Heritage: English. Born in Dover, Delaware, son of wealthy plantation owner. Grandfather emigrated from England to America soon after William Penn started settlement of Pennsylvania.

Religion: Christian. See quote below.

Education: A brilliant, self-educated man. Some tutoring in the home. Had no time for schools or colleges. Inherited his father's plantation in 1745 when just 17-years old. Had to devote his time to running business affairs.

Marriage: Unmarried.

Children: None. Never married.

Interesting Highlights: Opposed the tyrannical Stamp Act of 1765.

One of 56 men to sign the *Declaration of Independence*. Hancock was the *only* one to sign on July 4, 1776. Another 49 signed on August 2. Six signed at a later date – they were Richard Henry Lee, Gerry, McKean, Thorton, Wolcott and Wythe.

Described by a fellow Signer of the *Declaration of Independence* as *"an animated skeleton with a bandaged head."*

One of two bachelors to sign the *Declaration of Independence*. The other was Joseph Hewes of North Carolina.

Became Major General in the Continental Army in September, 1777.

Fought against the British in both Delaware and New Jersey.

Delegate to the Second Continental Congress that convened in the Philadelphia State House on May 10, 1775.

Quotable Quote: Instrumental in having this Article included in the *Constitution* of Delaware: *"Every person who shall be chosen a member of either house, or appointed to any office or place of trust ... shall ... make and subscribe the following declaration, to wit: 'I, _____, do profess faith in God the Father, and in Jesus Christ His only Son, and in the Holy Ghost, one God, blessed for evermore; I do acknowledge the holy scriptures of the Old and New Testament to be given by divine inspiration'."*

Heroic Deed: Signing the *Declaration of Independence*. Caesar Rodney knew that should the struggle for independence fail, an ignominious death by hanging would most certainly be his punishment.

Refused an offer of amnesty from British Governor Gage in June 1775.

Little Known Fact: Suffered since childhood with disfiguring, painful, unsightly cancer that was eating away his face. Covered this with a green silk scarf when in public. This is the reason he never tried to marry.

Price Paid for Signing: All the Signers, including Rodney, suffered monetary losses because of their connection with the cause. Some were brought to the brink of financial ruin, or even worse, abject poverty.

Almond-Maple Layer Cake – Mrs. McHenry's Supper Time Offering

1 cup butter	1-1/2 tsp baking powder
3 cups sugar	4-1/2 cups flour
10 egg whites, beaten	Bitter almond extract to suit
1 cup milk	Coconut to suit, grated
Powdered sugar to suit	

Cream butter and sugar in large wooden mixing bowl. Carefully stir in beaten egg whites. Blend in milk. Sift together baking powder and flour. Add to mixture in bowl. Flavor to individual taste with almond extract. When ingredients are thoroughly blended, pour batter into round buttered and floured cake pans. Bake in thin layers in moderate oven (350 degrees) for about 20 minutes or until done. Test for doneness by sticking toothpick in center of cake. It is done if toothpick comes out clean. Set layers on rack to cool. When cold, fill between layers with mixture of ¾ grated coconut and ¼ powdered sugar. Frost finished cake with the following:

1 cup maple sugar	1 tsp butter
2 tbls milk	1 egg white, beaten

Put maple sugar, milk and butter in saucepan. Cook until it hairs. Then stir in frothy beaten egg white. Continue stirring until mixture begins to cool. Then spread on top and sides of cake.

Margaret McHenry's Frosting Pointer

When beating whites of eggs for frosting, a pinch of salt will often aid in bringing them to a quick froth.

James McHenry (1753 – 1816)

Heritage: Irish. Born in Ballymena County Antrim, Ireland. Emigrated by himself from Ireland to America in 1771. Settled in Philadelphia. Family followed the very next year.

Religion: Devout Christian. President of the *Pennsylvania Bible Society*. Also see quote below.

Education: Highly educated in Ireland. Had only the best private tutors. Studied medicine in Philadelphia under the famed Dr. Benjamin Rush, who later Signed the *Declaration of Independence.*

Marriage: Wed Margaret Allison Caldwell in 1784. Nothing much is known about his wife or their marriage.

Children: Three children, two of whom survived him.

Interesting Highlights: Delegate from Maryland to the Continental Congress from 1783 to 1786.

Captured by British at Fort Washington, New York, late in 1776. Released in prisoner exchange in March of 1778.

Delegate to the Constitutional Convention that met in Philadelphia for a four month period from May 25 to September 17, 1787.

Missed many sessions due to family illness, but was seated when it came time to sign the document.

One of 39 men to sign the *Constitution.*

Pushed hard for ratification of the new *U. S. Constitution* in Maryland.

Served as a surgeon in the Continental Army, first on the staff of Washington, then under Lafayette until 1781.

Elected in 1781 to be the first Senator from Maryland under the new *United States Constitution*

Washington appointed this trusted friend to be his first Secretary of War.

Quotable Quote: *" ... the poor cannot be presented by the rich with anything of greater value [than the Bible]. ... It is a book ... fitted to every situation in which man can be placed. It is an oracle which reveals to mortals the secrets of heavens and the hidden will of the Almighty. "*

Heroic Deed: Vigorously supported the *Declaration*. James McHenry knew that should the struggle for independence fail, an ignominious death by hanging would most certainly be his punishment.

Refused an offer of amnesty from British Governor Gage in June 1775.

Little Known Fact: One of four Signers of the *Constitution* who were born in Ireland. The others were Butler, Fitzsimmons and Paterson.

Price Paid for Signing: All the Signers, including McHenry, suffered monetary losses because of their connection with the cause. Some were brought to the brink of financial ruin, or even worse, abject poverty.

Custard-Crème Layer Cake --
Samuel Adams' Enjoyed This Often

¾ cup butter	4 egg yolks, beaten
3.cups powdered sugar	½ cup milk
4 egg whites, beaten	1-1/2 tsp baking powder
	3 cups flour

Cream butter and powdered sugar in large wooden mixing bowl. Stir in separately beaten egg whites and egg yolks. Blend in milk. Sift together baking powder and flour and add last. When well blended, pour batter into round, buttered and floured cake pans. Bake in moderate oven (350 degrees) in thin layers for about 20 minutes or until done. Test for doneness by sticking toothpick in center of cake. It is done if toothpick comes out clean. Set layers on rack to cool. When cold, make filling and frosting as follows:

1 cup milk	2 tsp arrowroot starch
1 egg, well beaten	Cold milk to suit
½ cup sugar	1 tsp vanilla

Heat milk to boiling while beating egg and sugar until stiff. Wet arrowroot starch with little cold milk and stir into the boiling milk. Continue stirring until it becomes thick and custard-like. Take ½ cup of the custard out of pan and gradually blend it with beaten egg and sugar mixture. This will be frosting for cake. Let the custard cool. Then flavor it and frosting with vanilla. Spread custard between layers and the frosting over top and on the sides.

Samuel Adams (1722 – 1803)

Heritage: English. Born in Boston, Massachusetts. Ancestors were Pilgrims. Descendant of John Alden who sailed to America on the Mayflower.

Religion: Christian. He once said: *"The rights of the Colonists as Christians ... may be best understood by reading and carefully studying ... the New Testament."* Also see quote below.

Education: Tutored at the prestigious Boston Latin School for his college prep. Entered Harvard when 14 and graduated with honors in 1740 when only 18. Tutored in law for a short time.

Marriage: Twice married. In October of 1749, he married 24-year old Elizabeth Checkley. She died on July 25, 1757. On December 6, 1757, he remarried, this time to 29-year old Elizabeth Wells.

Children: He and his first wife had five children. Only two, Hannah and Samuel, Jr., lived to maturity.

Interesting Highlights: He and his cousin, John Adams, were two of the 49 men who signed the *Declaration of Independence* on August 2, 1776. Six others signed at a later date. They were Gerry, Richard Henry Lee, McKean, Thornton, Wolcott and Wythe. John Hancock was *only* man to sign on July 4.

Was for more than 20 years before the signing of the *Declaration of Independence* , a defiant, anti-British leader.

He once said: *"The right to freedom is a gift of the Almighty."*

Offered the resolution that called for the First Continental Congress. It was convened in Carpenter's Hall, Philadelphia, on September 5, 1774.

Best known as "The Father of the American Revolution."

Quotable Quote: After signing the *Declaration of Independence,* he declared: *"We have this day restored the Sovereign to whom all men ought to be obedient. He reigns in Heaven and from the rising to the setting of the sun, let His kingdom come."*

Heroic Deed: Signing the *Declaration.* Samuel Adams knew that should the struggle for independence fail, an ignominious death by hanging would most certainly be his punishment.

Little Known Fact: Samuel Adams made this statement: *"The Constitution shall never be construed ... to prevent the people of the United States who are peaceable citizens from keeping their own arms."*

Price Paid for Signing: He and John Hancock were the only men who were not offered amnesty in 1775 by British Governor Gage. They were to be captured and punished, perhaps hanged, because their *"offenses were of too flagitious a Nature to admit of any other Consideration than that of condign Punishment."*

Jelly Cake --
Made for the Floyd Family by Joanna

1 cup butter	4 egg yolks, beaten
2 cups sugar	1 cup milk
4 egg whites, beaten	1 tsp baking soda
3 cups flour	

Cream butter and sugar in large wooden mixing bowl. Add stiffly beaten egg whites. Stir in custard-like beaten egg yolks. Sift baking soda into flour. Gradually stir into mixture in bowl. When everything is nicely blended, pour thin layers of batter into shallow, buttered and floured baking pans. Bake in moderate oven (350 degrees) for about 20 minutes or until done. Test for doneness by sticking toothpick in center of cake. It is done if toothpick comes out clean. When cooled sufficiently, spread between layers and on top of cake with your favorite fruit jelly or jam. **NOTE:** *This cake is also excellent when baked as a loaf, and when cold, sliced lengthwise in ½ inch layers. Spread each layer with jam or jelly and stack one on the other.*

William Floyd (1734 – 1821)

Heritage: Welsh. Born in what is today known as Mastic, Long Island. Grandfather emigrated from Wales to America in 1680. Settled in Brookhaven Township on Long Island.

Religion: Devout Christian. See quote below.

Education: Only informal home schooling. Wealthy father saw to it that he had only the finest private tutors. Wanted William to have the best possible opportunity to acquire a useful education.

Marriage: Twice married. Wed Hannah Jones in 1760 or 1761. Little is known about Hannah other than her father was wealthy and from Setauket, Long Island. Hardship undermined her health and she died on May 16, 1781. General Floyd remarried in 1784. His new bride was Joanna Strong.

Children: First marriage resulted in two daughters, Mary and Catherine; one son, Nicoll. Second marriage produced a son, Abraham and a daughter, Ann (Some sources say two daughters, Ann and Eliza).

Interesting Highlights: Delegate to First Continental Congress that convened on September 5, 1774, at Carpenter's Hall in Philadelphia.

Returned as delegate to the Second Continental Congress that convened on May 10, 1775, at the State House in Philadelphia.

One of 56 men to sign the *Declaration of Independence*. Hancock was the *only* one to sign on July 4, 1776. Another 49 signed on August 2. Six signed at a later date – they were Richard Henry Lee, Gerry, McKean, Thorton, Wolcott and Wythe.

Quotable Quote: On June 12, 1775, this man spoke before the Continental Congress a short time after the Concord, Massachusetts, *"shot heard 'round the world."* He said this: *"It is recommended to Christians, of all denominations, to assemble for public worship, and to abstain from servile labor and recreations that day."*

Heroic Deed: Signing the *Declaration*. William Floyd knew that should the struggle for independence fail, an ignominious death by hanging would most certainly be his punishment.

Refused an offer of amnesty from British Governor Gage in June 1775.

Little Known Fact: Major General in the New York militia. Led a division and marched to where the British soldiers were disembarking from ships in preparation of invading Long Island. The invaders were driven back and quickly retreated to the safety of their ships.

Price Paid for Signing: After the Battle of Long Island in August of 1776, his beautiful mansion was pillaged and, used to stable horses. It was then burned to the ground. Acres of fine timber and his orchard of fruit trees were wantonly destroyed. They completely laid waste to his land.

Marble Cake --
Elizabeth Witherspoon's Best

Light Portion

½ cup butter   ½ cup cold milk
1 cup sugar   1-1/2 tsp baking powder
3 egg whites, beaten   2 cups flour

Cream butter and sugar in large wooden mixing bowl. Lightly stir in stiffly beaten egg whites. Sift together baking powder and flour. Add to mixture and blend thoroughly. Set aside and do next step.

Dark Portion

¼ cup butter   1-1/2 tsp baking powder
½ cup brown sugar   2 cups flour
3 egg yolks, beaten   ½ nutmeg, grated
¼ cup milk   1 tsp cinnamon
½ cup molasses   ½ tsp allspice

Cream butter and brown sugar in large wooden mixing bowl. Lightly stir in custard-like beaten egg yolks. Blend in milk, then molasses. Sift baking powder and flour together. Stir into mixture in bowl. Add spices. Blend everything well.

To Ready for Baking

Butter and flour 2 shallow baking pans if you wish to have a layer cake. Put in light and dark batters in alternate tablespoonfuls. Then bake in moderate oven (350 degrees) for about 20 minutes or until done. Test for doneness by sticking toothpick in center of cake. It is done if toothpick comes out clean. When sufficiently cooled, cover with boiled chocolate frosting to be made thusly:

8-1 ounce squares of   2 tbls arrowroot
  baker's chocolate   starch
1 cup milk   2 tsp vanilla extract

Blend all of ingredients with the exception of vanilla in small saucepan. Bring to boil and let boil a full 2 minutes while stirring constantly. Take from stove. Sweeten to individual taste with powdered sugar. Take care to make it sweet enough. Stir in vanilla. Immediately spread between layers and over top and sides of cake.

John Witherspoon (1722 or 1723 – 1794)

Heritage: Scottish. Born in a small village near Edinburg. Descendant of the Great Reformer, John Knox. Immigrated to America in 1768.

Religion: Christian. Son of a Calvinist clergyman who was pastor of a Scottish Church of Yester. Licensed preacher.

Education: Tutored in exclusive private school in Haddington. Theological studies at University of Endinburg when 14 years old. Masters degree in 1739. Divinity degree at age 20 in 1743.

Marriage: Twice married. First wife in 1783. She died in 1789. Wed again at 68 years in 1791 to a 24-year old widow.

Children: 10 children born in first marriage. Five died before the family immigrated to America. Had two more children with second wife.

Interesting Highlights: Signed the *Declaration of Independence* on August 2, 1776. Hancock was *only* man to sign on July 4.

One of the four Signers who had been trained for the ministry. The others were Hall, Hooper and Paine.

Held distinction of being the *only* active clergyman among the Signers.

One of the eight foreign born Signers. The others were Gwinnett, Lewis, Robert Morris, Smith, Taylor, Thornton and Wilson.

One of only two of the Signers to have been born in Scotland. The other was the distinguished James Wilson.

His colleagues in the Continental Congress were astounded at the versatility of his knowledge.

Had no superior or match as a theological writer and teacher.

Served on more than 100 committees in the Continental Congress.

President of the College of New Jersey (presently Princeton).

Quotable Quote: John Adams called him *"A true son of liberty. So he was. But first, he was a Son of the Cross."*

Heroic Deed: Signing the *Declaration*. John Witherspoon knew that should the struggle for independence fail, an ignominious death by hanging would most certainly be his punishment.

Refused an offer of amnesty from British Governor Gage in June 1775.

Little Known Fact: Oldest son, James, served in Continental Army as an aide to General Nash. Killed during the Battle of Germantown.

Second son, John, went down with a ship at sea in 1795.

Lost eyesight two years prior to his death. Had to be assisted to the pulpit. Still able to preach a sermon with all the vigor of his youthful years.

Price Paid for Signing: When the British occupied New Jersey in November of 1776, they used Princeton to billet their troops and stable their horses. Everything was wantonly destroyed and all library books were burned.

Lemon Layer Cake –
Daniel Carroll's Birthday Favorite

1-1/2 cups butter
    5 cups powdered sugar
    8 egg whites beaten
    8 egg yolks, beaten

2 tsp baking soda
2 cups milk
6 cups flour
2 lemons, juice and rind

Cream butter and powdered sugar in large wooden mixing bowl. Carefully stir in custard-like beaten egg yolks. Then fold in stiffly beaten egg whites. Dissolve baking soda in milk and stir into mixture. Gradually blend in flour. Stir in lemon juice and grated rind. Pour batter in two nicely buttered and floured square or oblong baking tins. Bake in moderate oven (350 degrees) for about 20 minutes or until done. Test for doneness by sticking toothpick in center of cake. It is done if toothpick comes out clean. When cold, frost with the following:

4 egg whites   2-1/2 cups powdered sugar
2 lemons, juice only

Beat eggs with powdered sugar until stiff. Lightly stir in lemon juice. Use mixture to frost the cake on top, sides and between layers.

Mrs. Carroll's Frosting Making Pointer: Mix powdered sugar with egg whites before beating. But to have a glossy effect on frosting, egg whites are to be thoroughly beaten before sugar is added.

Daniel Carroll (1730 – 1796)

Heritage: Irish descent. Born in Upper Marlboro, Maryland. Family emigrated from Ireland to America sometime in the late 1600s or early 1700s.

Religion: Devout Christian. Roman Catholic. See quote below.

Education: Born to a wealthy family, he was sent from age 12 to 18 to Flanders. There he was to study under the Jesuits at St. Omers (1742 – 1748). Prior to this he had been thoroughly home schooled with only the finest tutors.

Marriage: Wed Eleanor Carroll around 1749 or 1750. She was believed to be the first cousin of Charles Carroll of Carrollton. Not much more is known about their married life.

Children: Not known.

Interesting Highlights: Attended the Constitutional Convention held in Philadelphia for four months from May 25 and September 17, 1777.

Spoke more than 20 times during the debates over the *Constitution*.

One of the 39 men to sign the *Constitution.*

One of two Roman Catholics to sign the *Constitution*. The other Catholic Signer was Thomas Fitzsimmons of Pennsylvania.

One of five men to sign both the *Constitution* and the *Articles of Confederation*. The others were Dickinson, the two Morrises and Sherman.

One of the wealthiest Signers of the *Constitution*. Others were Jenifer and Mifflin. The richest was probably Robert Morris and George Washington.

Older brother, John, became first Roman Catholic bishop in America.

Voted favorably for moving the nation's Capitol to Washington, D.C. (District of Columbia) on the bank of the Potomac River.

Quotable Quote: One of the men chosen to develop the Maryland *Constitution*. He wrote in part: *"We the people of the state of Maryland, grateful to Almighty God for our civil and religious liberty ... no other test or qualification ought to be required, on admission to any office ... than such an oath of support and fidelity to this state ... and a declaration of a belief in the Christian religion."*

Heroic Deed: Strongly supported the *Declaration*. Daniel Carroll knew that should the struggle for independence fail, an ignominious death by hanging would most certainly be his punishment.

Refused an offer of amnesty from British Governor Gage in June 1775.

Little Known Fact: One of 12 Signers of the *Constitution* who owned slaves. The others were Bassett, Blair, Blount, Butler, Jenifer, Madison, both Pinckneys, Rutledge, Spaight and Washington.

Price Paid for Signing: All the Signers, including Carroll, suffered monetary losses because of their connection with the cause. Some were brought to the brink of financial ruin, or even worse, abject poverty.

13

Cake Varieties
Baked by Our Colonial Ancestors

Brandy Pound Cake –
Sarah Franklin Made it for Her Father

4 cups flour	1 nutmeg, grated
1-1/2 cups butter	1 tsp mace
¼ cup brandy	10 eggs
2 cups sugar	

Cream half the flour (2 cups) with butter in large wooden mixing bowl. Stir in brandy and various spices. Separately beat egg whites and egg yolks in another bowl. When yolks are smooth and custard-like, add sugar to them and blend. Then alternately fold in stiffly beaten egg whites. Add rest of flour to this mixture. When thoroughly blended, pour into mixing bowl with other ingredients. Beat steadily for about 30 minutes. Pour batter into buttered and floured loaf pans. Bake in slow oven (300 degrees) for about 45 minutes to an hour or until done. Test for doneness by sticking toothpick in center of cake. It is done if toothpick comes out clean.

Benjamin Franklin (1706 – 1790)

Heritage: English. Born in Boston. Father immigrated in 1682 to America from England and settled in Massachusetts.

Religion: Christian. A Puritan. Franklin said this on the eve of the American War for Independence in 1774: *"We think it is incumbent upon this people to humble themselves before God on account of their sins. ... so God may be pleased to continue to us the blessings we enjoy, and remove the tokens of His displeasure."*

Education: Could never afford private tutoring or prestigious schools. Read and studied on his own extensively. Taught himself five languages.

Marriage: Took a common law wife in September of 1730. She was Deborah Read, a 25-year old Philadelphia widow. Franklin was 24 at the time. Some sources say they were formally married, others dispute this.

Children: They had two children out of wedlock. Sarah was born in 1774. Their son died as an infant.

Interesting Highlights: The oldest Signer of the *Declaration of Independence* at 70, and of the *Constitution* at 83.

Founder of the University of Pennsylvania

Developed the first street lights in Philadelphia.

Organized the first postal system in America and was Deputy Postmaster General of the Colonies (1737-1752).

Organized the first volunteer fire department in America.

Was the fifteenth of seventeen children in his family.

Made a motion that Congress be opened each day with a prayer.

Last official act was making a recommendation to Congress that they formally abolish slavery.

Quotable Quote: *"In the beginning of the Contest with Great Britain, when we were sensible of the danger we had daily prayer ... for the Divine protection. Our prayers ... were heard, and they were graciously answered."*

Heroic Deed: Signing the *Declaration*. Benjamin Franklin knew that should the struggle for independence fail, an ignominious death by hanging would most certainly be his punishment.

Refused an offer of amnesty from British Governor Gage in June 1775.

Little Known Fact: Sickly and frail when he signed the *Constitution*, Franklin had to be carried in a chair from his home to the sessions of the Constitutional Convention. Prisoners incarcerated in the city jail were recruited to undertake this task.

Price Paid for Signing: All the Signers, including Franklin, suffered monetary losses because of their connection with the cause. Some were brought to the brink of financial ruin, or even worse, abject poverty.

Holiday Fruit Cake –
George Washington Loved This One

2 cups butter	4 cups flour
3 cups sugar	3 tsp baking powder
5 egg whites, beaten	½ tsp cinnamon
5 egg yolks, beaten	¼ tsp nutmeg
1 cup milk	2 cups raisins, floured

Handful citron, chopped and floured

2 cups hickory nuts, chopped

Cream butter and sugar in large wooden mixing bowl. Lightly stir in stiffly beaten egg whites. Then stir in custard-like beaten egg yolks. Add milk and blend well. In separate bowl, sift together flour, baking powder and spices. Stir mixture into first bowl. After ingredients are thoroughly blended, stir in citron and chopped hickory nuts. Line loaf pans with well-buttered paper. Pour batter into pans. Bake in very slow oven (275 degrees) for at least 2 hours or until done. Test for doneness by sticking toothpick in center of cake. It is done if toothpick comes out clean. **NOTE:** *Martha Washington's mother gave her daughter this special recipe on her wedding day. The family often enjoyed it during the Christmas holiday period.*

George Washington (1732 – 1799)

Heritage: English. Born in Wakefield Plantation, Virginia. The eldest of six children from his father's first marriage. Only 11 when father died.

Religion: Christian. Born and raised in a Godly home. His mother taught him the *Bible* and how to pray. His father taught him to know and to worship God.

Education: Was never formally taught school beyond the elementary level. Privately tutored for the most part.

Marriage: Married Martha Dandridge Custis, an extremely wealthy widow, who had two children from her previous marriage.

Children: He and Martha had no children. He brought up Martha's children as if they were his own.

Interesting Highlights: After the battles of Lexington and Concord, he was selected to be Commander-in-Chief of the Continental Army.

One of 39 men who signed the *Constitution*.

Chosen by the electoral college to be first President of the United States from 1789 to 1797.

One of the wealthiest men in the Colonies. Made numerous and generous loans of money to friends in need.

Had at least 166 head of prize cattle at Mount Vernon in 1765.

Known to be a workaholic, but was known to take time off to go fishing once in a while. His favorite fish was the shad.

Enjoyed chasing foxes through the woods while on horseback.

Described by Thomas Jefferson as being the most accomplished horseman in America.

Thoroughly denounced the idea that the Continental Army should take over the newly formed government.

Quotable Quote: *"Firearms stand next in importance to the Constitution itself. They are the American people's liberty teeth. ... The very atmosphere of firearms everywhere restrains evil interference."*

Heroic Deed: Refused to consider the offer of important men in the colonies who wished to appoint him king.

Refused an offer of amnesty from British Governor Gage in June 1775.

Little Known Fact: One of 12 Signers of the *Constitution* who owned slaves. The others were Bassett, Blair, Blount, Butler, Daniel Carroll, Jenifer, Madison, both Pinckneys, Rutledge and Spaight.

Price Paid for Signing: All the Signers, including Washington, suffered monetary losses because of their connection with the cause. Much of Washington's extensive fortune was lost due to financial sacrifices and long absences during the war.

Abigail Adams' Honey Cake –
Often Enjoyed by Her Husband, John

½ cup butter   1 tsp baking soda
1 cup honey   ½ tsp salt
1 egg, well beaten   ½ tsp cinnamon
2 cups flour   ½ cup sour milk

Using fork, cream butter in large wooden mixing bowl. Stir in honey and beaten egg. Sift together in separate bowl flour, baking soda, salt and cinnamon. Add alternately with sour milk, to mixture in first bowl. Blend thoroughly. Butter shallow baking pan. Pour in mixture. Bake in moderate oven (350 degrees) for 50 minutes or until done. Test for doneness by sticking toothpick in center of cake. It is done if toothpick comes out clean. Take from pan and set aside to cool. Meanwhile, make following frosting:

1 cup powdered sugar   1 tbls butter, melted
1-1/2 tbls warm milk   ½ tsp warm honey

Blend ingredients in small wooden mixing bowl. When ready, and cake has sufficiently cooled, spread frosting over top and sides of cake.

John Adams (1735 – 1826)

Heritage: English. Born in Braintree (now Quincy), Massachusetts. Direct descendant of John Alden who came to America on the Mayflower.

Religion: Christian. Considered going into the ministry. He said this: *"The Ten Commandments and the Sermon on the Mount contain my religion"*

Education: Graduated from Harvard College in 1775. Later studied law under a local lawyer.

Marriage: Married Abigail Smith on October 26, 1764, when she was 20. From a Christian family, both her father and grandfather were clergymen.

Children: Four children – three sons and one daughter.

Interesting Highlights: He and his cousin, Samuel Adams, were two of the 49 men who signed the *Declaration of Independence* on August 2, 1776. Six others signed the *Declaration* at a later date. They were Gerry, Richard Henry Lee, McKean, Thornton, Wolcott and Wythe. John Hancock was *only* man to sign on July 4.

He and Abigail's life together was one of history's everlasting love affairs. They were completely devoted to each other throughout their blissful marriage of 54 years.

A major force behind getting the various states to ratify the *Constitution*.

John Adams and Thomas Jefferson (1743-1826) were two of the last three Signers of the *Declaration of Independence* to die. Charles Carroll (1737-1832) was the last Signer to pass away.

America's second President (1797-1801) following George Washington.

Was the man most influential in getting George Washington appointed as Commander-in-Chief of the Continental Army.

Quotable Quote: Regarding the day the Continental Congress approved the *Declaration,* he said this: *"It ought to be commemorated, as a Day of deliverance, by solemn acts of devotion to God Almighty."*

Heroic Deed: Signing the *Declaration*. John Adams knew that should the struggle for independence fail, an ignominious death by hanging would most certainly be his punishment.

Refused an offer of amnesty from British Governor Gage in June 1775.

Little Known Fact: Worked with Franklin and Jefferson on a special committee to develop the *Declaration of Independence.*

Price Paid for Signing: The British put an especially high price on his head. He was able to elude capture, even though they hunted him down like a wild animal.

All the Signers, including Adams, suffered monetary losses because of their connection with the cause. Some were brought to the brink of financial ruin, or even worse, abject poverty.

Maple Syrup Loaf Cake –
Richard Henry Lee's Family Favorite

½ cup butter   2 tsp baking powder
½ cup sugar   ½ tsp baking soda
1 cup maple syrup   2/3 tsp ginger
2 eggs, well beaten   ½ cup water, boiling
2-1/2 cups flour   1 cup nuts, chopped

Cream butter and sugar in large wooden mixing bowl. Stir in maple syrup. Blend thoroughly. Add beaten eggs and stir well. Sift together in separate bowl the flour, baking powder, baking soda and ginger. Add this, a little at a time, alternately, with boiling water, to mixture in first bowl. Beat thoroughly after each addition. Stir in chopped nuts. Butter loaf pan. Pour in batter. Bake in moderate oven (350 degrees) for about 45 minutes or until done. Test for doneness by sticking toothpick in center of cake. It is done if toothpick comes out clean. When done, take loaf from pan and allow to cool. Meanwhile, make the following special frosting:

2 cups maple sugar   1 cup cream
1/8 tsp salt   ¾ cup nuts, chopped fine

Blend maple sugar, salt and cream in small kettle. Bring to boil. Allow to simmer until a little dropped into cold water forms soft ball. Then pour batter out into bowl. Stir in finely chopped nuts. Beat mixture until creamy. Allow to cool. Carefully spread over cake.

Richard Henry Lee (1732 – 1794)

Heritage: English. Direct descendant of early settlers un the Virginia Colony who had emigrated from England to America in the early 1600s.

Religion: A man of strong Christian convictions. Was known as a sincere practicing Christian. His character was above reproach.

Education: Father sent him to England as a young boy to get his education. Had the finest tutors and attended the most prestigious private schools. Returned to Virginia a polished scholar when nearly 19-years of age.

Marriage: Twice married. First married Anne Aylett in 1757. Her father was a close friend and advisor to General George Washington. Her mother and Martha Washington were first cousins. She died in 1767 at the age of 35 years. He remarried in 1769, this time to Anne Pincard.

Children: Had 4 children – 2 boys and 2 girls in his first marriage. His second wife bore him 5 more children – 3 girls and 2 more sons.

Interesting Highlights: First man in Virginia to publicly denounce the British StampAct.

One of 56 men to sign the *Declaration of Independence*. Hancock was the *only* one to sign on July 4, 1776. Another 49 signed on August 2. Six signed at a later date – they were Richard Henry Lee, Gerry, McKean, Thorton, Wolcott and Wythe.

His younger brother, Francis Lightfoot Lee, was also a signer of the *Declaration of Independence.*

He and fellow patriot, Patrick Henry, were the closest of friends

Lee and Henry, young America's greatest orator, opposed ratifying the *Constitution* unless specific Amendments were added.

Ludwell, one of Lee's sons, was on the staff of General Lafayette.

Lee became Virginia's first Senator under the new *Constitution*.

Quotable Quote: Regarding guns, he said: *"To preserve liberty, it is essential that the whole body of the people always possess arms, and be taught alike, especially when young, how to use them."*

Heroic Deed: Signing the *Declaration*. Richard Henry Lee knew that should the struggle for independence fail, an ignominious death by hanging would most certainly be his punishment.

Refused an offer of amnesty from British Governor Gage in June 1775.

Little Known Fact: He was the daring Colonial patriot who bravely introduced the first *Resolution for Independence* before the Continental Congress in July 2, 1776. John Adams immediately seconded it.

Price Paid for Signing: All the Signers, including Lee, suffered monetary losses because of their connection with the cause. Some were brought to the brink of financial ruin, or even worse, abject poverty.

Brandied Fruit Cake --
Delight of the McKean Family

2 cups butter	1 tsp cloves
2-1/2 cups powdered sugar	2 cups currants, floured
12 egg yolks, well beaten	3 cups raisins, chopped
4 cups flour	¾ cup citron, chopped
1 tbls cinnamon	12 egg whites, well beaten
2 tsp nutmeg	¼ cup brandy

Cream butter and sugar in large wooden mixing bowl. Add custard-like beaten egg yolks. Stir well. Blend in half the flour (2 cups) and then stir in spices and fruits. After everything is nicely blended, alternately stir in stiffly beaten egg whites and other two cups flour. Lastly blend in brandy. Pour batter into two large, deep baking pans carefully lined with buttered paper. Bake in slow oven (300 degrees) for at least 2 hours. Test for doneness by sticking toothpick in center of cake. It is done if toothpick comes out clean. **NOTE:** *According to Mary, Thomas McKean's first wife, this kind of cake, if kept covered and in a cool, dry place, will not spoil for months. They sometimes last for as long as a year.*

Cover cake with icing made as follows:

3-1/2 cups almonds	4 egg whites
Little rose water	2-1/2 cups powdered sugar

Blanch almonds by pouring boiling water over them. Then strip off skins. When dry, pound to paste, a few at a time. Moisten with rose water as needed. Beat egg whites with powdered sugar until stiff. Beat almond paste into egg whites. When finished, spread thickly on cake. When nearly dry, cover with coating of plain icing.

Thomas McKean (1734 – 1817)

Heritage: Scotch-Irish descendant. Born in New London, Pennsylvania. Second son of a tavernkeeper-farmer. Father emigrated to America from Ireland in the late 1600s or early 1700s.

Religion: Dedicated Christian. Not known if Catholic or Protestant. See quote below regarding what he and Read wrote in Delaware's *Constitution*.

Education: Attended common school close to home and had some tutoring as a child and young adult. Placed in the care for seven years under the Reverend Doctor Allison. He and fellow Signer, George Read, were both students at this time at Allison's prestigious Academy in nearby New London. Tutored in law by an attorney cousin who practiced in New Castle, Delaware.

Marriage: Twice married. Wed first wife, Mary Borden, in 1763. Her father was wealthy and a patriot in the freedom and independence movement. Mary lived only 10 years after their marriage. A year after Mary died, McKean married Sarah Armitage, a New Castle woman.

Children: First marriage produced six children – four girls and two boys. Three more children were born to Thomas and Sarah – two girls and one boy. The boy died as an infant.

Interesting Highlights: Delegate to the First Continental Congress that convened on September 5, 1774, at Carpenter's Hall in Philadelphia.

One of 56 men to sign the *Declaration of Independence*. Hancock was the *only* one to sign on July 4, 1776. Another 49 signed on August 2. Six signed at a later date – they were McKean, Gerry, Richard Henry Lee, Thorton, Wolcott and Wythe.

McKean's sister-in-law, Anne Borden, also married a man who would later sign the *Declaration of Independence*. His name was Frances Hopkinson.

Three time Governor of Pennsylvania (1799 – 1808).

Quotable Quote: *"Everyone appointed to public office must say: 'I do profess faith in God the Father, and in Jesus Christ His only Son, and the Holy Ghost one God and blessed forevermore. And I do acknowledge the Holy Scriptures of the Old and New Testament to be given by divine inspiration'."*

Heroic Deed: Signing the *Declaration*. Thomas McKean knew that should the struggle for independence fail, an ignominious death by hanging would most certainly be his punishment.

Refused an offer of amnesty from British Governor Gage in June 1775.

Little Known Fact: One of two members of the Continental Congress to join the Continental Army. The other was John Dickinson.

Price Paid for Signing: Hounded by the British military. Had to keep family in hiding. Everything he owned was confiscated or destroyed by the vengeful British. Died in rags.

Christmas Pound Cake –
Deborah Hart Made This for John

1 cup butter	2 tsp baking powder
1 cup powdered sugar	1 tsp vanilla
4 eggs	¾ cup apples, chopped
2 cups flour	¼ cup raisins
1-1/2 cups almonds, chopped	

Put butter and sugar in large wooden mixing bowl. Beat together until nicely creamed. Add eggs, one at a time, beating thoroughly. Sift together in separate bowl the flour and baking powder. Stir this in with ingredients in first bowl. Add vanilla, chopped apples, raisins and chopped almonds. Blend well. Set aside momentarily. Grease one large or two small loaf pans. Pour in batter. Bake in moderately slow oven (325 degrees) for about 1 hour or until done. Test for doneness by sticking toothpick in center of cake. It is done if toothpick comes out clean.

Note: *Many young girls in he Colonies were prone to slipping a small piece of this cake under their pillow on Christmas eve just before going to sleep. This was believed to make her dream of her future husband.*

John Hart (1711 – 1779)

Heritage: English. Born in Stonington, Connecticut. Family emigrated to America from England around 1710. First settled in New Jersey. John was born a year later.

Religion: Christian. Quaker who rejected his faith. See quote below.

Education: Very little formal education. Never attended college. Basic learning consisted of avid reading. Primarily self-educated.

Marriage: Wed Deborah Scudder in 1740 when he was 29-years old. Her parents settled on the Delaware River near Falls, Pennsylvania, in 1717. Deborah died on October 28, 1776, while John was still in hiding from the vengeful British.

Children: She bore him 13 children. All but one lived into adulthood.

Interesting Highlights: Delegate to the First Continental Congress that convened on September 5, 1774, in Carpenter's Hall, Philadelphia.

Delegate to Second Continental Congress that convened on May 10, 1775, at the State House in Philadelphia.

One of 56 men to sign the *Declaration of Independence*. Hancock was the *only* one to sign on July 4, 1776. Another 49 signed on August 2. Six signed at a later date – they were Richard Henry Lee, Gerry, McKean, Thorton, Wolcott and Wythe.

One of the most unbending patriots in the cause for independence.

Quotable Quote*: "I believe the Holy Bible is the inspired Word of God. It contains the only reliable rules of Christian faith and Godly practices. Yes, I certainly believe the Son of God is Jesus Christ – the Saviour of everyone who believes in Him."*

Heroic Deed: Signing the *Declaration*. John Hart knew that should the struggle for independence fail, an ignominious death by hanging would most certainly be his punishment.

Refused an offer of amnesty from British Governor Gage in June 1775.

Little Known Facts: A pacifist Quaker, Hart Loved dancing and many other social pleasures. As a result, he eventually turned away from his strict Quaker upbringing.

John Hart died during the gloomiest period of the war for independence. Sadly enough, he did not live to see the sunl;ight of independence and peace gladden the face of his his beloved new nation.

Price Paid for Signing: Home stripped and destroyed. British laid waste to his land. His wife lay dying. His 13 children fled to the woods. He was hunted down like an animal. Forced to live in caves. Finally returned home. Entire family had vanished. Never saw them again. Hart died a few weeks later of a broken heart.

All Signers, including Hart, suffered monetary losses because of their connection with the cause. Some were brought to the brink of financial ruin, or even worse, abject poverty.

Huckleberry Loaf Cake –
Eaten by the Lewis Morris Family

1 cup butter
2 cups sugar
5 egg yolks, beaten
1 cup milk
3 cups flour
1 tsp nutmeg

1 tsp cinnamon
5 egg whites, beaten
1 teaspoon baking soda
    (dissolved in hot water)
4 cups fresh huckleberries
    (thickly floured)

Cream butter and sugar in large wooden mixing bowl. Add custard-like beaten egg yolks and whip 5 minutes. Then blend in milk, flour and spices. Fold in stiffly beaten egg whites and baking soda. Lastly, lightly stir in huckleberries with wooden spoon or paddle so they do not get bruised. Pour batter into buttered and floured loaf pan. Bake in moderate oven (350 degrees) for 45 minutes or until done. Test for doneness by sticking toothpick in center of cake. It is done if toothpick comes out clean. **NOTE:** *If huckleberries are not available, simply use blueberries instead.*

Lewis Morris (1726 – 1798)

Heritage: French-English descent. Born at the Morrisania Estate located in Westchester County (presently the Bronx), New York. Family emigrated to America from England in the early 1700s or before.

Religion: Devout Christian as was his half- brother, Gouverneur Morris. See quote below

Education: Tutored (home schooled) as a child in religion and secular subjects. Attended Yale College when only 16-years old. He was primarily educated under the watchful eye of an excellent tutor, Reverend Clapp. Graduated with honors.

Marriage: Wed Harriet Mary Walton in 1749. She was a most capable young woman from a distinguished and wealthy New York family.

Children: 10 children. Three oldest sons fought in the Revolutionary War under George Washington.

Interesting Highlights: One of 56 men to sign the *Declaration of Independence*. Hancock was the *only* one to sign on July 4, 1776. Another 49 signed on August 2. Six signed at a later date – they were Richard Henry Lee, Gerry, McKean, Thorton, Wolcott and Wythe.

One of the first men in the Colonies to risk his reputation and his fortune by supporting the independence movement in both Virginia and Massachusetts.

Served in Continental Army as a Brigadier General.

Regarded by everyone in the Colonies as a totally unselfish patriot.

Saw that war with England was inevitable and boldly expressed his opinion while New York was still lukewarm with the idea of independence.

Delegate to the Second Continental Congress that convened on May 10, 1775, at the State House in Philadelphia.

Quotable Quote: Morris assisted Hamilton in developing the *Constitution* for New York. Here is the preamble Morris is credited with writing: *"We, the people of the State of New York, grateful to Almighty God for our freedom: in order to secure its blessings, do establish this Constitution."*

Heroic Deed: Signing the *Declaration*. Lewis Morris knew that should the struggle for independence fail, an ignominious death by hanging would most certainly be his punishment.

Refused an offer of amnesty from British Governor Gage in June 1775.

Little Known Fact: His younger half-brother, Gouverneur, was a Signer of the *Constitution*.

Price Paid for Signing: His wife, Mary, was forced to flee with their children when the British were on the way. Entire estate destroyed. Farm was left in smoldering ruin. Home sacked and burned to the ground. The British even stole his cattle and further despoiled his more than 1,000 acre forest.

Mrs. Hall's Fruit Cake Recipe – She Made it for Lyman

2 cups butter
3 cups brown sugar
6 egg whites, beaten
1 cup milk
3 tsp baking powder
4 cups flour

2 cups raisins,
      chopped and floured
2 handfuls cherries,
      chopped and floured
Cinnamon to suit
Nutmeg to suit

Cream butter and brown sugar in large wooden mixing bowl. Lightly stir in custard-like beaten egg yolks. Then fold in fluffy beaten egg whites. Blend in the milk. Sift together baking powder and flour. Stir into mixture. After ingredients are all thoroughly blended, add fruit and spices. Stir nicely. Pour batter into deep loaf pans or large shallow baking pans lined with well-buttered paper. Fruit cakes take longer to bake than do plain cakes. Bake in very slow oven (275 degrees) for at least 2 hours or until done. Test for doneness by sticking toothpick in center of cake. It is done if toothpick comes out clean. **NOTE**: *Mrs. Hall said that when making a fruit cake, it is always best to prepare materials the day before.*

Lyman Hall (1721 – 1784) or (1724 – 1790)

Heritage: English. Born in Wallingford, Connecticut. Father emigrated to America from England in late 1600s or early 1700s.

Religion: Devout Christian. See quote below regarding the words he and William Few chose while writing the *Constitution* of Georgia.

Education: Privately tutored as a child and young adult by an Uncle, Dr. Samuel Hall. Was to become a minister. At the age of 16, he commenced his study at Yale College. Graduated in 1747. Decided to study medicine under the watchful eye of a prominent local physician.

Marriage: Twice married. Wed lovely Abigail Burr of Wallingford, Connecticut, in May of 1752. She died in childbirth the next year, in May of 1753. Remarried in 1757, this time to Mary Osborne of Sunbury, Georgia.

Children: No children resulted from first marriage. Second marriage brought forth one child, a son.

Interesting Highlights: Delegate to the First Continental Congress that convened on September 5, 1774, at Carpenter's Hall in Philadelphia.

Delegate to the Second Continental Congress that convened on May 5, 1775, at the State House in Philadelphia.

Warmly supported and voted in favor of Richard Henry Lee's daring introduction of the first *Resolution for Independence* on June 2, 1776.

One of 56 men to sign the *Declaration of Independence*. Hancock was the *only* one to sign on July 4, 1776. Another 49 signed on August 2. Six signed at a later date – they were Richard Henry Lee, Gerry, McKean, Thorton, Wolcott and Wythe.

One of four Signers of the *Declaration of Independence* who were physicians. Others were Bartlett, Rush and Thornton.

One of four Signers of the *Declaration of Independence* who were trained for the ministry. Others were Hooper, Paine and Witherspoon.

Quotable Quote: *"We, the people of Georgia, relying upon the protection and guidance of Almighty God, do ordain and establish this Constitution."*

Heroic Deed: Signing the *Declaration*. Lyman Hall knew that should the struggle for independence fail, an ignominious death by hanging would most certainly be his punishment.

Refused an offer of amnesty from British Governor Gage in June 1775.

Little Known Fact: One of the earliest Southern patriots to openly and courageously lift his voice against British suppression.

Price Paid for Signing: All the Signers, including Hall, suffered monetary losses because of their connection with the cause. Some were brought to the brink of financial ruin, or even worse, abject poverty.

Lady Cake --
Mrs. Rachel Wilson's Best

1 cup butter	1 cup milk
2 cups sugar	1-1/2 tsp baking powder
8 egg whites, beaten	4 cups flour
8 egg yolks, beaten	Almond extract to suit

Cream butter and sugar in large wooden mixing bowl. Carefully stir in stiffly beaten egg whites. Then stir in custard-like beaten egg yolks. Blend in milk. Sift baking powder with flour and slowly add this.

or

¾ cup butter	10 egg whites, beaten
2 cups sugar	3 cups flour
Almond extract to suit	

Cream butter and sugar in large wooden mixing bowl. Carefully stir in stiffly beaten egg whites. Slowly blend in flour. Flavor either of above cake batters to individual taste with almond extract. Pour batter into square, not very deep, buttered and floured baking pan. Bake in rather quick oven (400 to 425 degrees) for about 30 minutes or until done. Test for doneness by sticking toothpick in center of cake. It is done if toothpick comes out clean. When cake has cooled, cover with caramel frosting made as follows:

1-1/2 cups brown sugar	1 tbls flour
½ cup milk	2 tbls ice water
1 cup molasses	½ cake baker's chocolate
1 tsp butter	Pinch of baking soda
1-1/2 tsp vanilla extract	

Beat first five ingredients in saucepan for 5 minutes. Then grate baker's chocolate and blend with mixture in saucepan. Bring to boil and cook until mixture is consistency of thick custard. Add pinch of baking soda. Stir well. Remove saucepan from stove.

When mixture is cold, flavor with vanilla extract. Spread on top and sides of cake. Set in open, sunny window to dry.

James Wilson (1742 – 1798)

Heritage: Scottish. Born at Carskerdo, near St. Andrews, Scotland. Emigrated to America from Scotland in 1765. Settled in Philadelphia.

Religion: Dedicated Christian. See quote below regarding what he and Rush wrote in Pennsylvania's *Constitution.*

Education: Tutored by some the finest teachers in Edinburg. Studied law under John Dickinson, fellow Signer of the *Constitution.* Awarded honorary Master of Arts degree from the College of Philadelphia (presently University of Pennsylvania) in 1766.

Marriage: Twice married. Wed first wife, Rachel Bird, in 1769 or 1772. She died in 1786. Remarried in 1793, this time to the beautiful Hannah Gray of Boston, daughter of a wealthy merchant.

Children: Rachel bore him five children – four sons and 1 daughter. Hannah had one boy who died as infant.

Interesting Highlights: One of 56 men to sign the *Declaration of Independence.* Hancock was the *only* one to sign on July 4, 1776. Another 49 signed on August 2. Six signed at a later date – they were Richard Henry Lee, Gerry, McKean, Thorton, Wolcott and Wythe.

Extremely active participant at the Constitutional Convention. Known to have spoken 168 times during debates.

One of 39 men to sign the *Constitution.*

One of six men who affixed their signatures to both the *Declaration of Independence* and the *Constitution.* Others were Clymer, Franklin, Robert Morris, Read and Sherman.

One of two Signers of the *Declaration of Independence* born in Scotland. The other was Witherspoon.

Almost arrested and tossed into debtors prison after the War ended.

Quotable Quote: *"We, the people of Pennsylvania, grateful to Almighty God for the blessings of civil and religious liberty, and humbly invoking His guidance, do ordain and establish this Constitution."*

Heroic Deed: Signing the *Declaration.* James Wilson knew that should the struggle for independence fail, an ignominious death by hanging would most certainly be his punishment.

Refused an offer of amnesty from British Governor Gage in June 1775.

Little Known Fact: One of eight Signers of the *Declaration of Independence* who were foreign born. The others were Gwinnett, Lewis, Robert Morris, Smith, Taylor, Thornton and Witherspoon.

Price Paid for Signing: All the Signers, including Wilson, suffered monetary losses because of their connection with the cause. Some were brought to the brink of financial ruin, or even worse, abject poverty.

Breakfast Jelly Roll --
Mrs. Hamilton's Concoction

1/3 cup water	1 cup flour, sifted
2 eggs	1 cup sugar
1 tbls butter, melted	1-1/2 tsp baking powder
1 tsp lemon extract	¼ tsp salt
	Powdered sugar to suit

Blend hot water with eggs, melted butter and lemon extract in large wooden mixing bowl. Into this mixture, sift together flour, sugar, baking powder and salt. Beat very hard until mixture is smooth. Pour batter into large shallow, well-buttered and heavily floured baking pan. The batter should be about ½ inch thick or less. Bake in moderate oven (350 degrees) for about 20 minutes or until done. Watch cake carefully while baking. It should be done but not brown in order to roll it successfully. Use wide spatula and gently work cake out of baking pan. While still warm, turn cake out on towel wrung out in hot water. Cut off any crisp edges. Spread cake thickly with soft, tart jelly or jam. Roll up lightly and quickly before it cools. Wrap cake with wet towel. Allow to remain in towel for 20 to 30 minutes so it will better hold together. Then remove towel and sprinkle cake with powdered sugar.

Alexander Hamilton (1757 -- 1804)

Heritage: Scottish-English-French. Born in the West Indies, the illegitimate son from a common law marriage. His mother was a planter's daughter of English-French descent. His father a Scottish traveling salesman who deserted his family.

Religion: Christian. On his death bed, he said: *"I have a tender reliance on the mercy of the Almighty, through the merits of the Lord Jesus Christ. I am a sinner. I look to him for mercy. Pray for me."*

Education: Most of his basic education came about through tutoring by a Presbyterian clergyman. A brilliant thinker, he taught himself to speak and write fluent French. Also studied law on his own and eventually opened a practice in Albany, New York. Attended King's College (presently Columbia University) in 1773 at the age of 16, but his formal schooling was interrupted by the Revolutionary War.

Marriage: Married Elizabeth Schuyler in 1780. She came from a filthy rich and politically powerful New York family.

Children: Eight children were born of this union.

Interesting Highlights: One of 39 men who signed the *Constitution*.

Unhappy as a child in the West Indies, he ran away and immigrated to America in 1772 when only 15-years of age.

Upon his arrival in the Colonies, he enthusiastically joined in the fight for American independence.

Although of modest origins, Hamilton rose to become one of the young Republic's brightest stars.

One of General Washington's closest friends and most trusted advisors during the Revolutionary War.

Served in every major campaign during the War in 1776 and 1777.

Hamilton's life ended tragically when he was mortally wounded in a duel with Aaron Burr, a man who was his deadly political adversary and a person he despised. Hamilton was hear to mutter: *"I have lived like a man, but I die as a fool."* He died in his late forties while in the prime of life.

Quotable Quote: *"The best we can hope for concerning the people at large is that they properly armed."*

Heroic Deed: Refused an offer of amnesty from British Governor Gage in June 1775.

Little Known Fact: Only man to sign the *Constitution* who was born in the West Indies.

Price Paid for Signing: All the Signers, including Hamilton, suffered monetary losses because of their connection with the cause. Some were brought to the brink of financial ruin, or even worse, abject poverty.

Sponge Cake –
Delightful Specialty of Ann Ross

12 medium eggs   1 lemon, juice
 1 pound sugar   and grated rind
          ½ pound flour

Beat egg whites in bowl until very stiff. Beat egg yolks in separate bowl until custard-like. Put beaten yolks in large wooden mixing bowl. Blend sugar in with them. Stir in lemon juice

and grated peel. Blend in flour, a little at a time. Very lightly fold in stiffly beaten egg whites. Line baking pan (any shape desired) with buttered paper, fitted neatly to sides and bottom. Pour in cake batter. Cover top with paper to prevent burning. Bake in moderate oven (350 degrees) for about 20 minutes or until done. Test for doneness by sticking toothpick in center of cake. It is done if toothpick comes out clean. **NOTE:** *Ann used to first weigh her eggs. Then she would and match their weight with sugar and weigh out ½ the weight of her eggs in flour.*

George Ross (1730 – 1779)

Heritage: Scottish. Born in New Castle, Delaware. Father immigrated to America from Scotland sometime during the late 1600s or early 1700s.

Religion: Christian. Father was highly esteemed Episcopal minister in New Castle, Scotland. Formerly an Anglican clergyman. See quote below.

Education: Brilliant student. Tutored at home by mother and private tutors. Proficient in Latin and Greek. Studied law in brother's office.

Marriage: Wed highly respectable Ann Lawler on August 24, 1751. She was from Lancaster, Pennsylvania. His sister, Gertrude, married George Reed, another Signer of the *Declaration of Independence.*

Children: Three – two sons and one daughter.

Interesting Highlights: Ardent supporter of Richard Henry Lee's *Resolution for Independence*, introduced as a motion before the Continental Congress on June 7, 1776. John Adams quickly seconded the motion. This was the spark that ignited the flame of freedom and independence.

Delegate to the First and Second Continental Congress, held respectively in Philadelphia's Carpenter's Hall and the State House on September 5, 1774 and May 10, 1775 respectively.

One of 56 men to sign the *Declaration of Independence*. Hancock was the *only* one to sign on July 4, 1776. Another 49 signed on August 2. Six signed at a later date – they were Richard Henry Lee, Gerry, McKean, Thorton, Wolcott and Wythe.

Well liked by his colleagues because of his eloquence as a speaker and his charming wit. A popular man at the sessions of the Continental Congress.

Made no significant contributions during the sessions he was able to attend of the First and Second Continental Congress.

Resigned from the Continental Congress in January of 1777 due to serious illness. Died in Philadelphia soon after when only 49-years of age.

Quotable Quote: *"For all my adult years, I have read and reread the Bible, the Scriptures each day. ...I need no more than God has revealed to me in the crucified Christ, the risen Christ and the ascended Christ."*

Heroic Deed: Signing the *Declaration*. George Ross knew that should the struggle for independence fail, an ignominious death by hanging would most certainly be his punishment.

Refused an offer of amnesty from British Governor Gage in June 1775.

Little Known Fact: Close friend of Benjamin Franklin who was also a Signer of the *Declaration of Independence* as well as the *Constitution.*

Price Paid for Signing: All the Signers, including Ross, suffered monetary losses because of their connection with the cause. Some were brought to the brink of financial ruin, or even worse, abject poverty.

Elegant French Cake –
One Elizabeth Braxton Dearly Loved

1 cup butter
2 cups sugar
4 egg yolks, beaten
4 egg whites, beaten
½ tsp baking soda

3 tbls milk
3 cups flour
Nutmeg to suit
Cinnamon to suit
2 cups raisins, floured

Cream butter and sugar in large wooden mixing bowl. Stir in beaten custard-like egg yolks. Carefully fold in stiffly beaten egg whites. Dissolve baking soda in milk and stir into mixture. Gradually blend in flour. Add spices and floured raisins. When everything has been thoroughly blended, pour batter into square, not very deep, buttered and floured baking pan. Bake in moderate oven (350 degrees) for about 20 minutes or until done. Test for doneness by sticking toothpick in center of cake. It is done if toothpick comes out clean.

Carter Braxton (1735 — 1797)

Heritage: English. Born in Huntington, Virginia. Family emigrated from England to America sometime between the late 1600s and early 1700s.

Religion: Devout Christian. His virtue and morality were above reproach. See quote below.

Education: Had only the finest of tutors as a child and young adult. Attended William and Mary College. Graduated when 19-years of age.

Marriage: Twice married. Wed lovely and extremely wealthy Judith Robinson in 1755. Came from prominent Virginia family. Judith died during childbirth when 21-years of age. Four years later, Carter remarried, this time to Elizabeth Corbin.

Children: He and Judith had two daughters – Mary and Judith. Braxton and Elizabeth produced 16 more children. Several died at birth.

Interesting Highlights: Delegate to the Second Continental Congress that convened on May 10, 1775, at the State House in Philadelphia. He was to fill the vacancy created by the untimely death of Peyton Randolph.

One of 56 men to sign the *Declaration of Independence*. Hancock was the *only* one to sign on July 4, 1776. Another 49 signed on August 2. Six signed at a later date – they were Richard Henry Lee, Gerry, McKean, Thorton, Wolcott and Wythe.

Had a wonderful talent for public speaking. Oratory was graceful, flowing and persuasive to the highest degree.

His mother had died during his birth.

Refused to condone violence to achieve independence from England's tyrannical rule.

Considered to be among the wealthiest men in the American Colonies.

Quotable Quote: *"I commend you to Jesus, to God, whom I serve to the best of my ability. God will never forsake me. Pray faithfully and God's spirit will never leave you."*

Heroic Deed: Signing the *Declaration*. Carter Braxton knew that should the struggle for independence fail, an ignominious death by hanging would most certainly be his punishment.

Refused an offer of amnesty from British Governor Gage in June 1775.

Little Known Facts: Originally against the idea of American independence. Arriving at the Continental Congress in Philadelphia, he took the floor and spoke sharply against it. Soon changed his mind as he carefully listened to the speeches of the other delegates.

Price Paid for Signing: His fleet of ships were utterly destroyed by the vengeful British. Had to sell all of his property and belongings to pay off his debts. Died a pauper.

14

Cookie Favorites
Before and During the Revolution

Sugar Cookies –
Dolly Served This Treat to James

2 cups butter	¾ cup milk
4 cups sugar	1 tsp baking soda
10 egg yolks, beaten	1 tsp cinnamon
10 egg whites, beaten	Flour to suit

Cream butter and sugar in large wooden mixing bowl. Stir in custard-like egg yolks. Follow this by lightly stirring in stiffly beaten egg whites. Add milk. Dissolve

 baking soda in a little boiling water and blend with other ingredients. Lastly add cinnamon and blend. If dough is not the right consistency to roll out, work in more flour as needed. When ready, place dough on floured board. Roll out into thin sheet about 1/4 inches or less thick. Cut cookies in any desired shapes. Place on shallow buttered baking sheets. Sprinkle sugar over them prior to putting in moderately quick oven (375  degrees) for 10 to 12 minutes or until done. Makes about 6 dozen.

James Madison (1751 – 1836)

Heritage: English. Born to a planter aristocracy in Port Conway, King George County, Virginia. Descendants immigrated to America from England sometime in the 1600s. May also have Scottish and Welsh relatives.

Religion: Christian. First considered becoming a minister and did postgraduate study in theology. Also see quote below.

Education: Home schooled by his mother and tutored by a variety of the best teachers. Also attended a number of prestigious private schools. Graduated from the College of New Jersey (now Princeton)

Marriage: Married Dolly Payne Todd in 1749. She was a widow and 16 years younger than James.

Children: No children of their own. Lovely and vivacious Dolly brought a son from a previous marriage.

Interesting Highlights: The oldest of 10 children in his family.

A slave owner all of his life, he was an active member of the *American Colonization Society*, a group dedicated to sending all slaves back to Africa.

One of the most influential members of the *Constitutional Convention*. Rarely absent, he almost totally dominated the proceedings.

Deservedly known today *as "The Father of the Constitution."*

His most important contribution as one of our Founding Fathers was his work on the writing of our *Constitution*.

One of 39 men who signed the *Constitution*.

He outlived all other Signers of the *Constitution*.

Collaborated with John Jay and fellow Signer of the *Constitution*, Alexander Hamilton, in writing a series of essays. They were published in newspapers in 1787 and 1788. These writings were later published as a book titled *The Federalist Papers*.

Quotable Quote: *"We have all been encouraged to feel in the guardianship of that Almighty Being, whose power regulates the destiny of nations."*

Heroic Deed: When the *Constitution* came up for ratification in Virginia, he had to defend the document against such great patriot orators as Patrick Henry, Richard Henry Lee and George Mason.

Refused an offer of amnesty from British Governor Gage in June 1775.

Little Known Fact: Madison was one of 12 signers of the *Constitution* who owned slaves. The others were Bassett, Blair, Blount, Butler, Daniel Carroll, Jenifer, both Pinckneys, Rutledge, Spaight and Washington.

Price Paid for Signing: All Signers, including Madison, suffered monetary losses because of their connection with the cause. Some were brought to the brink of financial ruin, or even worse, abject poverty.

Vanilla Wafers --
Mary Williams Baked These for William

2/3 cup butter
1 cup sugar
1 egg, well beaten
½ tsp baking soda

4 tbls milk
1 tsp cream of tartar
Flour to suit
1 tbls vanilla

Cream butter and sugar in large wooden mixing bowl. Stir in frothy beaten egg. Dissolve baking soda in milk and add. Sift cream of tartar with 1 cup flour. Blend this in with rest of ingredients. Lastly, stir in vanilla. After thoroughly beating mixture, blend in enough flour to make rather soft and pliable dough. It must be able to be rolled without sticking. Put dough on a floured board. Using rolling pin, roll out in ¼ inch thick sheet. Using floured cookie cutter or upside down drinking glass, cut into small round cookies. Butter baking sheet and neatly place cookies on it. Bake in rather quick oven (400 to 425 degrees) for 10 to 12 minutes or until done. Makes about 6 dozen.

William Williams (1731 – 1811)

Heritage: Welsh. Ancestors immigrated to America from Wales in 1630. Settled in Roxbury, Massachusetts.

Religion: Christian. Congregational. Father and grandfather were highly regarded clergymen. Grandfather was pastor of the Congregational Society in Lebanon, Connecticut, for more than 50 years.

Education: Home schooled and tutored. Entered Harvard when 16. Graduated at 20 in 1751 with honors. Studied theology under his father.

Marriage: Married Mary Trumbull in 1771. She was daughter of Jonathan Trumbull, Royal Governor of Connecticut. William was 40, while Mary was 25. She was a well-educated and an accomplished young woman.

Children: Three– two sons and one daughter. Lost oldest son in 1810. Unable to recover from the shock of this tragedy. Soon thereafter died.

Interesting Highlights: Enthusiastically supported Richard Henry Lee's June 7, 1776, resolution for independence.

Elected to be a delegate to the Second Continental Congress that convened on May 5, 1775, at the State House in Philadelphia.

One of 56 men to sign the *Declaration of Independence*. Hancock was the *only* one to sign on July 4, 1776. Another 49 signed on August 2. Six signed at a later date – they were Richard Henry Lee, Gerry, McKean, Thorton, Wolcott and Wythe.

Made many personal sacrifices for the good of his country. Sold his business at the beginning of the Revolutionary War so he could devote all of his time to the cause.

Quotable Quote: At the close of 1776 when the outlook in the Colonies appeared gloomy, Williams, at a gathering in his home made this comment: *"If we fail, I know what my fate will be. I have done much to prosecute the war; and one thing I have done which the British will never pardon – I have signed the Declaration of Independence; I shall be hanged."*

Heroic Deed: Signing the *Declaration*. William Williams knew that should the struggle for independence fail, an ignominious death by hanging would most certainly be his punishment.

Refused an offer of amnesty from British Governor Gage in June 1775.

Little Known Fact: In 1779, the Colonists lost confidence in the use of paper money. Supplies couldn't be purchased for the Continental Army. Williams loaned $2,000 to the government to buy the needed items. He was never repaid for his unselfish generosity.

Price Paid for Signing: All the Signers, including Williams, suffered monetary losses because of their connection with the cause. Some were brought to the brink of financial ruin, or even worse, abject poverty.

Christmas Gingersnaps –
Made for the Livingston Family

2/3 cup butter   2 tbls ice water
½ cup sugar   4½ cups flour
1 egg, well beaten   1 tbls baking soda
1 cup molasses   1 tbls ginger
1 tbls vinegar   1 tbls cinnamon

Cream butter and sugar together in large wooden mixing bowl. Blend in beaten egg, molasses, vinegar and ice water. Setting this aside momentarily, sift together flour, baking soda, ginger and cinnamon in separate bowl. Stir into first bowl as much of flour blend as possible. Knead in what ever is left of flour mixture. When finished, place dough on floured board . Using rolling pin, roll dough out to 1/8 inch thick sheet. Sprinkle with sugar. Cut into 2 to 3 inch round cookies with lightly floured cookie cutter or upside down drinking glass. Lay cookies on lightly buttered baking sheets. Bake in moderate oven (350 degrees) for 10 to 12 minutes, or until done. Makes about 5 to 6 dozen.

Philip Livingston (1716 – 1778)

Heritage: : Scottish-Dutch. Born in Albany, New York, to one of the wealthiest and most politically powerful families in the Colonies. Descendants emigrated to America from Rotterdam, Holland, sometime in the late 1600s.

Religion: Christian. Descendant of a Scottish minister.

Education: Tutored (home schooled) by his maternal grandmother. Attended Yale, as did his younger brother, William. Graduated with distinguished honors in 1737 when 21-years old.

Marriage: Wed to Christina Ten Broech about 1740. She was a woman of sturdy Dutch stock.

Children: Had nine children.

Interesting Highlights: Initially opposed independence.

Delegate to the First Continental Congress that convened on September 5, 1774, in Carpenter's Hall, Philadelphia.

One of 56 men to sign the *Declaration of Independence*. Hancock was the *only* one to sign on July 4, 1776. Another 49 signed on August 2. Six signed at a later date – they were Richard Henry Lee, Gerry, McKean, Thorton, Wolcott and Wythe.

One son, Henry, served as an aide to General Washington.

Abraham, their eighth child, served in the Continental Army. He was captured by the British and incarcerated in Charleston, South Carolina.

After State governments were formed, he was elected a member of New York's first Senate that met on September 10, 1777..

Quotable Quote: John Adams wrote of this man in his diary: *"Philip Livingston is a great, rough, rapid mortal. There is no holding any conversation with him. He blusters away – says if England should turn us adrift, we should instantly go to civil war among ourselves, to determine which Colony should govern all the rest."* Either Livingston changed his thinking, or else he had intentionally misled the young Bostonian, for when the time came, he placed his name of the historic document as did the others.

Heroic Deed: Signing the *Declaration*. Philip Livingston knew that should the struggle for independence fail, an ignominious death by hanging would most certainly be his punishment.

Refused an offer of amnesty from British Governor Gage in June 1775.

Little Known Fact: His younger brother, William, signed the United States *Constitution*.

Price Paid for Signing: Lost most of his business property, two homes and his family as a result of his unselfish devotion to his dream of a new America, an America free of British tyranny. He died a heart-broken man at the age of 62, still separated from his family by the Revolutionary War.

Sugar Thin Cookies –
Jenifer's Mother Fixed His Favorite

1 cup sugar   ¼ cup milk
¾ cup butter   Flour to suit
2 eggs, beaten   Pinch of salt
3 tsp baking powder   Nutmeg to suit
Cinnamon to suit

Cream sugar and butter in large wooden mixing bowl. Stir in thoroughly beaten eggs. Dissolve baking powder in little hot water. Add it, the milk and enough flour to make soft dough. Blend in salt. Add spices according to individual taste and blend well. Take rolling pin and roll out dough on floured board until sheet is about 1/8 inch thick. Using floured cookie cutter or upside down drinking glass of appropriate size, cut dough into small round cookies. Carefully place on  shallow, buttered baking sheets. Bake in rather quick oven (400 to 425 degrees) for 10 to 12 minutes or until done. Makes about 4-to 6 dozen.

Daniel of St. Thomas Jenifer (1723 – 1790)

Heritage: Swedish-English. Born near Port Tobacco in Charles County, Maryland. Family emigrated to America from Sweden and England sometime late in the 1600s or early in the 1700s.

Religion: Devout Christian. See quote below.

Education: Family utilized services of finest private tutors during childhood and as young adult. Very bright young man. Insatiably read books. Was self-taught in many areas of knowledge.

Marriage: Never married. Was wealthy, aristocratic bachelor.

Children: None.

Interesting Highlights: Delegate to the Continental Congress from 1778 to 1782.

Little known about his childhood other than he grew up on Stepney, the family estate near Annapolis.

A popular figure among the political leaders of his day.

Became close, personal friend of George and Martha Washington.

Initially reluctant to support the Colonial independence movement.

Seldom missed a session of the Constitutional Convention.

On the shy, retiring side, he seldom spoke during the debates while attending the Convention, and later, the Continental Congress.

Made little impact on the outcome of the Constitutional Convention.

One of 39 men who signed the *Constitution*.

One of three Signers of the *Constitution* who were lifelong bachelors. The others were Baldwin and Gilman. Two bachelors signed the Declaration of Independence. They were Joseph Hewes of North Carolina and Caesar Rodney of Delaware..

Among the wealthiest Signers of the *Constitution*. Others were Carroll and Mifflin. The richest were probably Robert Morris and Washington.

Quotable Quote: Brave immigrants from Sweden settled in America and started the first Lutheran Colony. According to Jenifer, who was of part Swedish descent: *"I have a very personal belief in and relationship with the Lord Jesus Christ, just as the founders did from the beginning.*

Heroic Deed: Refused an offer of amnesty from British Governor Gage in June 1775.

Little Known Fact: One of 12 Signers of the *Constitution* who owned slaves. The others were Bassett, Blair, Blount, Butler, Carroll, Madison, both Pinckneys, Rutledge, Spaight and Washington.

Price Paid for Signing: All the Signers, including Jenifer, suffered monetary losses because of their connection with the cause. Some were brought to the brink of financial ruin, or even worse, abject poverty.

Molasses Drop Cookies –
How Maria Williamson Made Them

2/3 cup butter	¼ tsp cloves
½ cup sugar	½ tsp salt
1 cup light molasses	2 tsp baking soda
1 tsp cinnamon	1 cup water, boiling
1 tsp ginger	4 cups flour

1 cup raisins, cut up

Using fork, cream butter and sugar together in large wooden mixing bowl. Stir in molasses, spices and salt. Dissolve baking soda in cup of boiling water. Stir into mixture already in mixing bowl. Fold flour in slowly, blending well with other ingredients, so as not to leave lumps in batter. Lastly work in raisins. Lightly grease some cookie sheets. Drop batter by tablespoonfuls onto sheets. Liberally sprinkle cookies with sugar. Bake in moderate oven (350 degrees) for about 12 to 15 minutes or until done. Makes about 4 dozen.

Hugh Williamson (1735 – 1819)

Heritage: Scotch-Irish. Born in West Nottingham, Pennsylvania, the oldest son in a large family. Parents emigrated to America from Scotland and Ireland sometime during the late 1600s.

Religion: Devout Christian. Visited and prayed for the sick as young man. Studied for the ministry. Licensed to preach after father died. Presbyterian clergyman. See quote below regarding what he wrote when he collaborated on developing North Carolina's *Constitution*.

Education: Tutored as a child and young adult. Attended a number of prestigious preparatory schools. Entered the first class conducted at the College of Philadelphia (now the University of Pennsylvania). Graduated in 1757. Went abroad in 1764 to study medicine in London, Edinburg and Utrecht. Received medical degree from the University of Utrecht.

Marriage: Wed to Maria Apthorpe in 1789. She was a wealthy young woman from a prominent and powerful Colonial family.

Children: Had at least two sons. Not much else is known.

Interesting Highlights: Delegate to the Constitutional Convention. One of the 39 men who signed the *Constitution*.

Worked tirelessly for ratification of the *Constitution* in North Carolina.

Witnessed the **Boston Tea Party**.

Brilliant and talented individual. Not only was he a minister at one time, but he was also a physician, scientist and writer.

Professor of Mathematics at the College of Philadelphia (presently the University of Pennsylvania).

Elected in 1789 to the first House of Representatives under the new *United States Constitution*. Served two terms.

Faithfully attended all sessions of the Constitutional Convention.

Quotable Quote: *"No person who should deny the being of God or the truth of the religion [Christian], or the divine authority of either the Old or New Testaments … shall be capable of holding any office, or place of trust …within this state."*

Heroic Deeds: Refused an offer of amnesty from British Governor Gage in June 1775.

Took an active part in the Revolutionary War. As a doctor at the Battle of Camden, he often crossed enemy lines to care for wounded British soldiers.

Little Known Fact: A brilliant scientist-inventor who often worked with his close friend, Benjamin Franklin, on many electrical experiments.

Price Paid for Signing: All the Signers, including Williamson, suffered monetary losses because of their connection with the cause. Some were brought to the brink of financial ruin, or even worse, abject poverty.

Maple Nut Christmas Cookies –
Prepared by Maria Hopkinson

½ cup butter   3-1/8 cups flour
1 cup maple syrup   2 tsp baking powder
1 egg, well beaten   1 tsp salt
1 cup walnuts, chopped fine

Cream butter in wooden mixing bowl. Add maple syrup and beaten egg. Stir. Sift together flour, baking powder and salt in a separate bowl. Add to ingredients in first bowl and blend thoroughly. Lastly, work in chopped nuts. Chill dough for 1 hour. Then get rolling pin and roll dough out on floured board to about a 1`/4 inch thick sheet. Cut into cookie shapes with floured cookie cutter or upside down drinking glass. Lay cookies on greased baking sheets. Bake in rather quick oven (400 to 425 degrees) for 8 to 10 minutes or until a delicate brown. Makes 8 dozen 2 inch cookies.

Francis Hopkinson (1737 – 1791)

Heritage: English. Born in Philadelphia. Family emigrated to America from England sometime in the late 1600s or early 1700s.

Religion: Devout Christian. Mother was daughter of England's Bishop of Worcester. Also see quote below.

Education: Home schooled (tutored) by his mother until ready to attend the College of Philadelphia (now the University of Pennsylvania). After graduation in 1757, was tutored in law by prominent attorney Benjamin Chew.

Marriage: Wed wealthy Ann Borden of Bordenton, New Jersey, on September 5, 1768. Father operated a stage coach line and boat business to transport Colonists between New York and Philadelphia.

Children: Nine. Three died as infants.

Interesting Highlights: Delegate to the Second Continental Congress that convened on May 10, 1775 at the State House in Philadelphia.

Was member of the Continental Congress for only a few months.

One of 56 men to sign the *Declaration of Independence*. Hancock was the *only* one to sign on July 4, 1776. Another 49 signed on August 2. Six signed at a later date – they were Richard Henry Lee, Gerry, McKean, Thorton, Wolcott and Wythe.

Credited with designing the Stars and Stripes in 1777.

Became the most widely known poet, musician, artist, satirical essayist and writer in the Colonies.

Drew caricatures of his colleagues during sessions of the Continental Congress in an effort to relieve his boredom and stay alert.

Wife was also a fervent patriot and an active member as well as leader of the ***New York Revolutionary Convention.***

Wife's sister, Maria, married Thomas McKean, a fellow Signer of the *Declaration of Independence.*

Quotable Quote: *"This land, America, was our Father's gift from heaven. It has been decreed to us by Divine Providence. There can be no other explanation."*

Heroic Deeds: Signing the *Declaration*. Francis Hopkinson knew that should the struggle for independence fail, an ignominious death by hanging would most certainly be his punishment.

Refused an offer of amnesty from British Governor Gage in June 1775.

Little Known Fact: Wrote a book titled **The Prophecy.** In it he predicted the adoption of the *Declaration of Independence.*

Price Paid for Signing: All the Signers, including Hopkinson, suffered monetary losses because of their connection with the cause. Some were brought to the brink of financial ruin, or even worse, abject poverty.

Raisin Drop Cookies –
Made by Rebecca Gorham for Holidays

1 cup butter   ½ tsp baking soda
1-1/2 cups sugar   Pinch of salt
3 egg whites,   1-1/2 cups raisins,
    beaten stiff   chopped fine
3 egg yolks,   ½ nutmeg, grated
    well beaten   Flour to suit

Cream butter and sugar in large wooden mixing bowl. Stir in stiffly beaten egg whites. Then stir in custard-like beaten egg yolks. Blend in baking soda, salt, chopped raisins and nutmeg. Lastly, add enough flour to make very thick batter. Batter should be stiff enough to roll out or mold. Spread in spoonfuls on baking sheet lined with buttered paper. Bake in rather quick oven (400 to 425degrees) for 10 to 12 minutes or until lightly browned. Makes 4 to 6 dozen cookies.

Nathaniel Gorham (1738 – 1796)

Heritage: English. Born in Charlestown, Massachusetts. Family came to America from England sometime in the late 1600s or early 1700s.

Religion: Devout Christian. See quote below for the kind of wording he and Rufus King used in drafting the *Constitution* of Massachusetts.

Education: No formal schooling. The only education he received was from tutoring at home by various family members. Apprenticed to a merchant in New York when 15 years of age. No college.

Marriage: Wed lovely Rebecca Call in 1763.

Children: Nine.

Interesting Highlights: Began career in government as a notary public in Boston.

Elected to Colonial Legislature and served from 1771 to 1775.

Delegate to the Constitutional Convention.

Influential at the Convention. Spoke often during debates.

One of 39 men who signed the *Constitution*.

Delegate to the State Constitutional Convention in Massachusetts. Firmly supported ratification of the United States *Constitution*.

Took his job as a delegate very seriously and was never known to miss a session of the Continental Congress.

Despite humble beginnings, he rose to become President of the Continental Congress from June of 1786 to January of .1787.

Quotable Quote: Any person elected to the Legislature or a State office must believe in and make this declaration: *"I _____, do declare, that I believe the Christian religion, and have firm persuasion of its truth."* In Part 1, Article 11: *"It is the right, as well as the duty, of all men ... to worship the Supreme Being, the Great Creator and Preserver of the Universe. And no subject shall be hurt, molested, or restrained ... for worshipping God in the manner ... most agreeable to the dictates of his own conscience."*

Heroic Deed: Refused an offer of amnesty from British Governor Gage in June 1775.

Little Known Fact: From humble beginnings. Quit his job after apprenticing six years with local merchant. Went into business for himself. Became one of the richest and most successful businessmen and landowners in Massachusetts.

Bankrupt when he died at the age of 58-years.

Price Paid for Signing: In retaliation for his deeds as a patriot, the British destroyed much of his land during the Revolutionary War. They burned his home and devastated his property.

Ginger Cream Cookies –
Special Treat on the Rutledge Table

4-1/2 cups flour	1 cup butter
3 tsp ginger	1 cup sugar
1 tsp baking soda	2 eggs, well beaten
1 tsp salt	½ cup dark molasses

Sift together flour, ginger, baking soda and salt. In separate bowl, using fork, cream together butter and sugar. Add to this beaten eggs, molasses and 1 cup of flour mixture from other bowl. Beat everything thoroughly until smooth and lump free. Then add remaining flour mixture and blend well. Put dough on lightly floured board. Make into 2-inch diameter rolls of dough. Wrap rolls in wax paper and set aside to chill. When rolls are firm, slice in pieces about 1 inch thick. Lay slices on lightly buttered cookie sheets. Bake in moderate oven (350 degrees) for 10 to 12 minutes or until done. Makes about 6 dozen cookies.

Edward Rutledge (1749 -- 1800)

Heritage: Irish. His father, a physician, emigrated to America from Ireland in 1775. First settled in Charleston, South Carolina.

Religion: Devout Christian. Strong convictions. Whether Catholic or Protestant is unknown. See quote below.

Education: Carefully tutored at home during his youth and had a good English and Classical education. Studied law at the Inner Temple in London.

Marriage: Twice married. First to Henrietta Middleton, age 24, in 1774. Daughter of Henry Middleton, President of the Provincial Council and Continental Congress. Father was largest land owner in South Carolina. Had more than 50,000 acres, 20 plantations and 800 slaves. She died in 1792. Edward later married his first love, a widow, Mary Shubrick. The parents of both had opposed their courtship when youngsters.

Children: First marriage produced two children – 1 son, Henry Middleton and 1 daughter, Sarah. No children from second marriage.

Interesting Highlights: Delegate to the First Continental Congress that convened on September 5, 1774, at Carpenter's Hall in Philadelphia.

Delegate to the second Continental Congress that convened on May 5, 1775, at the State House in Philadelphia.

One of 56 men to sign the *Declaration of Independence*. Hancock was the *only* one to sign on July 4, 1776. Another 49 signed on August 2. Six signed at a later date – they were Richard Henry Lee, Gerry, McKean, Thorton, Wolcott and Wythe.

One of 5 Signers of the *Declaration of Independence* of Irish descent. The others were Carroll, Lynch, McKean and Read.

Older brother, John Rutledge, was a Signer of the Constitution.

Quotable Quote: *"I find that I can agree fully with my good friend, Patrick Henry, when he said: 'It cannot be emphasized too strongly, or too often that this great nation was founded, not by religionists, but by Christians; not on religions, but on the Gospel of Jesus Christ'."*

Heroic Deed: Signing the *Declaration of Independence*. Edward Rutledge knew that should the struggle for independence fail, an ignominous death by hanging would most certainly be his punishment.

Refused an offer of amnesty from British Governor Gage in June 1775.

Little Known Fact: Youngest Signer of the *Declaration of Independence* at only 26. The oldest Signer was 70-year old Ben Franklin.

Price Paid for Signing: He and many others were captured by the British. Loaded on heavily guarded ship and transported to St. Augustine, Florida. Thrown into prison and kept there nearly a year.

Ginger Snaps –
Mary Carroll's Three Fine Recipes

1 cup butter	¾ cup milk
1 cup molasses	1 tsp baking soda
1 cup sugar	2 tsp ginger

Flour to make stiff dough

or

1 cup butter	1 tbls ginger
2 cups molasses	1 tbls allspice
¾ cup sugar	5 cups flour

or

¾ cup butter blended	1 tsp baking soda
with ½ cup shortening	dissolved in hot water
1 cup molasses	1 tbls ginger
1 cup sugar	1 tbls cinnamon
½ cup water	1 tsp cloves

Flour enough to make stiff dough

Melt butter (butter and shortening in last recipe). Put in large wooden mixing bowl. Blend into this all remaining ingredients in sequences given above. Take rolling pin and roll dough out until it is no more than 1/8 to ¼-inch thick. Using floured cookie cutter or upside down drinking glass, cut dough into small round cookies. Place each on nicely buttered cookie sheet. Bake in moderately quick oven ((350 to 375 degrees) for 12 to 15 minutes or until done. Makes about 6 dozen. **NOTE**: *Each of these old ginger snap recipes are good for making cookies that will keep fresh for weeks. Try all three of them.*

Charles Carroll (1737 – 1832)

Heritage: Irish descent. Grandfather, Daniel, emigrated from Ireland to America toward the end of the Seventeenth Century.

Religion: Christian. A leader in Maryland's Catholic community.

Education: Taken to France when 8-years old (1745) to attend a Jesuit college in St. Omers. More education followed in Paris and London until he graduated. Studied law in London. Returned to Maryland in 1765.

Marriage: Married distant cousin, Mary Darnell, on June 5, 1768. He was 31, she was 21. Mary died after 14 years of wedded bliss, at age 35 in 1782. Charles never remarried.

Children: Six daughters, one son. Four daughters died as infants or in early childhood. Children who lived were Mary, born in 1770; Charles born in 1775; and Catherine, born in 1778.

Interesting Highlights: One of 56 men to sign the *Declaration of Independence*. Hancock was the *only* one to sign on July 4, 1776. Another 49 signed on August 2. Six signed at a later date – they were Richard Henry Lee, Gerry, McKean, Thorton, Wolcott and Wythe.

The only Roman Catholic to sign the *Declaration of Independence*.

One of the largest landowners in America.

Believed to be wealthiest man in America when he died.

Passage on the notorious ***Stamp Act*** in 1765 arrested his attention. He immediately supported the patriot cause. At this time he became closely associated with numerous future Signers of the *Declaration of Independence*. These included Chase, Paca, Stone and others of like persuasion.

Appointed in 1776 to be a delegate to the convention that framed a Constitution for Maryland as an independent State.

Last survivor of the 56 who signed the *Declaration of Independence*.

Quotable Quote: B. J. Lansing said this: " *...he was the last vestige that remained upon earth of that holy brotherhood, who stood sponsor at the baptism in blood of our infant republic.* "

Heroic Deed: Signing the *Declaration of Independence*. Charles Carroll knew that should the struggle for independence fail, an ignominious death by hanging would most certainly be his punishment.

Refused an offer of amnesty from British Governor Gage in June 1775.

Little Known Fact: One of America's wealthiest men, Hancock asked if he would sign the *Declaration*. Carroll responded: *"Most assuredly."* When finished, he stepped back and said: *"Well, there go a few thousand."*

Price Paid for Signing: All the Signers, including Carroll, suffered monetary losses because of their connection with the cause. Some were brought to the brink of financial ruin, or even worse, abject poverty.

Deborah Franklin's Spice Cookies – Benjamin Enjoyed Nibbling on These

1 cup butter	½ tsp cloves
2 cups sugar	1 tsp nutmeg
3 eggs, well beaten	1 tsp baking soda

Flour to suit

Cream butter and sugar in large wooden mixing bowl. Stir in thoroughly beaten eggs and spices. Dissolve baking soda in little hot water and add to mixture in bowl.. Gradually work in sufficient flour (about 2 cups) to make soft, pliable dough – dough just stiff enough to roll out into sheet. Place dough on floured board. Take rolling pin and roll out to a ¼ inch thick sheet. Using a floured cookie cutter or upside down drinking glass, cut into small round cookies. Place cookies on shallow, buttered cookie sheet. Press raisin in middle of each cookie. Bake in rather quick oven (400 to 425 degrees) for 10 to 12 minutes or until done. Makes about 4 to 6 dozen cookies.

Benjamin Franklin (1706 – 1790)

Heritage: English. Born in Boston. Father immigrated in 1682 to America from England and settled in Massachusetts.

Religion: Christian. A Puritan. Franklin said this on the eve of the American War for Independence in 1774: *"We think it is incumbent upon this people to humble themselves before God on account of their sins. ... so God may be pleased to continue to us the blessings we enjoy, and remove the tokens of His displeasure."*

Education: Could never afford private tutoring or prestigious schools. Read and studied on his own extensively. Taught himself five languages.

Marriage: Took a common law wife in September of 1730. She was Deborah Read, a 25-year old Philadelphia widow. Franklin was 24 at the time. Some sources say they were formally married, others dispute this.

Children: They had two children out of wedlock. Sarah was born in 1774. Their son died as an infant.

Interesting Highlights: The oldest Signer of the *Declaration of Independence* at 70, and of the *Constitution* at 83.

Developed first street lights in Philadelphia.

Founder of the University of Pennsylvania.

Organized first postal system in America and was Deputy Postmaster General in the Colonies from 1737 to 1752.

Organized the first volunteer fire department in America.

Was the fifteenth of seventeen children in his family.

Made a motion that Congress be opened each day with a prayer.

Last official act was his recommendation to Congress that they should formally abolish slavery.

Quotable Quote: *"In the beginning of the Contest with Great Britain, when we were sensible of the danger we had daily prayer ... for the Divine protection. Our prayers ... were heard, and they were graciously answered."*

Heroic Deed: Signing the *Declaration*. Benjamin Franklin knew that should the struggle for independence fail, an ignominious death by hanging would most certainly be his punishment.

Refused an offer of amnesty from British Governor Gage in June 1775.

Little Known Fact: Sickly and frail when he signed the *Constitution*, he had to be carried in chair from his home to sessions of the Constitutional Convention. Prisoners incarcerated in the city jail were recruited to undertake this task.

Price Paid for Signing: All the Signers, including Franklin, suffered monetary losses because of their connection with the cause. Some were brought to the brink of financial ruin, or even worse, abject poverty.

Simple Molasses Cookies –
Abigail Adams Fixed These for John

1 cup butter   1 tsp cloves
2 cups molasses   1 tbls ginger
          Flour to suit

 Blend ingredients in large wooden mixing bowl. Use enough flour to make *stiff batter,* not dough. Mold with hands into small cookies. Place on shallow buttered cookie sheet. Bake in moderately quick oven (350 to 375 degrees) for about 12 minutes or until done. Watch cookies carefully as they tend to burn easily. Makes 4 to 6 dozen.

John Adams (1735 – 1826)

Heritage: English. Born in Braintree (now Quincy), Massachusetts. Direct descendant of John Alden who came to America on the Mayflower.

Religion: Christian. Considered going into the ministry. He said this: *"The Ten Commandments and the Sermon on the Mount contain my religion"*

Education: Graduated from Harvard College in 1775. Later studied law under a local lawyer.

Marriage: Married Abigail Smith on October 26, 1764, when she was 20. From a Christian family, both her father and grandfather were clergymen.

Children: Four children – three sons and one daughter.

Interesting Highlights: He and his cousin, Samuel Adams, were two of the 49 men who signed the *Declaration of Independence* on August 2, 1776. Six others signed the *Declaration* at a later date. They were Gerry, Richard Henry Lee, McKean, Thornton, Wolcott and Wythe. John Hancock was *only* man to sign on July 4.

He and Abigail's life together was one of history's everlasting love affairs. They were completely devoted to each other throughout their blissful marriage of 54 years.

A major force behind getting the various states to ratify the *Constitution*.

John Adams and Jefferson (1743-1826) were two of the last three Signers of the *Declaration of Independence* to die. Charles Carroll (1737-1832) was the last Signer to pass away.

America's second President (1797-1801) following George Washington.

Was the man most influential in getting George Washington appointed as Commander-in-Chief of the Continental Army.

Quotable Quote: Regarding the day the Continental Congress approved the *Declaration,* he said: *"It ought to be commemorated, as a Day of deliverance, by solemn acts of devotion to God Almighty."*

Heroic Deed: Signing the *Declaration of Independence*. John Adams knew that should the struggle for independence fail, an ignominious death by hanging would most certainly be his punishment.

Refused an offer of amnesty from British Governor Gage in June 1775.

Little Known Fact: Worked with Franklin and Jefferson on a special committee to develop the *Declaration of Independence.*

Price Paid for Signing: The British put an especially high price on his head. He was able to elude capture, even though they hunted him down like an animal.

All Signers, including Adams, suffered monetary losses because of their connection with the cause. Some were brought to the brink of financial ruin, or even worse, abject poverty.

Drop Sugar Cookies –
Elizabeth Served These to Alexander

2 cups flour   1 cup sugar
½ tsp baking soda   1 egg yolk, beaten
1 tsp salt   ½ cup sour milk
½ cup shortening   1 tsp vanilla extract
1 egg white, well beaten

Sift together flour, baking soda and salt in large wooden mixing bowl. Blend together shortening, sugar and custard-like beaten egg yolk in separate bowl. Then alternately blend a little flour mixture with sour milk until all is gone. Now stir in vanilla. Lastly, fold in stiffly beaten egg white. Drop by teaspoonfuls onto lightly floured and greased baking sheet. Flatten each cookie with spatula to about ¼ inch thickness. Lightly sprinkle each cookie with sugar. Place in moderately quick oven (375 degrees) and bake for 20 minutes or until done. Makes 4 to 6 dozen cookies.

Alexander Hamilton (1757 -- 1804)

Heritage: Scottish-English-French. Born in the West Indies, the illegitimate son from a common law marriage. His mother was a planter's daughter of English-French descent. His father a Scottish traveling salesman who deserted his family.

Religion: Christian. On his death bed, he said: *"I have a tender reliance on the mercy of the Almighty, through the merits of the Lord Jesus Christ. I am a sinner. I look to him for mercy. Pray for me."*

Education: Most of his basic education came about through tutoring by a Presbyterian clergyman. A brilliant thinker, he taught himself to speak and write fluent French. Also studied law on his own and eventually opened a practice in Albany, New York. Attended King's College (presently Columbia University) in 1773 at the age of 16, but his formal schooling was interrupted by the Revolutionary War.

Marriage: Married Elizabeth Schuyler in 1780. She came from a filthy rich and politically powerful New York family.

Children: Eight children were born of this union.

Interesting Highlights: One of 39 men who signed the *Constitution*.

Unhappy as a child in the West Indies, he ran away and immigrated to America in 1772 when only 15-years of age.

Upon his arrival in the Colonies, he enthusiastically joined in the fight for American independence.

Although of modest origins, Hamilton rose to become one of the young Republic's brightest stars.

One of General Washington's closest friends and most trusted advisors during the Revolutionary War.

Served in every major campaign during the War in 1776 and 1777.

Hamilton's life ended tragically when mortally wounded in a duel with Aaron Burr, a man who was his deadly political adversary and a person he despised. Hamilton was hear to mutter: *"I have lived like a man, but I die as a fool."* He died in his late forties while in the prime of life.

Quotable Quote: *"The best we can hope for concerning the people at large is that they properly armed."*

Heroic Deed: Refused an offer of amnesty from British Governor Gage in June 1775.

Little Known Fact: Only man to sign the *Constitution* who was born in the West Indies.

Price Paid for Signing: All Signers, including Hamilton, suffered monetary losses because of their connection with the cause. Some were brought to the brink of financial ruin, or even worse, abject poverty.

Almond Macaroons –
Jefferson's Family Ate These

1 pound almonds   ¾ pound powered sugar
3 eggs, whites only

Put almonds in small kettle and pour boiling water over them. Stir well and remove skins. Wash thoroughly with cold water. Dry with clean towel. Put almonds in food chopper and grind to fine consistency. Now put them in a large wooden mixing bowl and gradually beat in powdered sugar with good wooden mixing spoon. Lastly beat in egg whites, one at a time until smooth paste is obtained. Using teaspoon,  drop small nut-size paste balls on white paper. Bake in very slow oven (275 degrees) for 15 to 20 minutes or until done. Set aside to cool. Makes about 4 dozen.

Thomas Jefferson (1743 – 1826)

Heritage: Born in Virginia. Family was among the early immigrants to the Colonies. Ancestors were from Wales. Mother was of Scottish descent.

Religion: Christian (See quote below).

Education: Privately tutored in the classics as a young man. Attended William and Mary College. Graduated after only two years. Tutored in law by eminent attorney, George Wythe, who was a fellow Signer of the *Declaration.*

Marriage: Was 29 when he married independently wealthy widow, Martha Skelton. She was the 23-year old daughter of George Wales, an eminent Virginia lawyer. They were wed on January 1, 1772.

Children: Martha had one child that died as an infant during her first marriage to Bathhurst Skelton. She and Thomas had five more, the last born in November of 1779.

Interesting Highlights: One of 49 men to sign the *Declaration of Independence* on August 2, 1776. Hancock was *only* man to sign on July 4. Six others signed at a later date – they were Gerry, Richard Henry Lee, McKean, Thornton, Wolcott and Wythe.

Vice-President and President of the United States.

An accomplished scholar, he read several languages with ease.

Founded the University of Virginia and actually designed the buildings.

Died exactly 50 years after the adoption of the *Declaration of Independence* on July 4, 1826, as did fellow Signer, John Adams.

Those who knew him best said he *never ever* lost his temper

First man to propose laws in the Virginia legislature prohibiting the importation of slaves.

Quotable Quote: *"I am a real Christian, ... a disciple of the doctrines of Jesus. ... I am a Christian in the only sense in which He wished anyone to be, sincerely attached to His doctrine in preference to all others."*

Last words: *"I resign myself to my God, and my child to my country."*

Heroic Deed: Signing the *Declaration of Independence*. Thomas Jefferson knew that should the struggle for independence fail, an ignominious death by hanging would most certainly be his punishment.

Refused an offer of amnesty from British Governor Gage in June 1775

Little Known Facts: Skillful performer with a violin.

First President to serve meringue on pies for White House State dinners.

Price Paid for Signing: All the signers, including Jefferson, suffered monetary losses because of their connection with the cause. Some were brought to the brink of financial ruin, or even worse, abject poverty. Sadly enough, Jefferson was so desperately in need of money before he died that he had to sell his magnificent library to the government for a mere $30,000.

Caraway Seed Cookies –
Holiday Favorite of William Blount

13 cups flour
4 tbls caraway seeds
2 cups butter

2-1/2 cups sugar
1 tsp baking soda
2 eggs, well beaten

Put flour in large wooden mixing bowl. Blend in caraway seeds. Rub in butter, or what is better, chop it up in flour. Dissolve sugar in 2 cups cold water. Dissolve baking soda in little hot water. Add both to mixing bowl with other ingredients. Stir well. Then blend in thoroughly beaten eggs. Place dough on floured board. Take rolling pin and roll dough into thin sheet about ¼ inch thick. Cut into small square or oval-shaped cookies. Place in a shallow buttered baking pan. Bake in rather quick oven (400 to 425 degrees) for 10 to 12 minutes or until done. Makes 12 to 14 dozen cookies.

William Blount (1749 – 1800)

Heritage: English. Born on grandfather's Rosefield estate near Windsor, Bertie County, North Carolina. Great grandson of Thomas Blount who emigrated to Virginia from England around 1660. Settled on plantation in North Carolina.

Religion: Devout Christian. Episcopal, Presbyterian. See quote below regarding what he, Williamson and Spaight wrote in North Carolina's *Constitution*.

Education: Apparently had an excellent education. Studies undertaken mostly at home, primarily by the finest of private tutors. He was also an avid reader and did this whenever time permitted.

Marriage: Wed Mary Grainger [Granger] on February 12, 1778.

Children: Six children, all of whom reached adulthood. Three sons – Eliza, William and Richard; three daughters –Anne, Barbara and Mary Louisa.

Interesting Highlights: One of 39 men who signed the *Constitution*.

Was a close personal friend of George Washington.

Reluctantly affixed his signature to the Constitution in order as he said, to make it *"the unanimous act of the States in Convention."*

Described by a fellow Signer as: *"No speaker, nor does he possess any of those talents that make men shine."*

Elected as one of Tennessee's first Senators under the new U.S. Constitution. Served in this capacity from 1796 to 1797.

Expelled from the U.S. Senate on a conspiracy charge on July 8, 1797, by a vote of 25 to 1.

Impeached by the House of Representatives but all charges were dropped by the Senate in 1798.

Quotable Quote: *"No person who should deny the being of God or the truth of the religion [Christian], or the divine authority of either the Old or New Testaments, or who should hold religious principles incompatible with the freedom and safety of the state, shall be capable of holding any office, or place of trust ...within this state."*

Heroic Deed: Volunteered to serve during the Revolutionary War in the North Carolina militia as well as the 3rd Regimental Continental troops.

Refused an offer of amnesty from British Governor Gage in June 1775.

Little Known Fact: One of the 12 Signers of the *Constitution* who owned slaves. The others Bassett, Blair, Butler, Carroll, Jenifer, Madison, Charles and Charles Cotesworth Pinckney, Rutledge, Spaight and Washington

Price Paid for Signing: All the Signers, including Blount, suffered monetary losses because of their connection with the cause. Some were brought to the brink of financial ruin, or even worse, abject poverty.

15

Pie Crusts and Pastries
Made by Families of the Signers

Making Pastry –
12 Good Pointers Given by Mrs. Rush

1. *Keep cool* is a cardinal motto for pastry makers.

2. A marble slab is ideal for rolling out pastry. Next to this is a *clean* hardwood board.. A pastry board is never to be used for any other purpose.

3. Pastry dough should be used immediately after it is made.

4. This particular kind of dough is best when fresh.

5. Pie crust dough must always be thoroughly chilled before rolling it out. Chilling dough ball will make finished pie crust lighter and flakier.

6. It is harder to make good pastry in warm weather than cold.

7. In warm weather the butter has a tendency to oil. Thus, the crust is heavy and solid.

8. All scraps of dough left over when cutting edges around pie pan are to be reused to make another pie crust.

9. Pie crust dough should be handled as little as possible when making dough into ball.

10. Always push rolling pin away from body while making a series of quick light strokes.

11. Always use spoon, knife blade, or fingers to press down edges of a pie crust in a pan.

12. Few people know what really good pastry is like. Fewer still can make it. It has no inevitable resemblance either to putty or leather. It is light, crisp, flaky, beautiful to behold – and even more wonderful to taste.

Benjamin Rush (1745 – 1813)

Heritage: English. Born at Berberry, about 12 miles NE of Philadelphia. His father, an officer in Cromwell's army, emigrated to America from England during the late 1600s or early 1700s.

Religion: Christian. He explained: *"I have alternately been called an Aristocrat and a Democrat. I am neither, I am a Christocrat."*

Education: Attended prestigious West Nottingham Academy in Rising Sun, Maryland. Graduated with honors from the College of New Jersey (now Princeton) in 1760 when just 15-years old. Then returned to Philadelphia and began his apprenticeship with a prominent physician.

Marriage: Married Julia Stockton on January 11, 1776. She was oldest daughter of another zealous patriot, Richard Stockton, who would also later became a Signer of the *Declaration of Independence.*

Children: They had 13 children, all of whom survived him. Some sources say only six sons and three daughters survived him.

Interesting Highlights: One of 56 men to sign the *Declaration of Independence*. Hancock was the *only* one to sign on July 4, 1776. Another 49 signed on August 2. Six signed at a later date – they were Richard Henry Lee, Gerry, McKean, Thorton, Wolcott and Wythe.

At the age of 30, he was one of the youngest Signers of the *Declaration of Independence.*

Served his country as Surgeon General in the Continental Army. Resigned after a disagreement with General Washington.

Helped found the ***Pennsylvania Society for Promoting the Abolition of Slavery*** in 1787. Later served as the organization's President.

Cofounder of the ***Philadelphia Bible Society***, a group that strongly advocated the use of the *Bible* and *Scripture* in all public schools.

Quotable Quote: His last words before dying: *"... blessed Jesus, wash away all my impurities, and receive me into Thy everlasting kingdom."*

Heroic Deed: Signing the *Declaration.* Benjamin Rush knew that should the struggle for independence fail, an ignominious death by hanging would most certainly be his punishment.

Refused an offer of amnesty from British Governor Gage in June 1775.

Little Known Fact: In 1776, he suggested to Thomas Paine that he should write his famous book, ***Common Sense***. He even gave Paine the title and helped finance its publication.

Died during a typhus epidemic in 1813 at the age of 67.

Price Paid for Signing: All the signers, including Rush, suffered monetary losses because of their connection with the cause. Some were brought to the brink of financial ruin, or even worse, abject poverty.

Ordinary But Good Pie Crust –
Cornelia Paterson's Best

3 cups flour   ½ cup butter
½ cup lard   Pinch of salt

Sift flour into large wooden mixing bowl. Add salt and stir in sufficient ice water to make stiff dough. Use large wooden spoon for blending ingredients until this no longer possible. Using floured hands, form dough into ball. ***Handle as little as possible***.

To make finished crust flakier, lay ball of dough in very cold place for at least 15 minutes and as long as I hour before rolling out. Then lay cold lump on lightly floured board.

Now roll out dough into as thin a sheet as possible (use very little flour as while rolling). Always roll away from yourself with quick, light action. Butter pie tins. Lay sheet of dough in each and cut neatly around edges. Roll all left over pieces into another thin sheet. If pies are to have top crust, first fill the pies. Then lay sheet of dough over the top and cut to fit. Use spoon or knife blade to press edges together. The upper and lower crusts should be sealed in this manner to prevent leakage. **NOTE:** *All lard may be used in this recipe instead of a lard-butter combination as called for in the above recipe. This makes simple but delicious pie crusts.*

William Paterson (1745 – 1806)

Heritage: Irish. Born in County Antrim, Ireland. Family emigrated from Ireland to America in 1747 when he was two years old. Disembarked from ship in New Castle, Delaware.

Religion: Devoted Christian. Protestant or Roman Catholic not known. See quote below.

Education: Much of his youth spent in prestigious private schools. Attended College of New Jersey (presently Princeton). Studied law under the tutelage of Richard Stockton, a prominent attorney who would later affix his signature to the *Declaration of Independence.*

Marriage: Twice married. Wed Cornelia Bell in 1779. She died four years later. Remarried in about two years, this time to Euphemia White.

Children: Three with first wife, Cornelia. She died during childbirth. Not known if children were born to his second union.

Interesting Highlights: One of 39 men who signed the *Constitution.*

One of four Signers of the *Constitution* who were born in Ireland. The others were Butler, Fitzsimmons and McHenry.

One of seven foreign born Signers of the *Constitution,* four of whom were Irish. Those born elsewhere are as follows: Hamilton -- West Indies; Robert Morris – England; and Wilson – Scotland.

Appointed by President George Washington to be an Associate Justice of the Supreme Court. Served from 1793 to 1806.

First man elected to the United States Senate under the new *Constitution.* Served in this capacity from 1789 to 1790.

City of Paterson, New Jersey, was named after him.

Held commission as an officer in the New Jersey militia in 1777.

Quotable Quote: Paterson, Brearly, Dayton and William Livingston are credited with the development of New Jersey's *Constitution.* Here is what they wrote: *"We the people ... grateful to Almighty God for the civil and religious liberty which He hath so long permitted us to enjoy, and looking to Him for a blessing upon our endeavors to secure and transmit the same unimpaired to succeeding generations, do ordain and establish this Constitution."*

Heroic Deed: Refused an offer of amnesty from British Governor Gage in June of 1775.

Little Known Fact: Of the 18 members of his class at the College of New Jersey (presently Princeton), 12 went on to become ministers.

Price Paid for Signing: All the Signers, including Paterson, suffered monetary losses because of their connection with the cause. Some were brought to the brink of financial ruin, or even worse, abject poverty.

Pie Crust Recipe --
Used to Make Pies in Rebecca Lee's Oven

4 cups flour   1-1/2 cups butter
3 tsp baking powder   Ice water to suit

Sift flour and baking powder together twice. Then put in large wooden mixing bowl. With broad-bladed knife chop half the butter (3/4 cup) into flour until it looks like yellow sand. Gradually work in ice water until dough is stiff. Do with large wooden spoon until it is no longer possible to move spoon.

Make dough into ball with floured hands. Handle dough as little as possible. Lay on floured board and roll out with heavy rolling pin into very thin sheet. Always roll away from body with light quick roller action. When thin enough, take ¼ of remaining butter and stick tiny pieces in close rows all over sheet of dough. Use knife for this purpose rather than hands or fingers.

Lightly sprinkle flour over sheet of dough. Tightly roll up into close folds. Flatten. Take rolling pin and roll out dough second time. Baste again with another ¼ of the butter. Sprinkle lightly with flour as you did before. Roll dough up in folds, flatten, and roll out again in thin sheet. Baste a last time with tiny pieces of remaining butter. Again sprinkle with flour. Again fold up dough. Before rolling dough a final time, chill it for at least 15 minutes, and as much as 1 hour if time permits.

Finished pie crust will turn out flakier and firmer. After properly cooling dough, roll out into crust. Butter pie pans. Lay sheet of dough in each pan. Cut evenly around edge of each pan after neatly fitting dough sheet into it. All scraps may be reused by simply piling together and rolling them out into a thin sheet. The top crust (if one is used) is made by laying a dough sheet across filled pie and trimming edges to fit. The edges are then to be pressed together with knife edge, spoon, or fingers.

Francis Lightfoot Lee (1734 – 1797)

Heritage: English. Born in Virginia. Direct descendant of early settlers in the Virginia Colony. They emigrated to America from England sometime in the early 1600s.

Religion: Known as a man of extremely strong Christian conviction. Raised in strict Christian family. See quote below.

Education: Solely educated by a private tutor – an eminent Scottish clergyman, the Reverend Doctor Clapp. Never attended college because his father died before he was old enough to be sent abroad to study as was his brother, Richard Henry.

Marriage: Wed 19-year old socialite, Rebecca Taylor, in 1769. He was 35 at this time. Rebecca was an accomplished and popular young woman.

Children: They had no children.

Interesting Highlights: Delegate to Continental Congress.

One of 56 men to sign the *Declaration of Independence*. Hancock was *only* one to sign on July 4, 1776. Another 49 signed on August 2. Six signed at later date – they were Richard Henry Lee, Gerry, McKean, Thorton, Wolcott and Wythe.

Younger brother of fellow Signer, Richard Henry Lee.

Vigorously opposed the institution of slavery in the Colonies.

Not a fluent speaker as was his polished brother, Richard Henry.

Rarely took part in debates on the floor of the Continental Congress because of his shyness.

Caught the spirit of the Revolution from his most persuasive brother, Richard Henry, at the time of the "Stamp Act" in March of 1765.

Signed both the *Declaration of Independence* as well as the *Articles of Confederation*.

Quotable Quote: *"For one to sincerely believe in the Lord Jesus Christ, is to live happily and with little worry. This I do without reservation. I unquestionably enjoy the peace on mind He brings to me. I trust Him fully."*

Heroic Deed: Signing the *Declaration*. Francis Lightfoot Lee knew that should the struggle for independence fail, an ignominious death by hanging would most certainly be his punishment.

Refused an offer of amnesty from British Governor Gage in June 1775.

Little Known Fact: Relied almost totally on the judgment of his older brother, Richard Henry Lee. He admired Richard's polished manners and held him up as a role model.

Price Paid for Signing: All the Signers, including Lee, suffered monetary losses because of their connection with the cause. Some were brought to the brink of financial ruin, or even worse, abject poverty.

Transparent Pie Crust –
Made by the Mother of Joseph Hewes'

2 cups butter   1 egg yolk, beaten
                4 cups flour

Melt butter in saucepan set in another pan of boiling water. Stir gently until melted. While melted butter is cooling, beat egg yolk until thick as custard. Pour melted butter in, a little at a time, while beating it hard with the egg yolk.

When thoroughly blended, gradually stir in flour with large wooden spoon. Then flour hands and take dough from bowl. Form into ball and lay on floured kneading board. Using large, heavy rolling pin, roll dough out into very thin sheet no thicker than 1/8 inch. Always roll rolling pin away from body with quick, light action. Sprinkle sheet lightly with flour. Tightly roll up sheet of dough in close folds. Roll out a second time. Again flour and then roll or fold it up. Chill dough roll at least 5 minutes, preferably longer, before rolling it out again to make finished pie crust. After chilling period, roll dough out for final time. Cut into small tartlet shells. Bake in very hot oven (450 degrees) before filling shells. When lightly tanned, take from oven. Brush over entire shell with beaten egg. Allow to cool. **NOTE**: *Fill with properly prepared pie and tart fillings as covered in Chapter 16. This is an extremely rich crust and is fragile as well. It is not suitable for regular pies.*

Joseph Hewes (1730 – 1779)

Heritage: English. Born on small farm in Princeton, Jersey. Parents emigrated to America from England sometime in the late 1600s or early 1700s.

Religion: Christian. Quaker. Belonged to the *Society of Friends*. Had a very strict Christian upbringing. See quote below.

Education: Although the son of a well-to-do Quaker farmer, he attended his local school rather than a prestigious one. Went on to graduate from the College of New Jersey (presently Princeton). Then worked as an apprentice to a merchant where he learned the things he needed to know about successfully running his own business

Marriage: Lifelong bachelor.

Children: None. Never married.

Interesting Highlights: One of 56 men to sign the *Declaration of Independence*. Hancock was the *only* one to sign on July 4, 1776. Another 49 signed on August 2. Six signed at a later date – they were Richard Henry Lee, Gerry, McKean, Thorton, Wolcott and Wythe.

One of 2 bachelors who signed the *Declaration of Independence*. The other bachelor was Caesar Rodney of Delaware. Three bachelors signed the *Constitution*. They were Baldwin, Gilman and Jenifer.

Came under intense pressure from his Quaker church associates, friends and family members to refuse to sign *the Declaration*.

After much soul searching, and upon affixing his signature to the *Declaration of Independence*, this courageous Christian patriot said these immortal words: *"My country is entitled to my services, and I shall not shrink from the cause, even though it should cost me my life."*

Because of his signing, he was shunned by his unforgiving Quaker friends and family members up until the time of his death.

Quotable Quote: Just before dying, as he took his final breath, Hewes whispered to those nearby: *"Do not fret or worry in my going, for I have full confidence in the mercy and the goodness of God. Pray for me."*

Heroic Deed: Signing the *Declaration*. Joseph Hewes knew that should the struggle for independence fail, an ignominious death by hanging would most certainly be his punishment.

Refused an offer of amnesty from British Governor Gage in June 1775.

Little Known Fact: Sadly, his beloved wife-to-be died just a few days before their wedding. Embittered, he lived with a broken-heart for the rest of his life. This is the reason he never again considered marriage.

Price Paid for Signing: All the Signers, including Hewes, suffered monetary losses because of their connection with the cause. Some were brought to the brink of financial ruin, or even worse, abject poverty.

French Puff Paste –
Prepared by Mrs. Susan Dayton

4 cups flour   1 egg yolk, well beaten
1-1/2 cups butter   ½ cup ice water

Sift flour into large wooden mixing bowl. With broad-bladed knife, chop half the butter (3/4 cup) into flour until it looks like yellow sand. Stir custard-like beaten egg yolk into ice water. Gradually work mixture into flour until it makes very stiff dough. Stir with large wooden spoon until this is no longer possible. Flour hands and make dough into ball. Lay balls of dough on a floured board. Using rolling pin, roll dough out into very thin sheet. Always roll dough away from body with quick light action. When dough is thin enough, take another ¼ of remaining butter and stick  little pieces in neat rows all over sheet. Use knife for this instead of fingers. Sprinkle flour lightly over sheet of dough. Then tightly roll up dough. Flatten enough so rolling pin can take hold.

Roll out dough a third time as thin as the previous sheet. Take another ¼ or remaining butter and stick in rows all over sheet. Again sprinkle lightly with flour. Roll up dough once again. Flatten and once again roll out thin. Take last of the butter and place small bits all over sheet of dough. Lightly sprinkle with flour. Roll it a final time. Chill for 10 to 15 minutes or longer if possible. After cooling period, roll out into sheet for the last time. Cut into small tartlet shells.

Bake tartlet shells before filling. Place each one on buttered baking sheet. Bake in very quick oven (450 degrees) for six minutes. Then bake in slow oven (300 degrees) for 25 to 30 minutes. When lightly tanned, take from oven and brush over with beaten egg. Let cool and then fill with properly prepared fillings as covered in Chapter 16. **NOTE**: *This is an extremely delicate and delicious crust. It may be used for regular pies as well as tartlet shells*

236

Johnathan Dayton (1760 – 1824)

Heritage: English. Born in Elizabethtown (presently Elizabeth), New Jersey. Family emigrated to America from England sometime in the late 1600s or early 1700s.

Religion: Devout Christian. See quote below.

Education: Primarily tutored by mother. Ended up with a good, well-rounded education. Attended the College of New Jersey (presently Princeton). Graduated in 1776.

Marriage: Wed a young woman named Susan Williamson. Wedding date unknown as is anything about his chosen mate.

Children: Two daughters.

Interesting Highlights: Religiously attended every session of the Constitutional Convention.

One of 39 men who signed the *Constitution.*

One of three men in their twenties to sign the *Constitution.* Others were Spaight and Charles Pinckney.

Joined Continental Army upon graduation from college.

Captain in the Continental Army at the age of only 19.

Served in the Continental Army under the famed French General Lafayette as well as his father, General Elias Dayton.

Took part in the Battle of Yorktown and other military engagements.

Captured by British forces and held in prison for a period of time.

City of Dayton, Ohio, was named after this great American patriot.

Charged with treason because of his close association with Aaron Burr's attempt to take over Spanish land in the Southwest and create their own empire. Was indicted but never prosecuted.

Served in U.S. Senate under the new *Constitution* from 1779 to 1805.

Quotable Quote: Dayton wrote of how members of the Continental Congress responded to Benjamin Franklin's speech calling for prayer each day to open sessions: " *... never did I behold a countenance at once so dignified and delightful as was that of Washington at the close of the address; nor were the members of the convention generally less affected. The words of the venerable Franklin fell upon our ears with weight and authority ...* "

Heroic Deed: Refused an offer of amnesty from British Governor Gage in June 1775.

Little Known Fact: Youngest Signer of the Constitution at 26 years of age. The oldest Signer was 81-year old Benjamin Franklin.

Price Paid for Signing: All the Signers, including Dayton, suffered monetary losses because of their connection with the cause. Some were brought to the brink of financial ruin, or even worse, abject poverty.

16

Pie and Tart Fillings
Prepared by Women of the House

Pumpkin Pie –
George and Martha's Favorite

¾ cup sugar   1-1/2 cups pumpkin,
  1 tsp cinnamon   steamed and strained
  1 tsp ginger   3 eggs, beaten well
½ tsp salt   1 cup milk
    1 cup heavy cream
    1 tbls butter, melted

Put sugar in wooden mixing bowl. Blend in spices and salt. Stir in steamed and strained pumpkin, custard-like beaten eggs, milk, heavy cream and melted butter. Blend thoroughly. Pour into pastry lined pie pan. Bake in moderate oven (350 degrees) for about 45 minutes or until done. Set aside and allow to cool. Then serve. Sufficient for making 1 pie. **NOTE:** *The cooler a pumpkin pie is, the better it will taste plain. Especially good when served with whipped cream or ice cream.*

George Washington (1732 – 1799)

Heritage: English. Born in Wakefield Plantation, Virginia. The eldest of six children from his father's first marriage. Was 11 when his father died.

Religion: Christian. He once said: *"The people know it is impossible to rightly govern the world without God and the Bible."*

Education: Never formally schooled taught beyond the elementary level. Privately tutored and self-taught for the most part.

Marriage: Married Martha Dandridge Custis, an extremely wealthy widow, who had two children from her previous marriage.

Children: He and Martha had no children. He brought up Martha's children as if they were his own.

Interesting Highlights: After the battles of Lexington and Concord, he was selected to be Commander-in-Chief of the Continental Army.

Chosen by the electoral college to be first President of the United States from 1789 to 1797.

Freed his 123 slaves upon his death.

Switched from growing tobacco to grain in the 1760s.

Had at least 166 head of prize cattle at Mount Vernon in 1765.

Known to be a workaholic, but was known to take time off to go fishing once in a while. His favorite fish was the shad.

Described by Thomas Jefferson as being the most accomplished horseman in America. Loved to go fox hunting when time permitted.

One of 12 signers of the *Constitution* who owned slaves. The others were Bassett, Blair, Blount, Butler, Daniel Carroll, Jenifer, Madison, both Pinckneys, Rutledge and Spaight.

Quotable Quote: In his first inaugural address, he said: *"It would be peculiarly improper to omit in this first official act my fervent supplication to that Almighty Being who rules over the universe, who presides in the counsels of nations and whose Providential aid can supply every human defect."*

At another time, he mentioned his view on gun ownership by American citizens: *"When firearms go, all goes – we need them every hour."*

Heroic Deed: Refused to consider the offer of important men in the colonies who wished to appoint him king.

Refused an offer of amnesty from British Governor Gage in June 1775.

Little Known Fact: Supervised planning to relocate the government in the District of Columbia. Laid the cornerstone of the Capitol in 1793.

Price Paid for Signing: All the Signers, including Washington, suffered monetary losses because of their connection with the cause. Much of Washington's extensive fortune was lost due to financial sacrifices and long absences during the war.

Pumpkin Custard –
Favorite Filling of the Ellery Family

1 cup pumpkin
    stewed and mashed
3 eggs, well beaten
¾ cup brown sugar

½ tsp salt
Pinch of nutmeg
½ tsp cinnamon
  2 cups milk, scalded

1 cup heavy cream, whipped

Line pie pan with good crust. Put stewed and mashed pumpkin into large wooden mixing bowl. Blend in frothy beaten eggs, brown sugar, salt and spices. Stir in hot milk. Beat mixture thoroughly and hard. Pour into baked pie shell. Put in moderate oven (375 degrees) and bake for 25 to 30 minutes, or until firm. Set aside to cool. No top crust is needed. Serve when cold with whipped cream on top.

William Ellery (1727 – 1826)

Heritage: English. Born in Newport, Rhode Island. Family emigrated to America from England sometime in the late 1600s or early 1700s.

Religion: Devout Christian. See quote below.

Education: A brilliant student, he had the best tutors money could buy as a child and young adult. Attended Harvard College and graduated in 1747. Distinguished himself in learning to fluently speak and read Latin and Greek. Went on to study law under a prominent local attorney.

Marriage: Twice married. Wed Ann Remington in 1750 when she was 21 and he was 23. Highly educated, accomplished and a member of high society, Ann died in 1764 during childbirth. Ellery remarried three years later. His new bride, Abigail Carey, a lovely 25-year old, was his second cousin.

Children: Ann bore William seven children – four daughters and three sons. Abigail bore him eight more children. Only two lived beyond infancy.

Interesting Highlights: One of 56 men to sign the *Declaration of Independence*. Hancock was the *only* one to sign on July 4, 1776. Another 49 signed on August 2. Six signed at a later date – they were Richard Henry Lee, Gerry, McKean, Thorton, Wolcott and Wythe.

His home state of Rhode Island was the first to publicly announce its independence from Great Britain on May 4, 1776.

Quotable Quote: An 1848 textbook had these words to say about this brave American: *"As a patriot and a Christian, his name will ever be revered."*

Ellery believed that the most important part of the pledge taken by all Signers of the *Declaration* was where it stated, *" ... with a firm reliance on the protection of the Divine Providence ... "*

Heroic Deed: Signing the *Declaration*. William Ellery knew that should the struggle for independence fail, an ignominious death by hanging would most certainly be his punishment.

Refused an offer of amnesty from British Governor Gage in June 1775.

Little Known Fact: Ellery deliberately stood close to the table where each man came forth to affix his signature to the document. He simply wanted *"to see how they all looked when they signed what might have been their death warrants. Undaunted resolution was displayed on every countenance."*

Price Paid for Signing: During British occupation of Rhode Island, Ellery suffered great losses of property. Personal belongings, his library, furniture, pictures hanging on the walls and anything else of any value, were either stolen or burned by the vindictive British invader.

All Signers, including Ellery, suffered monetary losses because of their connection with the cause. Some were brought to the brink of financial ruin, or even worse, abject poverty.

Apple-Lemon Pie –
Enjoyed by the Blair Family

1-1/2 tbls butter   1 lemon
1 cup sugar   1 apple, finely chopped
1 egg, well beaten

Line pie pan with good crust. Cream butter and sugar in wooden mixing bowl. Grate lemon rind and add this. Peel all white inner rind off lemon and throw away. Cut lemon into small pieces and remove seeds. Chop entire lemon very fine. Stir in along with finely chopped apple pieces. Lastly blend in frothy beaten eggs. Pour mixture into unbaked pie shell. Place in very quick oven (450 degrees) and allow to bake for about 10 minutes. Then reduce heat to moderate (350 degrees) and bake 25 to 30 minutes longer. No top crust is required for this pie.

John Blair (1732 – 1800)

Heritage: Born in Williamsburg, Virginia. Member of a wealthy socially prominent Virginia family. Descendants sailed to America from England and arrived sometime in the early 1600s.

Religion: Devout Christian. Episcopal. Very active in church. Supported his church generously. See quote below.

Education: Attended only the finest private schools. Also tutored extensively. Graduated from William and Mary College. Went on to study law at the prestigious London's Middle Temple.

Marriage: A widower. His wife, Jean Balfour, died in 1792. He chose to honor the memory of his loving mate by not remarrying.

Children: None.

Interesting Highlights: One of 39 men who signed the *Constitution*.

Practiced law in Williamsburg, Virginia,

Father was a Colonial official.

His uncle, John, founded the College of William and Mary.

Involved in the patriot movement for independence as early as 1770.

Delegate to the Constitutional Convention in 1787.

Religiously attended every session of the Convention, but took part in none of the committees.

Never made a speech at the Constitutional Convention due to his inherent shyness. He was somewhat in awe of many other Signers.

Appointed by President George Washington in 1789 to be an Associate Justice of the United States Supreme Court.

Although a slave owner himself, Blair signed the **Virginia Association**, of June 27, 1774, which banned any further importing of slaves from England.

Quotable Quote: On January 11, 1786, Blair's legislation was adopted. It was called the **Virginia Statute of Religious Liberty**: *"Well aware that Almighty God hath created the mind free; that all attempts to influence it by temporal punishments or burdens, or by civil incapacitations ... are a departure from the plan of the Holy Author of our religion."*

Heroic Deed: Refused an offer of amnesty from British Governor Gage in June 1775.

Little Known Fact: One of 12 Signers of the *Constitution* who owned slaves. The others were Bassett, Blount, Butler, Carroll, Jenifer, Madison, both Pinckneys, Rutledge, Spaight and Washington.

Price Paid for Signing: All the Signers, including Blair, suffered monetary losses because of their connection with the cause. Some were brought to the brink of financial ruin, or even worse, abject poverty.

Potato Pie –
Made by Sarah Clark for Her Husband

1 pound potatoes	6 egg yolks, beaten
1 lemon, juice only	1 tsp nutmeg
1 cup butter	1 tsp mace
2 cups sugar	6 egg whites, beaten

Line pie pan with good crust. Boil potatoes until soft. Mash while still hot and rub through colander. Squeeze in lemon juice and mix well. Set aside. Cream butter and sugar in large wooden mixing bowl. Whip custard-like beaten egg yolks and spices in with butter-sugar blend. Beat in mashed and strained potatoes, little by little. Continue beating hard until batter is smooth and light. Fold in stiffly beaten egg whites. Fill your unbaked pie shell with this mixture. Bake without top crust in quick oven (450 degrees) for 12 minutes. Then reduce heat to moderate (350 degrees) and bake for 20 to 30 minutes longer. **NOTE**: *To tell if pie is done, insert knife blade halfway between middle and edge of pie. It should come out clean. This pie is to be eaten when cold. Recipe makes excellent pudding as well as pie filling. Just bake in well-buttered baking pan without bottom crust.*

Abraham Clark (1726 – 1794)

Heritage: English. Born on a farm in Elizabethtown, New Jersey. A descendant of settlers who emigrated to America from England sometime in the late 1600s or early 1700s.

Religion: Devout Christian. See quote below.

Education: Very little or no formal education. A brilliant young man, he studied law and mathematics on his own. Became a self-taught surveyor.

Marriage: Wed 21-year old Sarah Hatfield in 1749. He was 23.

Children: Ten. Two sons, Thomas and Isaac, officers in the Continental Army, were captured by the British.

Interesting Highlights: One of 56 men to sign the *Declaration of Independence*. Hancock was the *only* one to sign on July 4, 1776. Another 49 signed on August 2. Six signed at a later date – they were Richard Henry Lee, Gerry, McKean, Thorton, Wolcott and Wythe.

An enthusiastic Signer of the *Declaration of Independence*. Opposed ratification of the *Constitution*, and refused to sign, until a *Bill of Rights* was added to the document.

Delegate in the Continental Congress throughout Revolutionary War.

Best known in the Colonies as "the poor mans counselor." Although never a member of the Bar, he would accept produce or merchandise for his legal expertise from those who couldn't pay him.

Elected to be a delegate to the Constitutional Convention in 1787, but was unable to attend due to poor health.

Quotable Quote: *"The people of America are able to choose their own rulers. Providence has given us this right. Since we have a Christian country, it's the duty of every citizen to select only Christians for their leaders."*

Heroic Deed: Signing the *Declaration*. Abraham Clark knew that should the struggle for independence fail, an ignominious death by hanging would most certainly be his punishment.

Refused offer of amnesty from British Governor Gage in June 1775.

Little Known Fact: Both sons were captured and treated with exceptional brutality because their father had signed the *Declaration*. Both were incarcerated on the *Jersey*, a notorious, infamous, disease-ridden British prison ship.

Price Paid for Signing: Although he didn't personally suffer during the British occupation as did Hart and Stockton, neglect of his property made it lose much of its value. All Signers, including Clark, suffered monetary losses because of their connection with the cause. Some were brought to the brink of financial ruin, or even worse, abject poverty.

Sweet Potato-Brandy Pie –
James Smith's Holiday Favorite

1 pound sweet potatoes	1 tbls nutmeg
½ cup butter	1 lemon, juice
¾ cup sugar	and grated rind
4 egg yolks, beaten	¼ cup brandy
1 tbls cinnamon	4 egg whites, beaten.

Parboil (boil until partly cooked) sweet potatoes (the firm yellow ones are best). Let cool and then mash. If this is done while sweet potatoes are still hot, they will be sticky and heavy. Set aside. Cream butter and sugar in large wooden mixing bowl. Add custard-like beaten egg yolks, spices, lemon juice and grated rind. Whip sweet potatoes in by degrees. Continue beating hard until mixture is smooth and light. Stir in brandy. Gently fold in stiffly beaten egg whites. Line pie pan with good crust. Fill unbaked pie shells. Bake without top crust. Put in very quick oven (450 degrees) and bake 12 minutes. Reduce heat to moderate (350 degrees) and bake 20 to 30 minutes longer. **NOTE**: *To tell if pie is done, insert knife blade halfway between the middle and the edge of the pie. It should come out clean.*

James Smith (1719? -- 1806)

Heritage: Irish. Born in Northern Ireland. His father emigrated to America from Ireland with him in tow sometime in the early 1700s.

Religion: Devout Christian. Catholic or Protestant unknown. Was said to have *"faithfully practiced the holier precepts of Christianity."* Also see quote below.

Education: Schooled in Reverend Francis Allison's prestigious academy in New London, Pennsylvania. Acquired the ability to fluently speak and read Latin and Greek through private tutoring. Was also taught surveying. Studied law under prominent local attorney.

Marriage: Wed well-connected and extremely wealthy Eleanor Armor of New Castle, Delaware in 1745 or 1746.

Children: Five – three sons and two daughters.

Interesting Highlights: One of 56 men to sign the *Declaration of Independence*. Hancock was the *only* one to sign on July 4, 1776. Another 49 signed on August 2. Six signed at a later date – they were Richard Henry Lee, Gerry, McKean, Thorton, Wolcott and Wythe.

One of three Signers of the *Declaration of Independence* who was born in Ireland. The others were Taylor and Thornton.

One of eight Signers of the *Declaration of Independence* who was foreign born. The others were Gwinnett, Lewis, Robert Morris, Taylor, Thornton, Wilson and Witherspoon.

As early as 1774, he fearlessly made it clear that he was in favor of cutting the bond that chained the Colonies to the British throne.

Was convinced that reconciliation with Great Britain was out of the question and that war was inevitable.

Extremely popular with fellow Signers as he was always witty and had a wonderful sense of humor.

Quotable Quote: *"Religious liberty must always include religious responsibility. Together they give a lasting happiness to believers. I feel a profound reverence for God, the Bible and the Christian religion."*

Heroic Deed: Signing the *Declaration*. James Smith knew that should the struggle for independence fail, an ignominious death by hanging would most certainly be his punishment.

Refused an offer of amnesty from British Governor Gage in June 1775.

Little Known Fact: James Smith's date of birth was never recorded. Nor, if he even knew what it was, he couldn't be induced to let anyone know.

Price Paid for Signing: All the Signers, including Lee, suffered monetary losses because of their connection with the cause. Some were brought to the brink of financial ruin, or even worse, abject poverty.

Apple Custard Pie –
Made by Elizabeth Adams for Samuel

3 cups stewed apples	Nutmeg to suit
1 cup sugar	4 cups milk
6 egg yolks, beaten	6 egg whites, beaten

Line pie pan with good crust. After apples have been completely cooked, stir in sugar. Allow to cool. Then add custard-like beaten egg yolks. Season to taste with nutmeg. Gradually blend in milk and whip well. Lastly, fold in stiffly beaten egg whites. Fill unbaked pie crust and bake without top crust. Place in hot oven (450 degrees) and bake 12 minutes. Then reduce heat to moderate (350 degrees) and bake another 20 to 30 minutes. **NOTE**: *To tell if pie is done, insert knife blade halfway between the middle and the edge of the pie. It should come out clean.*

Samuel Adams (1722 – 1803)

Heritage: English. Born in Boston, Massachusetts. Ancestors were Pilgrims. Descendant of John Alden who sailed to America on the Mayflower.

Religion: Christian. He once said: *"The rights of the Colonists as Christians ... may be best understood by reading and carefully studying ... the New Testament."* Also see quote below.

Education: Tutored at the prestigious Boston Latin School for his college prep. Entered Harvard when 14 and graduated with honors in 1740 when only 18. Tutored in law for a short time.

Marriage: Twice married. In October of 1749, he married 24-year old Elizabeth Checkley. She died on July 25, 1757. On December 6, 1757, he remarried, this time to 29-year old Elizabeth Wells.

Children: He and his first wife had five children. Only two, Hannah and Samuel, Jr., lived to maturity.

Interesting Highlights: He and his cousin, John Adams, were two of the 49 men who signed the *Declaration of Independence* on August 2, 1776. Six others signed at a later date. They were Gerry, Richard Henry Lee, McKean, Thornton, Wolcott and Wythe. John Hancock was *only* man to sign on July 4.

Was for more than 20 years before the signing of the *Declaration of Independence* , a defiant, anti-British leader.

He once said: *"The right to freedom is a gift of the Almighty."*

Offered a resolution calling for the First Continental Congress that was convened in Carpenter's Hall, Philadelphia, on September 5, 1774.

Best known as ***"The Father of the American Revolution."***

Quotable Quote: After signing the *Declaration,* he declared: *"We have this day restored the Sovereign to whom all men ought to be obedient. He reigns in Heaven and from the rising to the setting of the sun ...."*

Heroic Deed: Signing the *Declaration.* Samuel Adams knew that should the struggle for independence fail, an ignominious death by hanging would most certainly be his punishment.

Refused an offer of amnesty from British Governor Gage in June 1775.

Little Known Fact: Samuel Adams made this statement: *"The Constitution shall never be construed ... to prevent the people of the United States who are peaceable citizens from keeping their own arms."*

Price Paid for Signing: He and John Hancock were the only men who were not offered amnesty in 1775 by British Governor Gage.. They were simply to be captured and severely punished because their *"offenses were of too flagitious a Nature to admit of any other Consideration than that of condign Punishment."*

Fresh Strawberry Pie –
Often Eaten by the Pinckney Family

Fresh strawberries to suit   Sugar to suit

Wash and carefully pick over fresh strawberries. Line pie pan with good crust. Put in layer of strawberries. Liberally sprinkle with sugar. Cover with another layer of strawberries. Again liberally sprinkle with sugar. Pack entire pie shell *very full* in this manner, because strawberries tend to shrink during baking. Cover with top crust. Pinch down edges. Place in rather quick oven (400 to 425 degrees) for about 40 minutes. **NOTE:** *Charles wife, Eleanor, often used blackberries, huckleberries, blueberries and other kinds of berries to make pies exactly as she did with strawberries in this receipt.*

Charles Pinckney (1757 – 1824)

Heritage: English. Born in Charleston, South Carolina. Ancestors emigrated to America from England in the early to mid 1600s.

Religion: Devout Christian. Never allowed to go to bed at night until after praying with his mother or father. Grace was always required before every meal. See quote below.

Education: From an aristocratic background, he had only the best tutors and attended only the most prestigious private schools as a youth. Studied law in the office of a prestigious attorney friend of the family.

Marriage: Wed to Mary Eleanor Laurens in 1778. She was the daughter of a wealthy South Carolina merchant and a socialite.

Children: At least three children were born of this union.

Interesting Highlights: One of 39 men who signed the *Constitution*.
Second cousin, Charles Cotesworth, also signed the *Constitution*.
Captain in the South Carolina militia.
Captured by the British when Charleston fell in 1780.
Remained a prisoner of the British invaders until June of 1781.
One of three men in their twenties to sign the *Constitution*. The others were Dayton and Spaight.
Second youngest delegate to the Constitutional Convention.
Although one of the youngest Signers, he often spoke and contributed much to the document's final draft.
Thomas Jefferson's Campaign manager during 1800 when he was running for President of the United States.

Quotable Quote: Helped his second cousin, Charles Cotesworth Pinckney, and John Rutledge, write South Carolina's *Constitution*. Here is one of the articles: *"All persons and religious societies who acknowledge that there is one God, and a future state of rewards and punishments, and that God is publicly to be worshipped, shall be freely tolerated. ... all denominations of Christian[s] ... shall enjoy equal religious and civil privileges."*

Heroic Deed: Served as a lieutenant in the Continental Army under General George Washington. Saw action during the Siege of Savannah, Georgia, in September and October of 1779.
Refused an offer of amnesty from British Governor Gage in June 1775.

Little Known Fact: One of the 12 Signers of the *Constitution* who owned slaves. The others were Bassett, Blair, Blount, Butler, Carroll, Jenifer, Madison, the other Pinckney, Rutledge, Spaight and Washington.

Price Paid for Signing: All Signers, including Charles Pinckney, suffered monetary losses because of their connection with the cause. Some were brought to the brink of financial ruin, or even worse, abject poverty.

Raspberry Cream Pie –
Served to Guests by Dorothy Hancock

Fresh raspberries to suit   Powdered sugar to suit

Wash and carefully pick over fresh raspberries. Line pie pan with good crust. Put in layer of raspberries. Sprinkle liberally with powdered sugar. Cover with another layer of raspberries. Again liberally sprinkle with powdered sugar. Continue until the pie shell is very full. Cover with top crust but *do not* pinch down edges. Bake in very quick oven (450 degrees) for 10 minutes. Then reduce heat to moderate (350 degrees). Bake 20 to 25 minutes longer. Some homemakers prefer to bake this pie in a very quick oven (400 to 425 degrees) for 40 to 50 minutes. While pie is baking, prepare you the following:

½ cup milk   1 tbls sugar
½ cup cream   ½ tsp corn starch,
2 egg whites   wet in cold milk

Blend milk and cream in small kettle. Heat to boiling. Beat egg whites with sugar until fluffy and stiff. Stir into boiling milk. Add cornstarch last. Allow mixture in kettle to boil for 3 minutes. Set aside to cool.

Remove pie from oven when it has finished baking. Carefully lift off top crust so as not to break it. When mixture in kettle is cold, pour over raspberries in pie. Place top crust back on and set aside to cool. Brush top crust with a little melted butter. Sprinkle with sugar. **NOTE:** *Mrs. Hancock also used this recipe for making strawberry cream pies.*

John Hancock (1737 – 1793)

Heritage: Born near Quincy, Massachusetts. Descendant of an English family who immigrated to America sometime in the late 1600s or early 1700s.

Religion: Devout Christian. Father and grandfather were Congregational ministers of note in Massachusetts. See quote below.

Education: Had only the finest tutors. Studied at the prestigious Boston Latin School. Graduated from Harvard College when 17 in 1754

Marriage: Married beautiful Dorothy Quincy on August 23, 1775. She was a relative of John and Samuel Adams. He was 38, she 28.

Children: Two. Daughter died as an infant and a son, John George Washington Hancock, died when 9 years old.

Interesting Highlights: Delegate to the First Continental Congress that convened on September 5, 1774, at Carpenter's Hall in Philadelphia.

President of the Second Continental Congress that convened on May 10, 1775, at the State House in Philadelphia.

His wife, Dorothy, also an ardent patriot, matched the enthusiasm of her husband when it concerned freedom and independence.

Dorothy's father, Judge Quincy, also a fearless patriot, strongly supported his son-in-law's fight for American independence.

The *only* man to actually affix his signature on the *Declaration of Independence*, July 4, 1776. There were 49 others who signed on August 2, 1776. Six signed at a later date – Gerry, Richard Henry Lee, McKean, Thornton, Wolcott and Wythe.

Boldly stepped forward, picked up the quill, and placed his name on the Declaration in large letters. Stepping back, he spoke those immortal words: *"There! His Majesty can now read my name without spectacles, and can now double his reward of 500 pounds on my head. That is my defiance."*

Quotable Quote: *"We think it is incumbent upon this people to humble themselves before God on account of their sins. ... so God may be pleased to continue to us the blessings we enjoy, and remove the tokens of His displeasure."* Spoken on the eve of the Revolution (October 1774).

Heroic Deed: Signing the *Declaration*. John Hancock knew that should the struggle for independence fail, an ignominious death by hanging would most certainly be his punishment.

Refused an offer of amnesty from British Governor Gage in June 1775.

Little Known Fact: As a Major General in the Massachusetts militia, he led an expeditionary force to oust the British from Rhode Island.

Price Paid for Signing: All the Signers, including Hancock, suffered monetary losses because of their connection with the cause. Some were brought to the brink of financial ruin, or ever worse, abject poverty.

Fresh Cherry Pie --
Mary Morris Made This for Robert

Fresh cherries, pitted   Sugar to suit

Line pie pan with good crust. Fill pan with fresh, ripe and pitted cherries. Sprinkle sugar over them. Cover with top crust. Pinch down edges. Bake in rather quick oven (400 to 425 degrees) for about 45 minutes. Eat when cold, with powdered sugar sprinkled all over top. **NOTE:** *Mrs. Morris made her blackberry, plum, raspberry and gooseberry pies in exactly the same way.*

Robert Morris (1733 – 1806)

Heritage: English. His father, a Liverpool merchant, emigrated to America sometime in the mid-1700s. Robert was left behind in the care of his grandmother. He was sent for at the age of 13-years.

Religion: Christian. His wife was the daughter of the late venerable bishop of Pennsylvania.

Education: Brilliant young man. Placed in private school in Philadelphia. Chided by his father for his slowness in learning, Robert replied: *"Why, sir, I have learned all that he could teach me."* The 15-year old was immediately placed in the exporting business. With no more formal education, he became a resounding success and one of the richest men in the Colonies.

Marriage: Wed to Mary White in 1769. He was 35, she 20. Mary was from a wealthy, socially prominent Philadelphia family. She was described as *"tall, graceful and commanding, with a stately dignity of manner."* They were happily married for 37-years.

Children: Five sons and two daughters. Some sources disagree and say they had only four children – three sons and one daughter.

Interesting Highlights: One of 56 men to sign the *Declaration of Independence.* Hancock was the *only* one to sign on July 4, 1776. Another 49 signed on August 2. Six signed at a later date – they were Richard Henry Lee, Gerry, McKean, Thorton, Wolcott and Wythe.

One of six men to sign both the *Declaration of Independence* and the *Constitution.* The others were Clymer, Franklin, Read, Sherman and Wilson.

One of five to sign both the *Constitution* and *Articles of Confederation.* The others were Daniel Carroll, Dickinson, Gouverneur Morris and Sherman.

One of only two men to sign all three of our nation's basic documents – the *Declaration of Independence, Constitution* and *Articles of Confederation.* The other Signer was Robert Sherman.

Quotable Quote: Astonished and indignant upon hearing about the Battle of Lexington, he said this: *"I vow to dedicate the rest of my life to the cause of freedom."*

Heroic Deed: Signing the *Declaration.* Robert Morris knew that should the struggle for independence fail, an ignominious death by hanging would most certainly be his punishment.

Refused an offer of amnesty from British Governor Gage in June 1775.

Little Known Fact: One of two Signers of the *Declaration of Independence* who was born in England. The other was Button Gwinnett.

Price Paid for Signing: All the Signers, including Robert Morris, suffered monetary losses because of their connection with the cause. Some were brought to the brink of financial ruin, or even worse, abject poverty.

Mince Meat Pie Filling –
Special Treat Enjoyed by Washington

5 pounds beef, ground	1 tbls nutmeg
1 pound beef suet, ground	½ tbls salt
4 pounds raisins	½ tsp pepper
1 tbls cloves	4 cups sugar
2 tbls cinnamon	1 lemon, juice and rind
1 tbls sugar	½ pound citron peel

8 cups apples, chopped fine

Cook ground beef in large kettle or pot. When cool, add all other ingredients. Blend everything thoroughly. Set aside and get large saucepan. Put following ingredients in saucepan, stir well, and bring to boil:

1 quart apple cider	1 quart of brandy

2 tbls butter

Pour mixture over other ingredients in kettle or pot. Stir well until blended and set aside to cool. When cold, pack in jars, cover, and store in cool dry place. Allow to stand at least 24 hours before using to make pies. This amount of mince meat will make from 8 to 10 delicious mince meat pies. **NOTE**: *George Washington had a definite weakness for pies of this kind. Martha found it to be well worth her while to have her cook make up a large batch of mince meat, for if planned wisely, it had to be undertaken only once each winter. But, she recommended not eating these pies at night before going to bed if the eater valued his or her own sound slumber.*

George Washington (1732 – 1799)

Heritage: English. Born in Wakefield Plantation, Virginia. The eldest of six children from his father's first marriage. Was 11 when father died.

Religion: Washington, *"Without making ostentatious professions of religion, was a sincere believer in the Christian faith."* These are the words of John Marshall, Chief Justice of the U.S. Supreme Court and close friend. Also see quote below.

Education: Was never formally taught school beyond the elementary level. Privately tutored for the most part.

Marriage: Married Martha Dandridge Custis, an extremely wealthy widow, who had two children from her previous marriage.

Children: He and Martha had no children. He brought up Martha's children as if they were his own.

Interesting Highlights: His letters and speeches are filled with references to the Almighty.

Everything he did, every decision he made, was guided by the highest standards of morality.

Delegate from Virginia to the First and Second Continental Congress.

He was the most popular man in the Colonies and most respected among his peers.

One of the wealthiest men in the Colonies. Made numerous and generous loans of money to friends in need.

Letters and speeches are filled with references to the Almighty.

While the Continental Army was headquartered in Newburg, New York, he instituted what he called a *"Badge of Courage."* This combat medal was the forerunner of today's *Purple Heart* and the *Congressional Medal of Honor.*

During his Presidency, the nation's capitol was moved from New York to Philadelphia (1790)

Quotable Quote: *"It is the duty of all nations to acknowledge the providence of Almighty God, to obey His will, to be grateful for His benefits, and humbly to implore his protection and favor."*

Heroic Deed: Refused to consider the offer of important men in the colonies who wished to appoint him king.

Refused an offer of amnesty from British Governor Gage in June 1775.

Little Known Fact: According to his will, all of his slaves were to be given their freedom upon his death.

Price Paid for Signing: All the Signers, including Washington, suffered monetary losses because of their connection with the cause. Much of Washington's extensive fortune was lost due to financial sacrifices and long absences during the war.

Appendix

I: Old Time Measurements
    and Today's Counterparts
II: About the Author
III: Historical Baking Recipe Notes

Appendix I

Old-Time Measurements and Today's Counterparts

Here is a list of some of the most interesting old-time measurements used by homemakers during the period of our great War for Independence. The measurement used in the original writing of the recipe so many long years ago is first given. It is then followed by its modern day equivalent.

1 wineglass full = 4 tablespoonful; ½ gill; 2 ounces; ¼ cup.

4 wineglasses = 1 cup

1 gill = ½ cup or 8 tablespoonful

1 teacup = ¾ cup

2/3 teacup = ½ cup

1/3 teacup = ¼ cup

1 kitchen cup = 1 cup; 2 gills

1 coffee cup = 1 cup; 2 gills

1 tin cup = 1 cup; 2 gills

1 tumbler = 1 cup; ½ pint

1 gram =1/5 teaspoon

1 dram liquid = 1 teaspoon

1 dessert spoonful = 2 teaspoons

2 dessert spoonsful = 1 tablespoon

Saltspoonful.= ¼ teaspoon; a pinch

4 salt spoons = 1 teaspoon

Pinch of salt = 1/8 teaspoon

Handful salt or sugar = ¼ cup

Handful flour = ½ cup

Dash of pepper = 3 good shakes; 1/8 teaspoon

Lump of butter = 1 well rounded tablespoon

Butter the size of an egg = 2 tablespoons; ¼ cup; 2 ounces

263

Butter the size of a walnut = 1 tablespoon; 1 ounce
Pound of butter = 2 cups; 1 pint
Pound of flour (sifted) = 1 heaping quart; 4 heaping cups
Pound of graham flour = 4-1/2 cups
Pound of wholewheat flour = 4 cups
Pound of sugar = 2 cups; 1 pint
Pound of powdered sugar = 2-1/2 cups
Pound of milk = 2 cups; 1 pint
Pound of cornmeal (coarse) = 2-2/3 cups
                (fine) = 4 cups
Pound of ground suet = 4 cups
Pound of eggs = 8 large eggs (without shells);
            10 medium eggs (without shells)
            14 small eggs (without shells)
Quart of eggs = 16 large eggs (without shells)
            20 medium eggs (without shells)
            24 small eggs (without shells)
Cup of eggs =   4 large eggs
Pint of eggs =   2 cups
             8 large eggs (without shells)
          10 medium eggs (without shells)
          12 small eggs (without shells)
I/2 pint eggs = 1 cup
          4 large eggs (without shells)
          5 medium eggs (without shells)
          6 small eggs (without shells)
4 old-fashioned teaspoonsful = 1 modern tablespoon
40 drops of liquid = 1 old-fashioned teaspoonful
4 blades of mace = 1 teaspoon powdered mace

Oven Temperatures

Very Slow (275 degrees)……….. Moderately Quick (375 degrees)
Slow (300 degrees)……………....Rather Quick (400 to 425 degrees)
Moderately Slow (325 degrees)….Quick (425 degrees)
Moderate (350 degrees)………….Very Quick (450 degrees)

Appendix II

About the Author

Robert W. Pelton is a member of SONS OF THE REVOLUTION, a premier organization made up of men whose ancestors fought in the Continetal Army under General George Washington during the Revolutionary War. He has been writing and lecturing for more than 30 years on a great variety of historical and other subjects. He has published hundreds of articles and numerous books.

Pelton has carefully mined every imaginable source for old historical cooking and baking recipes from the early days of America. He has perused innumerable old cook books as well as yellowed and tattered handwritten receipt ledgers from both private and public archives and libraries. Through all this, he has been able to skillfully recreate these treasures of the past for use in kitchens of today.

Pelton speaks to groups all over the United States. Tom R. Murray offers this: "Mr. Pelton puts together rare combinations of intellectual energies as a writer and speaker that will captivate an audience."

Pelton may be contacted for convention speaking engagements or speaking before other groups at:

Freedom & Liberty Foundation
P.O. Box 12619
Knoxville, TN 37912-0619
Phone (toll free): 1-877-289-2665
Fax: 865-633-8398
E-mail: ChristianAmerica@yahoo.com

Appendix III

Historical Baking Recipe Notes

_____

_____

_____

_____

_____

_____

_____

_____

_____

_____

_____

_____

Historical Baking Recipe Notes

_____

_____

_____

_____

_____

_____

_____

_____

_____

_____

_____

_____

_____

_____

_____

_____

_____

_____

_____

_____

_____

_____

_____

Historical Baking Recipe Notes

_____

_____

_____

_____

_____

_____

_____

_____

_____

_____

_____

_____

_____

_____

_____

_____

_____

_____

_____

_____

Index

Another Title in the Pelton Historical Cookbook Series:

Civil War Period Cookery contains recipes favored by people who lived and loved and prayed during the period of the tragic War Between the States. Included are the favorite dishes of many men and women who fought for both the Union and the Confederacy. Here you will find such recipes as **Brown Sugar Cookies** eaten by General Ulysses S. Grant; a **Pork and Parsnip Stew** dish enjoyed by Medal of Honor winner, Mary Edwards Walker; the **Molasses Pie** made by the mother of Nathan Bedford Forrest; and that special pan of **Giblet-Cornmeal Turkey Stuffing** as it was served to the family of Abner Doubleday. All of these individuals were devout Christians. An enlightening biographical sketch follows each unique historical recipe.

Illustrated

168 pages $13.95 + $4.50 S&H ISBN 0-7414-0971-2

**Standard 40% Discount When Purchasing for Resale
Free Shipping on Orders of 20 or More Copies.**
*Available from Infinity Publishing
1094 New DeHaven Street #100
West Conshohocken, PA 19428-2713
Toll free: 1-877-289-2665*

Another Title in the Pelton Historical Cookbook Series:

Revolutionary War Period Cookery is a collection of unique recipes enjoyed by many signers of the *Declaration of Independence* and military leaders in the *Revolutionary War*. It contains the favorite dishes of numerous figures from the Colonial period of our glorious history. Included are such recipes as the one for Alexander Hamilton's **Blood Bread** dinner favorite; the **Walnut Bread Pudding** so loved by the great French General Lafayette; the **Ale Fritters** as cooked for George Washington; and the **Chicken and Oysters** dish prepared for John Adams. An enlightening biographical sketch follows each recipe.

Illustrated

180 pages $13.95 + $4.50 S&H ISBN 0-7414-1053-4

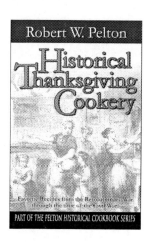

Another Title in the Pelton Historical Cookbook Series:

Historical Christmas Cookery is a collection of recipes enjoyed by signers of the *Declaration of Independence* and heroes of the *Revolutionary War*. Included are the favorite dishes of many men and women who wore both the Blue and the Gray during the *War Between the States*. Here will be found the recipe for Benjamin Franklin's **Mashed Turnip and Potato** dish; those **Sour Cream Cookies** so eagerly eaten by the great Jefferson Davis; Patrick Henry's special **French Flannel Cakes**; and the **Boiled Custard** made for Lincoln as a boy by his step-mother. An enlightening biographical sketch follows each unique historical recipe.

Illustrated

215 pages $15.95 + $4.50 S&H   ISBN 0-7414-1088-5

**Standard 40% Discount When Purchasing for Resale
Free Shipping on Orders of 20 or More Copies.**
*Available from Infinity Publishing
1094 New DeHaven Street #100
West Conshohocken, PA 19428-2713
Toll free: 1-877-289-2665*

Another Title in the Pelton Historical Cookbook Series:

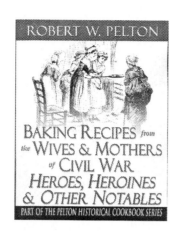

Baking Recipes from the Wives & Mothers of Civil War Heroes, Heroines & Other Notables contains recipes favored by people who lived and loved and prayed during the period of the tragic War Between the States. Included are the favorite dishes of many men and women who fought for both the Union and the Confederacy. Here you will find such recipes as the one for **Custard Pie** as made for General Robert E. Lee; **Whole Wheat Bread** as eaten by General W.T. Sherman; a cast iron skillet of **Spider Corn Cake** as served to the family of Abraham Lincoln; and **Early Morning Yeast Rolls** enjoyed by Confederate President Jefferson Davis. Each unique historical recipe is followed by an enlightening biographical sketch. Profusely illustrated.

352 pp - 8-1/2 x 11 - $23.95 + $4.50 S&H
ISBN 0-7414-2589-0

Standard 40% Discount When Purchasing for Resale
Free Shipping on Orders of 20 or More Copies.
Available from Infinity Publishing
1094 New DeHaven Street #100
West Conshohocken, PA 19428-2713
Toll free: 1-877-289-2665